THE ULTIMATE GUIDE TO
CROSSBOW HUNTING

THE ULTIMATE GUIDE TO
CROSSBOW HUNTING

How to Successfully Bowhunt Big and Small
Game across North America

Joe Byers

Skyhorse Publishing

Visit our website at www.skyhorsepublishing.com.

10 9 8 7 6 5 4 3 2 1

Library of Congress Cataloging-in-Publication Data is available on file.

Cover design by Tom Lau
Cover photo credit Joe Byers

Print ISBN: 978-1-5107-1275-1
Ebook ISBN: 978-1-5107-1276-8

Printed in China

Table of Contents

Chapter 1

Introduction: What's Crossbow Hunting Like? A Tale of Two Bucks

Horizontal archery levels the playing field in all measures of arrow pursuit. Gone is the need to hold high-poundage bows at full draw, the risk of slapping your arm with a bow string, or the need for hours of instinctive shooting practice. The crossbow allows a new shooter to gain proficiency quickly and enjoy the confidence of accurate arrows, whether you are a three-year-old with your first toy or a senior archer who can no longer shoot a heavy bowhunting weight.

Whitetail deer, especially bucks, are large animals with great stamina. A quality crossbow is capable of pushing a broadhead through both shoulders and lungs.

The crossbow is opening doors for many men, women, and children to enjoy archery. For many years, archers believed that crossbows would jeopardize the extended hunting seasons they enjoy or generate new hunting regulations that would become a burden on vertical archers. However, decades of crossbow hunting in states such as Ohio have shown that not to be the case. Buckeye archers have the option of vertical or horizontal gear, and the choice between the two has been evenly split. Crossbows have not given hunters a significant advantage in the field over vertical archery, and both forms have been embraced.

Vicki and Ralph Cianciarulo smile behind two great bucks taken with crossbows. Crossbows are an equal-opportunity excitement generator.

The purpose of this book is to open new doors to excitement and a lifetime of recreational enjoyment. I shot my first groundhog with a longbow at age twelve. The wooden shaft plunked it and bounced off, and the woodchuck raced down its hole, wiser and probably as confused as I was. I didn't know about broadheads at that young age; nor did I have any body of experience to draw upon. My family was passionate about hunting all types of game: pheasants, grouse, deer, squirrels, and others. Only they never used archery gear. I wouldn't enter the archery arena until my late twenties. What a liberating experience it was!

Back in the day, Maryland had a rather liberal bowhunting season that opened in mid-September and continued until the end of January. My deer hunting, though, had been confined to one week after Thanksgiving: the Maryland firearm season. I knew little about rubs, scrapes, and whitetail behavior during the rut. Even though deer hunting for me was primarily a waiting game, I loved it. After bagging my first buck at age sixteen, I strapped it across the hood of my old 1957 Chevy and drove down Interstate 70 beaming with pride. I could barely see over the hood with the monster four-pointer tied down, but that didn't matter. It was my first buck, and I was hooked.

A decade would pass before I began bowhunting. It was an endeavor I often considered, yet for which I had no firsthand access to information. Google was nothing but

The author hunted with a compound bow for nearly thirty years before switching to a horizontal format. Although equipment is very different, many hunting strategies and techniques are very similar.

a large number in those days, and not until I began working with the Wilson family of teachers did I seriously take up bowhunting.

Normally the Labor Day holiday was a chance to go dove hunting. Yet after practicing most of the summer with a recurve, I arose before dawn and drove half an hour to my hunting club to begin the fall scouting program. At dawn I saw a whitetail buck in velvet, bedded in an open field, and other deer moving from feeding to bedding areas. I'd never watched whitetail deer in their natural environments, and excitement began to build for opening day ten days later.

I scouted out areas I'd never been allowed to hunt, because more senior hunters had claimed them during the rifle seasons. Yet in September, I had the mountain to myself. I scouted out trails, found several excellent tree-stand locations, and returned home as if I'd just seen Disney World for the first time. No pumpkin army, animals moving in natural manner, and lots of deer. Wow!

Whether you are an experienced archer or a novice to hunting and shooting, you can go through the same metamorphosis. The world of archery hunting is wildly exciting and this book will help you become more successful at the craft.

A TALE OF TWO BUCKS

The whitetail deer is one of the grandest animals on the planet. Americans should be proud of our wildlife heritage and how well hunters have managed wild things in our

This buck was pushed toward the author, who hid in dense brush with his Aimpoint sights ready and his finger on the trigger.

country. The United States is number one in the world in wildlife management, thanks to the conservation efforts of hunters who gladly pay up to an 11 percent tax on all sporting equipment to support wildlife management and the shooting sports. Every bow, broadhead, and arrow you purchase has this Pittman-Robinson tax built-in, which is one of the prime reasons hunting in the United States is world-class.

In any state but Alaska or Hawaii, there is probably a huntable population of white-tail deer near your home. A crossbow, some gear, and effective practicing can put some of this delicious and healthy protein on your table this fall. (Venison is lower in fat than turkey and almost as low in fat as fish.)

The technical crossbow information in this book is very recent and up-to-date, while many of the hunting strategies and tactics have been honed over the last fifty years. Along the same lines, you can become a proficient shot with your gear fairly quickly, but the broader hunting skills will take years—if not decades—and game animals will still teach you a lesson or two every time out. This book is written to be equally informative to vertical archers and rifle hunters, since effective hunting skills, strategies, and techniques cross all equipment boundaries.

Two of my most exciting bucks came from a Native American reservation in South Dakota, ironically during the firearm season. I was hunting with a group of friends during the muzzleloader season and had the good fortune of drawing a double license: one for black powder and one for archery.

One particular river bottom draw had great potential for a deer drive. Several hunters moved slowly along the river bottom, while four hunters posted above a mixing bowl of cedars and tangles, where deer milled around before making a break across the open prairie. Normally, the bucks picked their spots to escape carefully, taking advantage of brushy cover and small ravines that allowed them to readily escape. Also, they often turned back into the drive and were rarely seen going the opposite way.

What if I posted in that mixing bowl of thick cover with my crossbow? Our hunt lasted a week, and on the third afternoon, we drove to the river and organized the drive. I had been talking about the strategy for two days, so I didn't have to ask about where I'd post.

Part of successful bowhunting is developing patterns for effective shooting. When you set up, be sure you can swing the bow and shoot without touching nearby twigs or branches.

The author smiles behind his great ambush buck, taken during a deer drive in a muzzle-loading season.

Two hunters watched the normal escape routes with muzzle-loading rifles, while I slid down a steep bank, looked quickly for a place to hide, and got settled in. I wore total camo, including a head net, and sat against a small tree in a turkey-hunting stance.

I loaded an arrow, worked the safety of my Mission bow, made sure the red-dot sight was properly illuminated, and tried to control my excitement. After less than a minute, I heard a stick snap and saw brown legs moving under the cedars. A heavy white rack came to the edge of one cedar bush fifteen yards away and stopped. I slowly raised the bow, anticipating the buck would move forward. But it swung its head from side to side, tested the wind, and held its ground. Would it bolt away, turn and run, or redirect? My heart pounded as the big deer stood stoically behind a wall of vegetation.

Suddenly, it turned hard right and chose a path that would give me a tiny window at a broadside shot. As the buck moved through the thickets, I followed it with the red dot, and the instant it stepped into my shooting lane, I squeezed. Actually, the buck saw my location and perhaps a flash of fletching as it left the bow, but its vigilance was a second too late. As the beast turned to flee, my shaft zipped through its shoulder, and it raced up the steep hill.

Despite the buck's departure, I felt confident that the hit had been lethal and that it would expire in seconds. As I sat in the afterglow of my success, another, larger buck suddenly emerged and headed right for me. It spotted my form at ten steps, whirled, and ran back into the drive. Somehow none of the drivers saw that deer.

When my buddies reached my position, I tried not to be too excited and searched in vain for the arrow. The powerful bow had sent a HellRazor broadhead completely through both shoulders, and the blood trail was easy to follow.

I'll cover trailing game extensively in later chapters, but suffice it to say that everything looked like we'd have a quick and sure recovery. I had a solid rest, the deer was standing still, the sight picture was steady, and no limbs or branches were in the path of the arrow.

The buck climbed a steep bank twenty-five feet high, crossed fifty yards of open prairie, and dropped into a small ravine. The blood trail was steady, and fifty yards further we came upon the big deer. The 3-½ -year-old buck had tall tines and a heavy, white, eight-point rack. Despite an extremely lethal hit, the 160-pound buck had moved until its last breath, and two strong men had to help me drag it back to the vehicle.

The buck was a beauty. The venison would be tasty, and my equipment worked flawlessly. But the greatest enjoyment came from the plan that came together. For nearly a year I had anticipated that post, and the strategy concluded exactly as planned.

Last Minute Opportunity

If the plan had worked once, would it work again? If I'd been excited the previous year, the anticipation was exponentially greater this next season. Again, hunting with a large group, we couldn't make the drive until the last day of the hunt, and the wind was totally wrong. I went to the same spot; the drivers moved in the same direction, yet the wind swirled badly in the bowl. I saw the rack of a big buck, but it broke back before it reached my position and sneaked past another archer standing forty yards away. This may sound impossible, but big whitetail deer don't grow old by being stupid. This could have been the same animal as the second deer I'd busted the previous year.

If a trophy buck is your quest, a crossbow can help you hunt longer seasons than firearm hunters. Once you get into bowhunting, you will get hooked.

My week of archery hunting would end without filling a tag, but the license was good until the end of the year, and I planned to return for the rifle season. As you will learn during this book, I'm a passionate hunter in many forms. I embrace hunting across all methods and have taken dozens of species with bullets, broadheads, and muzzle-loading projectiles.

Later the next month, that rifle hunt ended successfully with just one day to spare, as I intentionally filled the rifle tag so my archery tag would get another opportunity. Tagging a good whitetail after the firearm season had been in for two weeks would take some craft and a bit of luck, but I was anxious to try.

The Way of the Prairie

The hunt began with a big mistake. I had set up a ground blind during the October archery season, and a buddy had seen several good deer from that spot. On one occasion a bruiser ten-point was headed right for him, when a coyote suddenly showed up and spooked the buck.

Normally, approaching a blind from a circular route with the wind in your face is a wise move, but not this time. As I sneaked across the open prairie to reach the blind, I saw numerous fleeing deer. Although the blind was tucked in a deep cedar-choked ravine, the deer approached the stand from their morning feeding across the prairie. I saw a few

How you approach a tree stand or ground blind is very important. If you are approaching in daylight, be alert for fresh sign such as this scrape.

does from the spot, but one-third of my last day expired without incident.

Around noon I met with my Native American guide, and we discussed the best course of action during midday, when most deer were bedded. One option was to check out a deep draw that led to a fence-post rub. Since South Dakota deer often feed and live in agricultural fields, finding a tree to vent their frustrations on is difficult for a rutting buck. So one animal had found a fence post and rubbed half an inch from the near-solid cedar post. The force needed to shave this weathered staff took real muscle, and I knew it had to be a mature buck.

We drove past the post in a vehicle and headed for a high point, where we could glass for bucks on the prowl. Reaching a high, remote spot, my guide quickly pointed to the far ridge, where a buck was standing near a patch of chokecherry branches. The big deer's antlers were easily visible, and I wondered if it was the fence-post buck, since the location was just half a mile away.

The Stalk Begins

Bailing out of the vehicle, I had to make a large semicircle, drop into the bottom of the ravine, and stalk uphill to keep the wind in my face. The first fifteen minutes went smoothly. Yet once in the bottom, I had no way of seeing where the deer were or what my location was relative to the last sighting.

When in doubt, move slowly. I took one step at a time, estimating my location. Reaching a patch of pines, I paused and debated whether to sneak above or below them. Thinking that the wind was better with the lower route, I inched around the pines and slowly sneaked up hill. Suddenly, a doe burst from the pine thicket and raced away with another deer in pursuit.

Although many deer hunters are successful by ambushing deer, stalking can work too.

After a dejected climb back to the truck, I reached my guide, who greeted me with wide-eyed excitement. He had watched the entire stalk unfold and saw the buck chase the doe right to the pine thicket. "If you had gone above the pines, it would have been twenty yards away," he lamented. "Even if it saw you, it probably wouldn't have run away from the doe."

Last, Last Chance

As I took a breather in the truck, we got a call that another hunter had shot a mule deer and needed help. After taking time for that assist and a few photos, I returned to the cabin around four o'clock, with about an hour of daylight left. Not one to give up easily, I knew of a good ambush spot behind the cabin, about a ten-minute hike away.

This spot was the crest of a hill that overlooked a deep ravine, and sitting on its top made for a *terra firma* tree stand of sorts. As I approached, I noticed a single line of large tracks—apparently a big buck searching for does—leading directly to my ambush point.

I sat against a small pine tree to cover my silhouette and went through my usual ranging ritual, until I knew several reference objects without further ranging. As I waited through the last rays of sunset, I saw deer feeding onto the prairie four hundred yards away, but no bucks moving.

Suddenly, I saw movement below and a heavy-horned buck moved through the tree line and circled behind the bluff. This was a shooter deer for sure, yet I only got a glimpse of its movement. Perhaps the buck would circle behind me and jump the fence where its trail had led earlier. I moved ten yards backward and watched that track intently for about ten minutes, ready to shoot as soon as the buck appeared.

Assuming it had gone elsewhere, I returned to my elevated post just as the sun dropped below the horizon. "Thirty more minutes," I thought, and then I saw movement again. The buck had returned and was headed for the bottom of the ravine directly below me. As it entered the tree line again, I switched off the safety and sighted on the first available shooting opportunity.

The buck continued through the trees at a steady pace, and when it stepped into a

Crossbow hunting need not be a sedentary challenge. Mule deer bucks, like the one shown, are equally challenging as whitetails and usually involve much more movement.

small opening, I vocally *urrrped*. The buck instantly looked directly at me, but the bolt was already on its way, catching it squarely in the shoulder.

Wait or Trail

The shot felt good and looked good, although the arrow flew so fast that I could not see it hit, and the buck whirled and ran without going down in my sight. Half sliding down the steep hill, I found the deer's tracks in the six inches of snow, but only a few spots of blood. Following for about ten yards, I found a broken bolt as the meager blood trail continued. "When in doubt, always wait," is my theory. Even though we'd have to return in complete darkness, the snow cover would be a great asset in following tracks and the blood trail.

My mind was a swirl of mixed emotions as I hurried back to the cabin for help and better lights. Several hunters arrived soon afterwards, and we decided to eat dinner and

The author took this big eight-point during the last hour of daylight on the last day of the hunt. Even with the rifle season going full force, a bowhunter can still score. Crossbow hunters need not make a huge investment to be successful. The author took his buck with a Mission MXB-320, a mid-price bow that showed excellent performance.

then go track the deer. They were starved after hunting in the cold all day, and allowing more time in cold weather was the wisest course of action.

Three men and I took the short cut to the shooting point, pulling an ice sled to retrieve the deer. Dragging a big buck through brush is always difficult and the friction reduction of a sled over snow can make the chore much easier. Of course, we had to find the buck first.

We quickly picked up the trail and began following by flashlight, with one person constantly marking "last blood." In any trailing activity, having multiple people is always a plus. Despite the promise of a lethal hit, the trail was surprisingly sparse. Finally, we saw a place where the buck had lain down, probably twenty to thirty seconds after the shot. Tracks led to a five-foot-deep, dry stream bed, and one fellow said, "Hey, maybe it fell into there."

It had.

What a celebration! The buck would be one of the largest eight-points taken during the rifle season, and it fell to a crossbow. Under further investigation, the arrow had struck squarely in the center of the shoulder but had barely penetrated the far

The author took an ice sled when searching for his buck.
Luckily he had a full load on the way back.

shoulder. The big expandable broadhead had done its job well on the inside, yet with only a tiny exit hole, the blood trail was very sparse.

LESSONS LEARNED

My goal in this chapter was not to speak about achievement, but to relate a detailed account of two hunts that ended successfully. As you progress through the remainder of the book, I'll return to elements of these two hunts as illustrations. Hopefully, I communicated the excitement of hunting with a crossbow on our most popular and populous game animal, and you are anxious to turn the page.

Chapter 2

Which Bow Is for You? A Look at Five Great Choices

Don't skimp on cheap equipment. You will be hunting for trophy animals, and you want your gear to perform well under difficult circumstances.

"*Crossbow Magazine* is released five times per year, with fifty thousand annual subscriptions," says publisher Todd Bromley. "We've been around since 2011, and our numbers keep growing each year. The magazine started as print, and now we have online issues as well, at www.crossbowmagazine.com."

Crossbow Magazine is the largest magazine in the world dedicated to crossbows, and Bromley wears many hats in the production of the periodical. As an information source, he tries to handle questions on a regular basis from subscribers and readers online. In many ways, he's a publishing jack-of-all-trades and sometimes takes on "too much," he says with a laugh. "It's a bit overwhelming."

As a key information source, one would expect that he answers many questions, as readers are anxious for crossbow knowledge. "Generally, people don't know about crossbows," Bromley says.

Their first question is usually, 'What crossbow should I buy?' They often go in blind and buy the cheapest model, which isn't the best idea. A $200 crossbow may only last a year if you are lucky. I try to find out what their budget is and where they will hunt. Even for those who have a healthy budget, they don't want to spend the money. I try to steer them into bows in the $300–500 range. Cheap bows may last a week and have no customer service, and a lot of the overseas stuff doesn't stand up.

Since crossbow stores are not that abundant, Bromley suggests newcomers go to a box store like Dick's, Cabela's, or the like, where they can get their hands on a bow and shoot it. Then they should buy something they find they can really shoot well, or maybe find it cheaper online or begin with a used bow in decent shape. "The key is to get a lot of bows into your hands and shoot them. Most newcomers have no experience and find a bow that is too heavy, too loud, or they just don't like it."

GOT THE BOW: NOW WHAT?

Once customers settle on a bow, next they want arrows. "Do I need custom arrows, or are the ones at the store OK?" is a common question, according to Bromley.

Crossbow Magazine reaches fifty thousand readers each year and reviews a host of crossbow gear and hunting tactics. The author is featured in this edition.

"I recommend they go to a pro shop where they will receive arrows spined properly and according to the manufacturer's specifications," he says. He finds that most customers are good to go from there on, and a quality bow will last for several years.

Broadheads

Few things in bowhunting are more controversial or opinion-driven than identifying the "best" broadhead. Bromley has his own personal preferences, but he usually recommends expandables, especially for newer hunters. They require less maintenance and usually hit point-of-aim. A quality broadhead target is the next recommendation, so archers can experiment with what types of broadheads fly best from their equipment.

Bromley finds a troubling theme among new crossbow shooters. "They want two big things: speed and distance," he says. "They want to shoot 1,000 mph and launch a mile-and-a-half," he adds with a laugh. "These are usually hunters who don't have the bowhunter mentality, and I urge them to keep their shots close, control human scent, and not take shots out past thirty yards. They want fast, fast, fast, and the same is true on the vertical side." Bromley finds that speeds of 330–350 fps represent the best tunable range. At this speed, vibration is managed, arrows are more easily pulled from targets, and equipment seems to function better.

Bolts or Arrows?

One quirky term among crossbows is the word for the ammo used. Do they shoot a bolt or an arrow? During the Middle Ages, bolts were made of metal to pierce armor. Arrows have vanes or feathers. So today's "bolt" is really a short, stout arrow.

Bromley believes that crossbows are very basic and much easier to master than vertical bows.

You can practice a couple of days and become very proficient, very quickly. Some guys are

New crossbow readers will have many questions about gear, especially broadheads. Normally, mechanical heads, as shown, are a good option for powerful bows.

getting technical and breaking down arrows and tweaking crossbows, yet crossbows work simply, and there's not much to play with. Vertical-bow shooters feel they have reached mastery when they can hold a three-inch group at twenty yards, while most of today's crossbows will do that, or even better.

This year's bows have just been introduced, but they may not be at your dealer's just yet, so here's an overview of the latest brands in crossbows and a few words about each. As you would expect, each manufacturer offers glowing accolades about how their new product is the buzzword in horizontal archery. Before getting to the details about the various brands, I'd like to introduce a young man from Africa, a child really, and tell his story. Do you need the fastest, highest poundage, most whiz-bang bow to succeed? Meet Connor and his amazing accomplishment:

"The hand that rocks the cradle (and cocks the crossbow) rules the world." OK, maybe that's a stretch, yet the phrase emphasizes the importance of introducing the enjoyment of shooting and hunting at an early age. Young Connor was barely walking when his father, Steve, bought him a toy crossbow, a device the youngster quickly mastered. Perhaps Connor had archery in his DNA; he was the offspring of one of Africa's most successful archers. By age thirty Steve Kobrine had taken all twenty-nine species, including the Big Five, with stick and string.

The terms "bolts" and "arrows" are often used interchangeably, although crossbow bolts are shorter and stiffer than compound bow arrows.

Kobrine owned a five-thousand-acre game ranch and culled animals with a bow, such that Connor learned to follow blood trails practically from the time he could walk. As Connor's fourth birthday approached, he began asking his dad when he could shoot an animal with his crossbow.

Impressed with Connor's abilities to shoot the toy bow and rubber-tipped arrows, Steve bought a more advanced toy crossbow and crafted a sturdy arrow and small broad-head. He tweaked the string, arrows, and broadhead until he felt confident the shaft would penetrate well. After practicing on life-size, paper targets, Steve believed Connor was ready, and they sneaked within ten yards of a nyala bull. Connor aimed carefully and squeezed the trigger, and the arrow penetrated deeply into the crease behind the shoulder, a shot placement he and his dad had discussed many times. The broadhead entered the heart and the animal expired in a matter of seconds. Talk about a celebration! It was hard to tell who was happier, father or son!

I tell this story to celebrate the success of a young archer and to temper the lust that the crossbow fraternity has for speed and power. Certainly, today's modern bows are marvels of engineering, yet Connor's tale should help you wade through the hype and make better, informed choices.

FIVE BRANDS PERSONALLY TESTED

Five manufacturers were kind enough to physically loan equipment for field tests, and they have been used in the field extensively, especially on the African crossbow safari that you'll read about later. The benefit of having a bow to shoot and test is the depth of understanding you can achieve and the ability to discern hyperbole from actual performance.

Excalibur Micro 335

I own three Excalibur bows: the powerful Matrix 406, the modest Matrix 310, and the new, current model, the Micro 335. In some ways this is like the "three bears" bows, with the 406 by far the most powerful. Yet the 310 is anything but a baby bear.

Excalibur bows are recurve models by design. The "wheelless" engineering is much simpler and far more durable than bows with compound components. The Matrix 310 mentioned above shot as fast as any compound bow I can draw, yet was so durable it didn't have an anti-dry fire device. The company won't say this, but I suspect it's because the bow has been fired repeatedly without an arrow and suffered no damage.

Excalibur bows have other advantages. They all can have their draw relaxed by using a cocking rope. Instructions for this method are widely available on YouTube and explained in the operator's manual. In addition, changing the string on the Excalibur is easy, allowing you to always carry an extra string in case a broadhead inadvertently slices the string or there is some other calamity in the field. You don't need to drive to a professional shop; you can do it in minutes almost anywhere.

The Micro 335 is a very light and compact model that's ideal for all types of hunting. I first fired it at the Archery Trade Association (ATA) Show and got a perfect Robin Hood on the first shot. Excalibur offers bolts that are shorter and lighter than most models, but recommends 150-grain field tips for better Front of Center (FOC) balance and better accuracy. The Diablo bolts have two-inch vanes and flat nocks, allowing them to be loaded quickly, without regard to cock-feather orientation. The smaller vanes help reduce drag and maintain velocity at longer distances.

The Micro 335 is designed for sixteen-inch arrows, but I've fired twenty-inch aluminum shafts with full fletching, and the bow is so versatile that they shoot the same horizontally, with only the vertical impact changing due to increased arrow weight. The bow is very versatile and shoots a variety of broadheads and arrow configurations with ease.

A friend bought one as a Christmas present for his ten-year-old son. The lad was jubilant about the gift on Christmas morning, despite the fact that neither he nor his dad had shot a crossbow before. Dad was an experienced rifle hunter, and he set up a 3-D target for his son to practice. Within a few days, the lad was putting arrows precisely behind the shoulder of the target, and the weekend after the holidays, father and son went hunting. The second night out, a buck came by at twenty-five yards, and the new hunter put the 150-grain broadhead exactly in the boiler room. It was not just any buck, but a solid eight-point, which made for quite the celebration.

The Excalibur Micro 335 is light, compact, and very fast for its size.

Draw Weight 200 lbs.
Power Stroke 10.87"
Mass Weight 5.1 lbs.
Arrow Length 18"
Arrow Weight 350 Grain Min.
Trigger Pull Appx. 3 lbs.

The Matrix 310 is a fast-shooting, extremely durable crossbow.

The new Micro 335 is ideal for hunting in ground blinds or tight cover. It's quiet, smooth to shoot, accurate, and like all Excalibur crossbows, it's built to weather the very toughest hunting conditions for decades of flawless service. The Micro features the new Feather-Lite skeletonized stock, including rubber grip inserts for extra control and feel, and it comes with an ambidextrous cheekpiece and an oversized trigger guard for cold weather hunting. MSRP $899. www.excaliburcrossbow.com.

Mission

If you are new to archery, the Mission brand may be new to you, but you've probably heard of Mathews, one of the most innovative and effective archery companies in the world. Mathews bows are of excellent quality, yet they also come with a high-end price, and so the Mission line was created to provide archery gear in the mid-price range.

As an example, my new Mission Sniper Lite costs just $699 as a full kit (arrows, quiver, scope, the works), which is half the price of some of its competitors. After shooting a Mission for two seasons, they deliver maximum performance without expensive bells and whistles.

Just as Excalibur bows don't have wheels, Mission bows don't have cocking stirrups. At first this may seem impractical, yet the bows have been engineered to place your left or right foot on a riser at the base of the limbs, giving you much better leverage when cocking the bow. I'm of average height, and having the anchor foot low to the ground allows the bow to be cocked using leg muscles as well as force from my back and

The Mission Sniper Lite offers a combination of speed and light weight.

Mission bows are mid-priced but built with the quality and reputation of the Mathews brand. They perform well at a modest price.

shoulders. I can cock the bow with one quick, easy upward motion and readily hear the bow kick the safety from "fire" onto "safe."

As you will see, the Sniper Lite has a tactical look with the stock vented to reduce weight and help the bow to be more maneuverable. The fore-end grip has an excellent shield to protect your hand or fingers from being caught by the string. The longer frame of the bow has sling-swivel studs at each end so that the bow carries easily with a standard rifle or shotgun strap.

I've hunted two elk seasons in Wyoming with the bow and found it to be very durable and versatile. Each morning I'd leave my tent in the dark, climb a thousand feet toward likely ambush spots, and cock the bow when shooting light arrived. I'd hunt with it the rest of the day and return to camp, where I fired the bow. Every time, the scope and bow performed exactly on target. Getting close to an elk was a different matter, yet I hunted on my own without a guide and couldn't blame the bow for lack of opportunity.

Although the Mission MX didn't account for an elk, it was a magic charm on whitetail deer, taking two big bucks, mentioned previously, in firearm season. It's an excellent bow at a very reasonable price. www.missionarchery.com.

TenPoint/Horton

My first Wyoming elk hunt introduced me to the TenPoint brand, which includes Horton and Wicked Ridge. TenPoints are clearly the Cadillac of crossbows, and I was privileged to use them in a variety of hunting situations. Shooters can opt for the most unique cocking systems in the industry with the TenPoint and Horton lines.

TenPoint carries a bit of status factor, and some of my physician friends often remark about their TenPoint crossbows with a bit of superiority. In many ways, TenPoint has built its brand's prestigious recognition by marketing and supporting the industry. TenPoint doesn't just manufacture a product; they support the industry by lobbying for increased hunting opportunities and the overall good of the sport. TenPoint was the only crossbow manufacturer represented at the Safari Club International Convention in a recent year. With a gathering of thousands of the world's most successful hunters, they alone spoke up for horizontal hunters. Barb Terry represented the company. Ms. Terry is a retired US Army Captain and gives seminars across the country on crossbow safety and how to shoot bows effectively.

Barb Terry and Dave Robb posted information on TenPoint's patent-driven development on www.bowhunting.com. This innovation gives them a leg up on the competition. Here's what they posted:

Patented Trigger Technology

TenPoint has two triggers designed to match up with the performance characteristics of the models that use them. Our premium bow models (the Phantom CLS, Pro Elite HP, and Blazer HP) feature the patented 3½-pound machined PowerTouch trigger, made with MIM (Metal Injection Molded) action components. It is the finest crossbow trigger made today.

The remaining models are equipped with our innovative five-pound RollerTouch trigger (patent pending). The RollerTouch features a double-roller system installed at the top of the trigger finger that allows the finger to roll off the string latch's sear surface rather than to slide off. This rolling action significantly reduces the friction between the two parts.

Patented DFI (Dry-Fire Inhibitor)

In 1996, TenPoint introduced the DFI, which prevents dry firing our crossbows when no arrow is loaded on the flight deck. The addition of this technology to our entire crossbow lineup has virtually eliminated the potentially severe damage and/or injury that can be caused by a dry fire.

Patented ACUdraw and Patented ACUdraw 50

TenPoint's convenient and user-friendly cocking aids have made our models the crossbows of choice for those who can not or do not wish to manually load today's heavier draw weights. Compare TenPoint's ACUdraw or ACUdraw 50 to other cocking aides available today. Lightweight and fully integrated into the butt stock, they have no dangling parts. They load the crossbow consistently every time, and they auto-retract after each use. Check pages 24 and 25 of our catalog for details.

The Horton Legend Ultra Lite offers special cocking options, such as the ACUdraw and ACUdraw 50. It cocks easily and has special hand protection on the fore-end.

Patent Pending GripSafety

Installed in the foregrip of all TenPoint models with PowerTouch triggers, the GripSafety prevents pulling the trigger without first depressing and holding this secondary safety in place with your foregrip thumb. It helps prevent potentially severe injury by keeping thumbs and fingers in proper position on the foregrip and below the barrel's flight deck. Installed on a standard basis for right-handed shooters, left-handed installation is available at no charge when placing a new bow order.

Limb Pocket Technology

In 2004 we introduced the OTT (Over-the-Top) limb-pocket suspension system to our TenPoint Series models. Using Dupont Zytel suspension pads to lift and separate the limbs, this technology isolates the limbs from the riser and then securely captures the entire assembly with a machined aluminum outer-limb pocket. The OTT system dramatically increases limb stability and slashes noise and vibration levels by 50 percent.

As you will read later in the book, crossbows have been successfully used on animals much larger than whitetail deer.

Our 6 Point Series models (Slider and Pro Slider) are equipped with an equally effective and innovative Complete Capture limb-pocket suspension system. First, a polypropylene sleeve cushion fits securely inside the machined aluminum limb pocket or glove. The limbs slip inside the cushion, and the Complete Capture assembly lodges securely on the riser's custom-machined surface grid, where it is bolted in place. The end result is an ultra-secure and remarkably quiet system, which isolates the limbs from any contact with metal parts.

Limb Technology

TenPoint now offers four limb configurations specifically designed for optimum performance on the models that use them: TL-4 Limbs

TenPoint purchased Horton, and the company has merged many of the most popular features into the Horton line.

for 165-pound models, HL Limbs for 175-pound models, ST Limbs for the Pro Elite HP, and the new twelve-inch, 185-pound IsoTaper Limbs (patent pending), featured on our new Phantom CLS model. With a performance-matched limb for each crossbow design, combined with a performance-matched trigger, you can count on consistently superior accuracy, durability, and dependability up and down the entire lineup.

Barrel Technology

The TenPoint Series' ACRA-ANGLE and the 6 Point Series' UL TriLoc barrels are the key to the unparalleled shooting accuracy of TenPoint crossbows. Both are designed to allow shooters to load the bowstring with their hands resting against the barrel, thereby promoting accurate loading, which is essential to crossbow shooting accuracy. And both are designed to create arrow-launching platforms with unsurpassed dimensional integrity for accurate, repeatable arrow flight.

HP and MR Cam Stability Bushings

TenPoint's new Cam Stability Bushings, while simple in concept, perform several important functions. First, they provide an ultra-stable sleeve to support and stabilize the axles. Second, they help eliminate wheel lean when loading the crossbow. And third, they help establish precise string tension on the barrel surface, to promote accurate arrow flight and to reduce serving wear.

Horton now fills the mid-price line under the TenPoint brand. When the Horton brand was sold to TenPoint, it had many loyal followers who wondered what the new parent company would do. I learned that answer firsthand with the test of Horton's Legend Ultra Lite compound crossbow. Specs included 175-pound draw weight, 330 fps arrow speed resulting in just under 100 foot-pounds of kinetic energy, with a price point of $919.00. It also includes Horton's new ABX (Adjustable Bullpup Crossbow) stock for personalized comfort and handling.

Some of the most beneficial elements of TenPoint crossbows are the built-in cocking systems mentioned above: the ACUdraw and the ACUdraw 50. The ACUdraw consists of a cranking system that allows the heavy bow-draw weight to reach full cock with the turn of a crank. Best of all, the crank nests into the stock so that you don't have to fumble through your pockets or backpack to find it. Cranking the bow makes a clicking sound, so you will want to cock your bow before encountering game, but I've hiked all day with the cocked bow on my back without worry. The solid safety secures the

This monster 8-pointer fell to a perfectly made shot from a TenPoint crossbow.

bow against accidental firing, and of course, it should always be unloaded while hiking.

The ACUdraw 50 device uses a standard cocking rope, but the handles of the rope and the cord retract into the butt of the stock. The device uses magnets so the handle and hooks fit snugly against the stock. This allows you to shoot and recock the bow in seconds, potentially getting a second shot at game. The more time you spend with crossbows, the greater the appreciation for this cocking benefit. You'll never forget the rope again; you'll always know where it is. www.tenpointcrossbows.com.

The ACUrope is a handy cocking device for any bow. It uses magnets to keep the device in a pocket-size package.

Barnett

This line offers three engineering options: CarbonLite models, Core models, and those with reverse limbs. Variety is the key to this line, which offers more than two dozen models with a wide range of features. The Razr variations offer arrow speeds from 300–400 fps, giving all the gusto needed for those who love speed. Of the carbon models, the Razr is one of the newest and features a 43 percent lighter riser with their patented carbon riser technology. Other features include:

*   Finger reminders and pass-through foregrip
*   CNC machined ⅞" Picatinny rail
*   Custom composite laminated limbs
*   Retractable underarm support
*   Integrated skinning knife
*   Adjustable butt pad
*   String suppressors
*   20" axle to axle

Core Models include the Brotherhood with these features:

*   Magnesium STR riser
*   Finger reminders and pass-through foregrip

Horton's new ABX has an adjustable stock.

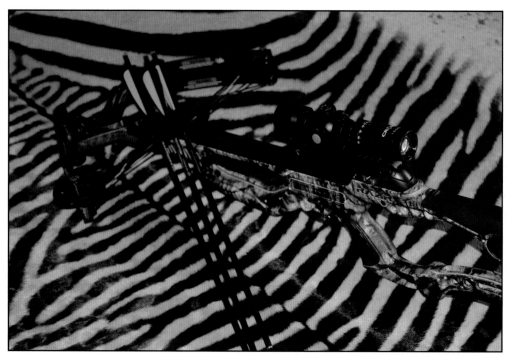

Shown is the new Razr, one of Barnett's hottest bows.

- CNC machined ⅞" Picatinny rail
- Lightweight composite stock
- Crosswire string and cable system
- High-definition camo finish
- 19" axle to axle

If you want a crossbow that is suited to your build, strengths, and personal needs, Barnett makes a model that will fit you like a tailored suit. While some companies manufacture one or just a few models, Barnett builds dozens. Regardless of age, strength, or physical status, researching on their website will scratch your itch.

The reverse-limb models are ideal for tree stand hunting, since the limbs become very compact and work very well in tight spaces. These bows use a special cocking rope with a "dead sled" attachment that allows the string to be drawn in at a sharp angle, simplifying a process that would be very difficult if hand cocking. www.barnettcrossbows.com.

PSE TAC Elite and RDX 365 Dream Season

If you like tactical firearms, you'll love the Elite, which features a fully adjustable stock and a crisp trigger. The PSE TAC Elite takes the original TAC 15i design to a whole new level and has been designed to be more accurate, more efficient, and more durable than ever before!

This bow is bigger and badder than the competition, as the numbers below will show. It has the longest power stroke, shoots longer bolts, and has all the feel of a tactical firearm.

Speed	405–395 fps (425-grain arrow)
Kinetic Energy	155 foot-pounds (425-grain arrow)
Peak Weight	150 lbs.
Overall Width	22" (measured from cam-to-cam)
Axle to Axle	17" at brace
Powerstroke	17-¼"
Finish	Hard anodized aluminum for maximum durability
Mass Weight	9 lbs.
Length	41-½"–45"

PSE has teamed with Drury Outdoors to deliver the RDX 365 Dream Season, built on an independent, machined aluminum barrel and composite stock that are mounted together to create a well-balanced, accurate shot. The field-serviceable RDX also features a reverse-draw cam system and a crisp trigger with a three-pound pull that fires the crossbow at an amazing 365 fps.

RDX packages include:

- String stops
- 3x32 scope with illuminated reticles
- Anti-dry fire & auto safety trigger (three-pound pull)
- Five-bolt quiver
- Three 20" Charger carbon bolts
- Three 85-grain bullet points
- Sling
- Cocking rope
- Rail lube
- Foot stirrup

I've had occasion to hunt with the Drury's over the years, so their Dream Season model had a special attraction. I'm field testing a Vortex scope and mounted the two together, which gave the bow a sniper look. The scope is designed to shoot accurately

PSE has teamed up with the Drury brothers for their signature Dream Season model.

out to seventy yards and includes a tactical turret, where you range a target, dial the scope to that distance and hold "dead-on."

My one caution with the list of products would be to change the 85-grain target points, since bolts usually fly better with a heavier 125-grain head. This provides a better FOC and usually tighter groups. Also, the Picatinny rail on the Dream Season is sensitive to abuse. I had one bow tip over, and the rail changed the impact of the scope. Mount your scope to the rear of the rail to avoid this issue. www.pse-archery.com.

Chapter 3

Crossbow Myths and Misconceptions

Crossbows may have some of the same parts as rifles, but they shoot very
differently. There's little comparison between a rifle cartridge and an arrow.

Crossbows are the fastest grow segment of the outdoor hunting market, yet along with
increased interest comes a host of myths and misconceptions. Here's a look at eleven
rumors, taken with the old Dragnet TV approach: "Just the facts."

Despite a rise in popularity, crossbows are still controversial in many communities.
To help support the sport, here are eleven common misconceptions that complicate
outdoor enjoyment. They won't solve the dilemma of which broadhead or bow is best,
but they will keep your facts on target with reality. See if you agree.

1. Crossbows shoot like rifles.

Crossbows have similar characteristics to rifles, including a stock, forend, safety, trigger,
and often a scope. However, the comparison ends when the trigger is pulled. A .30-06
deer bullet weighs about 160 grains and travels at nearly three thousand fps. It strikes
with such force that fluids in the animal's body respond to hydrostatic shock, which may

drop the animal in its tracks. A crossbow shoots a 400-grain arrow one-ninth as fast, so it falls rapidly and depends upon hemorrhaging for lethality.

If you are new to the world of crossbows, this comparison may seem plausible, especially as you raise the bow to your shoulder for the first time and look through a clear scope with a reticle. Is it accurate? Certainly. Does it shoulder like a rifle? You bet. However, terminal performance is dramatically different. Yet you can use a familiarity to firearms as a bonus. You already know about operating a safety, how to squeeze a trigger, and accuracy tips like using a rest, all skills that will help you quickly become proficient with your new bow.

Conclusion: Myth

2. Crossbows can kill a deer at one hundred yards and therefore should not be allowed in archery seasons.

Here's how this scenario plays out:

> Will a crossbow shoot an arrow 100 yards? *Yes*
> Will it kill a deer at 100 yards? *Possibly*
> Will a .270 Winchester shoot a bullet a mile? *Yes*
> Will it kill a deer at a mile? *Possibly*

Crossbow shooters may have more of an ethical challenge than compound shooters. Shooting a vertical bow takes consistent and extensive practice, and archers learn their effective range by trial and error. After you lose a few $20 arrows shooting at a fifty-yard target, the "error message" blinks in your mind. However, because a crossbow can be shot from a rest, it can fire very accurately at fifty to seventy-five yards. Of course, like in the illustrative conversation above, what will the game animal do while the arrow is in the air? Paper and 3-D targets don't "jump the string" (react to arrow-release noise) or take another step. Crossbow hunters must be accurate and keenly aware of animal behavior on even moderate-range shots. A well-placed arrow should have most animals dead on the ground in twenty seconds or less. When my time comes, I hope my maker is as compassionate.

Conclusion: Myth

Crossbows can shoot an arrow one hundred yards, but that doesn't mean it's ethical to shoot game animals at that distance.

3. Crossbows will deplete the deer herd, resulting in shorter archery seasons.

Michael Tonkovich, PhD and Wildlife Biologist for the Ohio Department of Natural Resources, conducted a study of Ohio's thirty-year history of crossbow use in general archery seasons and concluded:

> Contrary to predictions, legalization of the crossbow had no measurable impact on the deer resources in Ohio, and there is no reason to expect anything different in the future. Furthermore, I have no reason to believe that the crossbow has had a negative impact on any segment of our hunting population, including those initially opposed to the crossbow.

Maryland, a state with a brief history of crossbow use in general archery seasons, saw a one percent increase in archery harvest in 2011–2012 for both vertical and crossbow hunters. Obviously, this change had little impact on the deer herd. However, it may have had an impact on hunter-generated benefits.

Crossbows have had little impact on deer herds when used in archery seasons. Ohio has had equal opportunity hunting for decades, and archers are about evenly distributed between vertical and horizontal bows.

An increase in hunting license sales is a good thing on a wide variety of fronts. First, every bow, arrow, broadhead, and other hunting item incurs an 11 percent tax at the manufacturer's level, with the proceeds going to the states in the form of Pittman-Robinson funds. Many states use this money to fund their wildlife conservation and natural resource budgets.

Secondly, more licenses mean a greater diversity of hunters afield. If AARP was more positive toward hunters, you'd see a special discount at sporting goods stores. Young people are equally enthralled with archery and crossbows, thanks to the popularity of trendy movies where heroes use crossbows in their quests to save the world.

Finally, the more involved the general public becomes with hunting and wildlife, the more political power we enjoy. Organizations such as the Humane Society of America want hunting banned in all forms. Each year they spend millions of dollars trying to force their personal agendas on the American public, instead of saving shelter animals as their ads suggest. Some call it "pet porn," where donations are solicited to rescue an animal shown in misery. Yet the same organizations spend millions of dollars each year supporting anti-hunting projects.

Conclusion: Myth

4. Crossbows are more accurate than a compound bow.

In the accuracy department, crossbows have the advantage of optical sights and the ability to shoot from a rest. From an offhand position, an archer can shoot just as accurately with either type of bow. In quick-shooting situations, the vertical archer who practices a quick or instinctive release will score well on game, because he has the advantage of a second arrow. Crossbows usually have a trigger pull of four pounds or greater, which requires considerable practice to master and can make offhand shooting less accurate. Finally, the crossbow can be shot from a dead rest, even a gun rest, and therefore can be more accurate for the average shooter.

As you will see in this book, all archery is good, and there is no reason to polarize people into vertical and horizontal camps. I love shooting both kinds of bows, and do so to the best of my physical ability. Recurve and long bows are simpler and usually less expensive than a crossbow, so there is every reason to involve youngsters in the "mystical flight of the arrow," as Ted Nugent likes to say.

Conclusion: Misconception

Compound bows and crossbows are equally accurate. Crossbow users can sometimes use a rest, which is very helpful.

5. Crossbows are not appropriate for big game like elk.

Wyoming is the only state that allows the use of crossbows during big game archery seasons, so anecdotal evidence is sparse. Many proponents of big game hunting recommend heavy arrows, and the crossbow has an advantage here, since most bolts are at least 400 grains. Compounds and recurves are usually lighter and easier to carry in high-mountain situations than crossbows, and getting off a second shot is significantly easier and faster with a vertical bow. Archers in Africa must carry bows with kinetic energy of 100 foot-pounds or greater, and most crossbows meet—and many well exceed—this threshold.

Although Western outfitters and wildlife agencies have been slow to embrace crossbows in regular archery seasons, this has not been the case in South Africa. Former US Army Captain Ken Moody is an African outfitter and gleefully relates these two stories from his camp:

"LT, do you want to join our Africa safari next week?" his buddy asked over a friendly brew.

"Africa? Next week? But I've never hunted in my life," said the young man in total astonishment.

"One of our group had to cancel and you can take his place… it will be great fun."

No doubt the plane flight from Washington, D. C. to Johannesburg, South Africa was filled with hunting stories, as the group tried to school the adventurous LT and prepare him for what lay ahead. "The young man had never hunted, but he was quick to learn," said Ken Moody, who outfits safaris in several African countries. "We had an Excalibur crossbow in camp, and LT was quick to master it. By the second day, he too went out to a blind."

Moody caters to archers and has constructed blinds that attract animals to close range. Each enclosure is very dark so an archer can draw or raise a bow without spooking game. Also, each blind contains pictures of the various game species so hunters can make accurate identification, since first-time hunters often can't identify the more than two dozen species available.

"A big nyala bull drinks at this water hole every morning, but you want to think about shooting it, as it's the most expensive animal on the property," said Moody as he left LT in the blind just before daylight.

Good News . . . Bad News

Not long after, Moody's radio crackled. It was LT, who reported shooting a "big, shaggy goat." Moody knew of no such creatures, on his concession, but he soon greeted the excited hunter and followed a very short blood trail. "I've got good news and bad news,"

An African hunter who used a crossbow for the first time took a great nyala bull, similar to this trophy.

Crossbows are similar to muzzleloaders in that participants can enjoy special seasons. However, most archery seasons are much longer.

said Moody with a wry smile. "You just shot a very high-scoring nyala, and the hit was perfect. On the down side," he continued, "you've expended your entire package allotment."

Expensive or not, the new hunter was ecstatic with the trophy and soon made bank arrangements so that he could keep on hunting. He went on to take six animals with 100 percent recovery and had a fabulous time.

Moody had a similar experience with a group of bowhunters from Wisconsin. "Everybody's gear arrived but one," Moody remembers. "By the second day, the client was really discouraged, until I offered him the crossbow. As an experienced archer, he quickly grasped the crossbow concept and nailed bull's-eyes repeatedly on the camp target."

On the fourth day, the bow case finally arrived in camp, yet the crossbow convert was hooked. "He not only took a full bag of animals, but wanted to buy the bow, since it was his first safari," smiled Moody. "He stayed with the crossbow and really had a lot of fun."

Conclusion: Misconception

6. Crossbows are "the new muzzleloaders."

Just as "modern muzzle-loading" allowed center-fire rifle hunters to adopt a new hunting technology that was similar to their regular deer rifle, so too are center-fire folks taking to crossbows. Whereas a muzzleloader increased the average hunter's time afield by a week or two, the crossbow may provide months of extra hunting time, an exciting prospect. Muzzleloaders fire 300–500-grain bullets that are lethal and effective at two hundred yards, while the maximum range of many crossbows is fifty yards. A 500-grain muzzle-loading bullet travels at 2,000 fps, while a 500-grain arrow fired from a crossbow averages just beyond 300 fps, barely a comparison.

That said, many sporting men and women are taking up crossbows for the same reason as muzzle-loading hunters: extended seasons. Archery seasons in many states are quite long, with many beginning in early September and lasting until the end of January of the next year. In this way, hunters can enjoy the early season, rut, and postseason for greatly expanded quality time afield.

Conclusion: True

7. Crossbows make hunting easy.

Many hunters would argue that the "real hunting" occurs long before an arrow is launched. Pre-season scouting, selecting a stand, using calls effectively, practicing scent elimination, and woodsmanship are all important elements of hunting success that have little to do with arrow launch. We all know of a hunter who climbed into a stand and five minutes later a big buck walked by. Luck happens, yet most hunters make their own luck, whether with firearm, bow, or crossbow.

Can I say, "Amen!" to this myth? I've hunted the past three years in Wyoming, hoping for a shot at a bull elk. So far, twenty-one days spent camping, hiking, and climbing in the wilderness yielded one shot: a miss. However, those same twenty-one days were spent in a state of paradise and total enjoyment. Whether you are after whitetail deer, wild turkeys, or any other big game species, bowhunting is challenging. Wonderful, yet what a challenge.

Conclusion: Myth

8. Crossbows can be dangerous.

Crossbows can be more dangerous than a compound bow, since they store two- to three-times the energy of a sixty-pound (draw weight) compound. String slap on the arm is a common complaint among new vertical archers, especially with bows that have a short brace height. Crossbow shooters must be extremely careful of thumb placement, as firing a bow with a thumb on the rail can nearly sever it. For this reason, most modern crossbows have shields installed that make catching a thumb or fingers in the release nearly impossible. Also, a dry fire of a crossbow can destroy it, although anti-dry fire devices have solved this problem as well.

Since Ohio first legalized crossbows in 1976 through the 2003–04 season, there were nineteen accidents involving crossbows. Fifteen of these incidents were self-inflicted. There were twelve longbow incidents during the same period, with seven of these being self-inflicted. When this accident information is combined with the estimated number of hunting trips made by longbow and crossbow hunters in Ohio, the rate of accidents for both types of hunting implements is well below one incident per one million trips for each type of bow. Clearly, hunters are at far higher risk when driving to their hunting spots than when they are in the field with any type of archery equipment. (Source: Ortman, W. M.)

The biggest danger to most hunters, regardless of method, is falling from a tree stand. Be safe up there!

Conclusion: True

Crossbows can be dangerous, but following simple safety rules can make them safe and fun for people of any age.

9. A crossbow shoots an arrow faster and farther than a compound.

Power stroke is the key to understanding this misconception. Crossbows usually have a heavier draw weight than a compound bow; however, the power stroke of a horizontal bow is much shorter. If you take a compound bow with a thirty-inch draw and reduce the draw length to twenty-five inches, arrow speed is reduced because the power stroke of the bow is lowered by 15 percent. For this reason, a 150-pound crossbow with a twelve-inch power stroke may shoot a 400-grain arrow at the same speed as a sixty-pound compound bow with a twenty-eight-inch draw length.

This topic will be discussed at length in later chapters, yet it suffices to not pit crossbow hunters against vertical hunters. If you prepare ethically for the hunting season, you will learn your effective range for accuracy and the penetrating power of your bow. If you can shoot an arrow with a broadhead and have difficulty removing it from a foam target, you have the energy to kill a deer at that distance. We'll cover arrows, broadheads, and effective range in later chapters.

Conclusion: Doesn't matter

10. Crossbows are loud on release and complicated to maintain.

When an arrow is launched from any type of bow, the stored energy in the limbs passes into the arrow. Greater stored energy leads to greater vibration and can lead to a louder

Crossbows and compounds can shoot arrows at blistering speeds. Although the draw weight of a compound is usually less than a crossbow, its power stroke is much longer.

release and excessive vibration. Crossbows can be louder than compounds. However, using a significantly heavier arrow along with vibration-reducing aides such as those offered by LimbSaver can quiet the release. Crossbows require modest lubrication of the rail, and string wax, as do compound and recurve bows.

Alex Shifler is a recently-married man with two small children and a challenging job—not a situation that allows for extensive archery practice. However, his uncle Steve had an Excalibur crossbow that was about fifteen years old. Alex took the bow to an archery pro-shop, where they replaced the string. After a few brief practice sessions, the young man shot a coyote at thirty-five yards while deer hunting. Not much in the venison department, but a thrilling trophy and a memorable hunt.

Conclusion: Semi-myth

11. Crossbows should only be used by the disabled.

Illinois allows anyone sixty-two years old or older to use a crossbow during archery seasons, whereas West Virginia requires a physician's statement that a person is basically incapable of drawing a bow. Crossbows are fun to shoot, and youngsters and non-archers

Crossbows can be used in a host of exciting hunts. Luckily, less-able hunters can take advantage of this resource.

are quickly brought into archery with initial success. State legislatures would be wise to follow the Illinois example, because senior citizens may have less keen eyesight, arthritis, or muscles issues that limit practicing with a compound. Because a person has the physical strength to draw a fifty-five-pound draw weight does not mean that he or she has the stamina to do so repeatedly and become an effective shot. A host of other health concerns can make traditional bowhunting difficult or impossible for seniors, while a modern crossbow allows them to stay in the game.

Conclusion: Don't knock it if you haven't tried it.

Chapter 4

Entering the Archery Arena: Firearms to Crossbows

Transitioning from firearms to crossbows is challenging, yet exciting. Prepare to experience many new things at close range.

Learning to bow hunt is a terrific idea. States like Iowa, Illinois, Pennsylvania, and New York offer about two weeks of firearm deer hunting, while archers in those same states enjoy bow hunting for months. Maryland, for example, allows an annual archery limit of two bucks and ten does September 8th through January 31st, making for nearly a 150-day season. Talk about opportunity!

A BOW THAT SHOOTS LIKE A GUN

This topic was touched upon in the last chapter, yet it warrants a closer look, especially for those individuals tackling archery gear for the first time. A crossbow requires many of the skills that rifle hunters already possess. The crossbow has a stock like a gun, a trigger like a gun, a scope or sight like a gun, and, at twenty yards, you put the crosshairs on the target and squeeze . . . like a gun. Crossbows are similar to center-fire rifles, yet they have important differences and limitations. First, crossbows are a short-range device with a practical hunting range of fifty yards, with some espousing a maximum range of thirty yards. You will see articles or videos where some crossbows shoot accurately at a hundred yards, yet so do compound bows in the hands of an expert archer. Crossbows shoot stout, heavy

A crossbow has elements of a center-fire rifle, yet the terminal velocity of its "ammo" is very different.

arrows that limit their effective range. Secondly, arrows don't kill like bullets. There is no hydrostatic shock, and an archer must be careful to place his arrow in the vitals of an animal where hemorrhaging caused by the broadhead will bring about a quick, humane demise.

Cocking is another "similar difference." Crossbows must be cocked with the safety in the "off" position. To cock your rifle, you cycle the bolt, lever, or hammer, but a crossbow must be physically cocked with your hands, a specialized rope, crank, or other accessory. Although a strong person can cock a bow with his hands, doing so tends to misalign the center of the string, and the bow will lose accuracy. Ropes require moderate arm and back strength, while cranks require little effort, yet take longer.

Once you load your crossbow with an arrow, you can remove the arrow, but un-cocking a compound crossbow is nearly impossible, and doing so with a recurve can be dangerous if done incorrectly. This problem may be resolved with future technology, but for now, you must fire an arrow to relax the bow limbs. Also, a "dry fire" (discharging the bow

Cocking a crossbow effectively and safely is an important skill best mastered before you leave the archery shop.

without an arrow) can be catastrophic and crack a limb or burst a cable. Most modern bows are equipped with an "anti-dry-fire" device to prevent this problem, yet it's one more way crossbows and guns differ.

Make practice fun, and include your whole family. Taking turns shooting a bow is lots of fun, and you can coach each other for improvement.

FUN AND EFFECTIVE PRACTICE

The simplicity of practice is a huge benefit to crossbows. Shooting your rifle requires a trip to the range, where you could wait in line or shoot at distances and targets that don't excite you. Archery is quite the opposite, since you can practice in your back yard or even a basement. "Know your backstop," as arrows can miss, pass through, or deflect, yet you'll quickly get on target and learn to vary your shooting stances and range. You should practice all of your traditional rifle stances, but be sure to practice offhand most often, since a deer at close range won't stand still for long. Crossbows often have greater penetration than compounds, yet many targets work well for both.

You'll begin with target points when practicing, but as the season draws near you need to confirm the impact of your hunting broadheads. Welcome to the world of controversy. If you think disagreement about .30-06 vs. .270 vs. AR is interesting, just wait until you ask for opinions on broadheads. Like belly buttons, everybody has one. Two main trains of thought involve "cut-on-contact" broadheads and "mechanical heads" that expand on impact. The former usually provides better penetration, but it may not impact at the same point as an arrow with a target point. The mechanical heads impact more consistently, but because they are mechanical, there is the possibility of failing to open on impact. Since crossbows have high impact energy, the mechanical heads should open, and they will fly more like your target points, in my humble opinion.

WHY I SWITCHED

I grew up as a rifle shooting fanatic. As a young farm boy, I didn't get to play team sports, so when the hay was made and the wheat harvested, I grabbed my .22 and went groundhog hunting. One summer I killed one hundred groundhogs, all at close range by spotting and stalking. At sixteen, I was legally old enough to hunt deer, and I loved it, except that our season offered just two Saturdays and seemed to be over in a heartbeat.

At age thirty, a work buddy introduced me to bowhunting, and I'll never forget that immersion in a world of deer hunting I'd never known before. The bow season opened on September 15th, and I got up early on the Labor Day holiday. I was at my hunting grounds at daylight, where I sneaked around and spotted bucks with velvet antlers in bachelor groups. Who knew? I scouted for deer trails and travel corridors and selected a stand that would offer a shot on opening day. Later, as the leaves turned and fell, I saw the emergence of rubs and the formation of scrapes, signs I'd always encountered during the rifle season, yet never as a work in progress. I became so confident that I set a six-point minimum for my first deer. But I quickly realized how difficult that would be.

On Thanksgiving morning, I climbed a mountain in the dark, shinnied up a tall poplar tree with a self-climbing stand, and as dawn broke I downed a spike buck at twenty yards. Despite the tiny antlers, it remains one of the most memorable hunts of my life. I had the entire thousand acres to myself. No pumpkin army to avoid, and my rifle tag was still valid later in the month.

The first time the author tried archery hunting, he was instantly hooked. It would be a few years before he killed a buck with a bow, but his time afield soared exponentially.

Don't leave the archery shop without all the gear you need. Rail lube will help preserve your strings and cables.

HOW TO GET STARTED

Buy your first crossbow like you would a quality rifle: at a local archery shop so you can test it before you leave. You'll need to tweak the scope at home, yet most bows are well sighted right out of the box. The shop staff can match the brand of bow and design to both your pocket book and physical size. Some bows take significant strength to cock, so a professional can assure you are well suited.

Don't overlook a used crossbow from a shop or a trusted friend. Like cars, some guys need to have the latest model each year, and they are willing to take a discount on the value of their current model to "trade up." The pro shop owner can assure that there are no cracks in the limbs, frayed strings or cables, or any faults in other things that may wear on a bow.

Don't leave the shop without at least half a dozen bolts (arrows), target points, rail lube, sling, and a target. This way, you can bring your bow home, zero the scope, and instantly have fun. A soft carrying case is handy, but not necessary. Manufacturers list their suggested bolt length, weight, and nock configuration in the owner's manual and online. Previously, flat nocks have been adequate, yet manufacturers have recently moved to a nocking system similar to traditional arrows, where the nock "captures" the string. Mission recommends half-moon (concave) nocks, while TenPoint offers the Omni-Nock that protects against a misfire, with the string launching the arrow but pushing over or under the nock. This would put stress on the bow and cause erratic arrow flight. If this occurs, the fletching on the arrow gets a "bacon-like" look that's wavy and inappropriate to shoot again.

Targets are worth a special mention, as you will need more than one. Your first target should be a bag type. These stop arrows very well and usually allow bolts to be removed with little effort, but they are designed only for target points. Always use two hands to remove a bolt: one holding against the target face and the other holding the arrow next to the fletching and pulling straight back and perpendicular to the target face. Aluminum shafts can be easily bent if removal is done improperly. Eventually you'll need to test with broadheads, and a foam target is best for this purpose. Some are made especially to be shot with broadheads. A small "discharge target" is also great for unloading your bow after a hunt. Finally, you should practice on a 3-D deer target, whether it is one you purchase, a friend's, or an animal replica at a range. Learning the anatomy of your big game species is a must to be an ethical hunter.

SKILLS TO BECOME AN ARCHER

Once you've purchased crossbow gear and learned to use it, the next step is preparing for the season. For a rifle hunter, this may sound like heresy, but many bowhunters don't go hunting on opening day. They may have months to hunt and want conditions to be right before they begin. Perhaps they don't like warm weather, haven't scouted sufficiently, or would prefer to wait until the rut kicks in, when the biggest bucks are most vulnerable.

Hunting with archery gear means getting close to game animals, usually with a tree stand or ground blind. You may be able to hunt from the same stands you used in rifle season if animals typically pass within thirty yards of that location. Or you could use observations from previous years to pinpoint a closer ambush spot.

As October turns to November, deer in the Northern Tier enter their mating phase, and bucks become much more active, indicating their presence by rubbing the bark from trees and making scrapes. Posting a tree stand downwind of a rub line or series of

Specialized equipment such as an Aimpoint scope can help you become a more effective shooter.

scrapes is an excellent tactic. Calls can greatly help you by luring deer close to your hiding place. Grunt calls often cause bucks to investigate, and doe calls can lure in roaming bucks.

Crossbow hunters have the advantage of being able to stop deer with a standard grunt call, a trick you should practice. Either use your voice to make a grunting *urp* or tuck a grunt call in the side of your mouth as you aim. Usually the sound of a grunt will stop a buck in its tracks.

Rattling and scent lures are two other successful rut tactics. Banging deer antlers together to simulate a buck fight has a low probability of success, yet it only has to work once. Estrous lures can scare does away, but one whiff may bring a buck directly to the spot. Many archers use non-threatening scents, such as raccoon urine, to cover their entrance trail to a stand or blind. You'll quickly learn that a deer's sense of smell is extremely keen, and avoiding detection requires a lot of gear, thought, and work.

SPECIAL GEAR TO BOOST SUCCESS

Judging distance with a .30-06 in a woodlot is often immaterial, but hitting a deer properly with a crossbow is very different, and you should know the range to the animal within a yard or two. Laser range finders are excellent for determining distance and teaching you to judge on your own. Whenever climbing into a blind or stand, buckle in and immediately range rocks, trees, and other reference points you can remember.

Watch archery videos and TV shows to hone your archery knowledge. Remember that many products sponsor the series, so take all claims with a grain of salt. Dart makes a wonderfully realistic video game in which you use your hunting gear to compete. Check their website to find local shops that offer a range, and team up with friends for the most fun and greatest challenge.

Trail cameras have revolutionized a hunter's ability to know the deer in a particular area. Whether you want a tender doe or a special big buck for the wall, placing cameras in likely crossing and congregation areas will give you pictures of animal movement day and night. Plus, you'll get a look at bears, coyotes, and other creatures in your hunting area.

Binoculars are ideal to identify deer and to enjoy your sit. Unlike rifle season, where you'll be posted for a few days, use your binoculars to scope out the creatures in a wide area. The magnification may allow you to pinpoint specific crossing points to help in relocating stands. They can also bring great enjoyment of nature, as you watch a squirrel eat a nut at close range or a hawk chase it around a tree.

In a nutshell, learning to hunt with a crossbow is an enjoyable and fulfilling experience. Once you become proficient and know your bow well, like with a good rifle, you can practice intermittently and concentrate on hunting through the greatly expanded season. If you hunt the same areas during firearm season, you'll have a much greater understanding of the area and the game it harbors, making that season more special as well.

Binoculars are an important bowhunting tool. Unlike hunting with firearms, you will see many animals that are out of range.

TEN TIPS TO GET STARTED

Crossbow hunting has many adventures, but they begin with the basic knowledge of gear and technique. Get the basics before you leave the shop.

1. **Take charge**. Cock the bow, load the arrow, and shoot a shaft or two before leaving the shop. Be sure you master the routine while someone is there to assist.

2. **Ask about dry fires**. It may not sound possible that you could shoot the bow without an arrow, but you will, and it's important to know how to correct that situation.

3. **Think service**. Buy string wax and rail lube so that your bow is well serviced. You'll also need an extra cocking rope or crank.

4. **Double-check safety**. Make triple sure that you hold the fore-end properly, with no possibility of thumb or finger contact. Like checking a firearm to see if it's loaded, make this a habit.

5. **Learn to shoot off-hand**. At close hunting range, you can quickly become proficient. Resting the bow can cause excessive vibration from the stand or possibly cause limb interference.

6.   **Cock in good light**. Don't cock your bow in a tree stand or in the dark. Use a pull-up rope to raise your cocked bow into your stand.

Learn to load and shoot your bow carefully. Developing good shooting habits will aid you in times of great excitement.

7.   **Buckle up**. With gun, bow, crossbow, or camera, always fasten your safety harness first.

8.   **Practice judging distance**. Pass time on the stand by mentally guessing distances. Develop a ten-yard mental picture, and then use it to estimate farther distances.

9.   **Learn animal anatomy**. Bulls-eyes on bag targets are great for developing accuracy and shooting routines, but anatomically correct 3-D targets will increase your lethality. Become a "heart-and-lung specialist."

10. **Walk before running**. Take a doe at the first opportunity. The venison is excellent, and it will allow you to develop confidence before the antler pressure arrives.

Bonus   **Have fun out there**. Pace yourself. Unlike firearm seasons, you may have months of hunting ahead, so enjoy your newly found outdoor recreation.

MORE ON THE SUBJECT: BULLETS TO CROSSBOWS

Crossbows are the perfect transition from center-fire hunting to the challenging, close-range action of bowhunting, and they offer a ticket to a world of outdoor adventure beyond your wildest dreams.

As a boy, hunting was a passion: quail, pheasants, wild turkeys, and especially deer. Yet seasons were short and passed in a few weekends. Then, a buddy introduced bowhunting, and my horizons expanded from weeks to months, with incredible action month after month. With almost no hunting pressure, every day afield seemed like opening day. Since then, I've taken bears, elk, antelope, mule deer, and other challenging creatures, thanks to liberal seasons and special opportunities offered only to archery hunters.

If you've never hunted early-season whitetails when antlers are fresh from velvet and bucks feed in predictable patterns, or watched a scrape line develop past your favorite stand as the rut approaches, or taken the western challenge of bugling elk, decoying antelope, or scouting monster muley bucks in bachelor groups, you are missing tremendous excitement and magazine-style hunting adventures. Mastering a traditional or compound bow takes dedication and moderate athletic ability, yet the advent of crossbows in archery seasons makes bowhunting attainable for those eight to eighty, tall, short, male, and female. If you can hunt with a rifle, you can hunt with a crossbow, and you'll soon learn why the forty-yard maximum range is a blessing rather than a handicap.

If you are an avid hunter, crossbow hunting will greatly expand your pleasure afield. It doesn't guarantee success, but opportunity abounds.

ELEPHANT GUNS FOR DEER

Center-fire bullets are loaded with powder and testosterone. Face it, for many of us, there is something very manlike about carrying a magnum rifle, even when a .30-30 will do the job. Macho men, take note: Crossbows are powerful. Really powerful. Many recurves and compound bows deliver about sixty foot-pounds of energy, sufficient to push an arrow through a deer's vitals and adequate for elk, bears, or possibly moose. A modern crossbow, however, can produce kinetic energy of one hundred foot-pounds or more, a level sufficient for Cape buffalo and elephant. Who knew?

The incredible stored energy of a crossbow can be both a benefit and a problem, as will be discussed in a moment. Yet when that kraken is unleashed and strikes an animal's vitals, the arrow and broadhead do their work quickly and with great lethality. Center-fire rifle users will enjoy some of the similarities crossbows have with hunting rifles, like a safety near the trigger, a trigger, a fore-end to hold and aim the device, a stock that fits the shoulder like a hunting piece, and most importantly, a scope that functions much like a hunting scope. Doug Mongon, my local pro-shop archery tuner, says a customer can walk into his shop and he'll have the person shooting a crossbow comfortably in about ten minutes.

Unleashing an arrow is much different than firing a rifle cartridge, yet the impact on the animal can be just as lethal.

With so many benefits, one might ask, "Where have crossbows been? Why weren't they popular previously, especially with the archery fraternity?" Ironically, the very fact that a crossbow is so simple to use can be threatening to dedicated archers who live to shoot a longbow, recurve, or compound. If crossbows were made legal in archery seasons, would the response be so great that seasons would be shortened and special hunts eliminated? These concerns still prevail in a number of states, but thanks to the prolific nature of whitetail deer, game departments welcome any means of controlling populations. The jury is still out on this issue, yet so far, legalization of crossbows has not negatively impacted special archery seasons.

TIPS FOR EFFECTIVE SHOOTING

Testing your compatibility to a crossbow is as easy as visiting a local pro-shop or sporting goods store. Unlike with a firearm, you don't need hearing protection, and you can usually shoot several models right in the store. If you buy one, there's no FFL (Federal Firearms License) or waiting period, so you can take it right home and start practicing. Many national brands have support videos and information online, and it's important to read the owner's manual thoroughly for peak performance.

Mongon sells and repairs hundreds of crossbows each year and sees the "need for repetition" to be the biggest challenge for gun-to-broadhead newbies. Archers know that arrows, broadheads, nocking points, release methods, etc., must be exactly the same for consistent performance, yet these may be unfamiliar

Your performance in the field will depend upon the quality of your gear and how well you can use it.

terms to rifle hunters. In a nutshell, here are a few of Mongon's pointers that he passes along to all new customers:

- Always use the same cocking device, usually a rope, so that the arrow seats consistently each time.
- Use the same arrows (bolts) for practice and hunting.

- Use mechanical broadheads for hunting, because they fly more consistently and impact the same as target points of the same weight.
- Select nocks (flat or crescent) recommended by the manufacturer, although Mongon prefers flat nocks.
- Recurve limbs are more durable and less complex for beginners.
- Check for tightness. The significant amount of stored energy creates vibration, which can cause bolts to loosen quickly. Always check for tightness before each hunt or practice session.
- Shoot at various distances to become accustomed to multiple aiming spots in the scope. A 400-grain arrow sighted at twenty yards requires a different sighting point for thirty yards. Practicing at forty yards tends to increase skill levels at shorter distances.

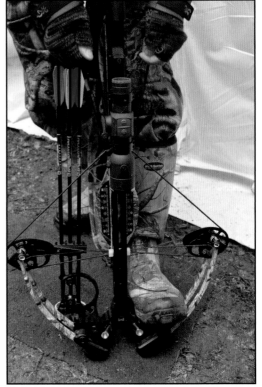

According to Doug Mongon, good performance begins with a consistent cock of the bow.

- Finally, practice realistically: offhand, down-angle, through a blind window, etc. Seeing game up close can cause nervous mistakes, so practice until you are confident of a perfect shot every time.

THINK SAFETY, LIKE A HANDGUN

Crossbows point like a rifle, yet the analogy to a standard handgun is a useful comparison. A crossbow with an arrow in place is "loaded" like a gun, and even with the safety on, you should never point toward a person or be in a vehicle. As with any form of hunting or shooting, always use common sense operating procedures.

Unlike a firearm, once cocked, crossbows cannot simply be "un-cocked." A compound bow can be brought to full draw and then let down with hand pressure. But crossbows have so much stored energy that you must shoot an arrow to relax the limbs. Dry firing (shooting the crossbow without an arrow) even once may break a string or crack a limb. For this reason, many models have an anti-dry-firing feature which will not allow the bow to fire without an arrow. It's a key safety element for you and the bow, but be sure you know how it works.

Crossbows point like a rifle, yet safety tips are more analogous to a handgun.

Tree stands are excellent locations to ambush whitetail deer, yet care must be taken. Many archers cock their bow on the ground (to avoid the prospect of falling). They then attach the bow to a pull-up rope and raise the bow after securing themselves with a safety harness. Once in the tree, they can pull up the bow and load an arrow. At the end of the day, the arrow is removed, the bow is lowered with the rope, and the archer climbs down. Once on the ground or back at camp, the bow should be unloaded into a discharge target, using a special discharge arrow or just an old non-hunting arrow.

When aiming from a tree, be aware of limb movement. If the bow limb rests against the tree, firing could push you off balance or knock the bow (and you) to the ground.

GETTING IT RIGHT: IMPORTANT CROSSBOW GEAR AND POINTERS

- Laser range finder: Knowing the exact distance is critical, and today's easy-to-use models give you an exact reading. Range in reference rocks and trees while you are waiting, so you will know the distance in advance.
- Carry extras: Stash an extra cocking rope, Allen wrench, string wax, and other backup gear in your coat or daypack.
- Buy a portable, quality crossbow target for practice and discharging at the end of the day. I take a practice shot, even if I have to do it using the headlights.
- Hunt with a buddy to hone your tracking skills: Arrow kills almost always require following a blood trail.
- Study deer anatomy: A double-lung hit is an archer's best shot.
- Read about the subject.
- Finally, join the Crossbow Hunters of America or other support group: Follow your bow company's comments online to get tips on gear and hunting strategies. Most of all, shoot and practice a lot. Crossbows are flat-out fun.

Chapter 5

Crossbow Safety: Don't Shoot Your Thumb Off

When that big buck comes along, have your safety and shooting habits well practiced so you make a quality, ethical shot.

The rub line that passed the stand was so hot, you could almost see smoke rising from the slash marks on trees at four inches in diameter. Dusk turned to darkness that first evening, and instead of lowering my gear, I left it in the blind where it would be safe and dry. The next morning, an hour after daylight, the whopper buck came ambling along as if sucked in by a Star Trek tractor beam. The beast had high points and three main beams (as I'd learn later). What a trophy!

With the buck at fifty yards, I lowered my binoculars and raised the crossbow, ready to shoot. He kept coming and stopped thirty yards away. This buck was dead, practically hanging on my wall, except that my scope was totally fogged. Not the inside, but the outside of the glass. I hastily rubbed the lens with my sleeve as the buck continued on its rutting trek. As it passed the blind window, I took a hasty shot, catching the edge of the opening and sending the bolt who knows where. The buck burst up the hill, looked as confused as I was befuddled, then continued on with not a hair out of place.

Talk about a BOO-BOO! I was sick, as much from the mental mistake as from the actual miss. Rule number one with a bow, rifle, or crossbow: As soon as you are securely belted in, simulate a shot. Pick up the bow from its hanger (if you use one), swing it through all shooting lanes, including hard right if you are right-handed. Work the safety; check the scope. Like a pilot approaching takeoff, be sure all systems are go. This works for ground blinds or just sitting on the ground. Since the limbs will burst forward, be sure that you have enough clearance that they can fly free. Also, you can help prime your shooting pump by anticipating the approach of game and making sure that you have your off shoulder (the arm holding the bow) facing in that direction. In this way the buck, elk, or bird can approach with quite a margin of error, and you'll still have an accurate shot.

I've been a bowhunter for forty years and hate to brag, but I've made some fantastic mistakes. I'm talking Pope & Young class, some even Boone & Crockett. I highlighted the first of the ten deadly slipups. Here's how to avoid nine more:

Whenever you begin a hunt, go through a series of safety checks, making sure that the safety works properly and that you have an arrow loaded in the bow.

PRACTICE REALISTICALLY

You may be able to Robin Hood an arrow at thirty yards from a solid rest, yet that's probably not the shot you'll get on a savvy buck. As the season draws near, replicate the hunting situation as much as possible, and practice that way: from a tree stand, out the window of a blind, or stalking. Practice shooting offhand on windy days, early in the morning with the sun in your eyes, and without a rest. Practice doesn't make perfect; realistic practice does. Rifle hunters always seek a rest since their game is often way out there. However, crossbow hunters usually get close shots, especially if you follow the tips in this book. For this reason, practice offhand and used Bob Foulkrod's approach ("Is the pin on the target?") to help maintain concentration.

Practice realistically, using a variety of positions. You can probably shoot more effectively offhand than you think.

GEAR UP

Always carry an extra cocking device, whether it's a crank or a rope, and know where you store it. It's really frustrating to walk an hour in the dark, finally reach your honey hole, and find you can't cock the bow. (Not that I'd know, of course.) Even if you can cock it by hand, using a rope makes for more accurate shots. Normally, I use the same backpack for all of my hunts and store specific gear in specific places. This helps me remember what I have and where it is, so that when my headlamp battery dies, as it often does, I can feel my way through the pack for replacements. The farther away you hunt from your camp or vehicle, the more important this becomes.

PRACTICE WITH BROADHEADS

Practice with broadheads to make sure your bolts fly true and strike point of aim. If your bolts impact the same with field points as they do with broadheads, practice with one of each, using the broadhead as the first shot. Any doubt about accuracy can deflate confidence and spoil the Moment of Truth. If you dislike shooting multiple bolts at one target, purchase a target with various shooting spots and fire one arrow at each. Always number your bolts so that you can identify one that flies poorly or won't group with the others. Sometimes you can fix this "flier" by rotating the nock so that the spine of the shaft matches the rest in your quiver.

MAINTAIN YOUR BOW

If you are a gun hunter just switching to a crossbow, learn about waxing strings and checking servings for wear. Check your owner's manual on how to lubricate the rail and inner parts with the appropriate lubricant. Crossbows generate significant vibration upon release, and screws can quickly work loose. Make a habit of checking these screws regularly, and carry an Allen wrench with your extra cocking device.

Traveling with a crossbow can put your strings and cables at risk, since a single nick or cut can ruin your day. Primos makes an excellent bow cover for compound bows that slips over the cams and protects the string. But unfortunately this doesn't exist for crossbows as of this writing. Covers will do the job, but they are often bulky and impracticable. One trick I've learned is to zip my outer jacket over the bow, using the limbs like a coat hanger. I can lay the bow in the back of the truck or walk through heavy brush with the

Your bow will come with safety warnings and directions. Read and follow them to the letter.

bow and strings padded and protected. Additionally, this prevents a bolt from being inadvertently pulled from the quiver.

USE A DISCHARGE TARGET

Discharge targets are inexpensive and will pay for themselves with the money saved on bolts and broadheads. Store one in your vehicle, tent, or camp. Use the discharge as a practice shot at the end of the day in your vehicle headlights. Aim carefully to show that your bow is still zeroed in. Listen to the sound of the discharge for any unusual vibrations. Pretend that those monster horns are right in your face, and then reaffirm your best trigger squeeze.

I took eight bolts on my last elk hunt, and by the time I went hunting, I was down

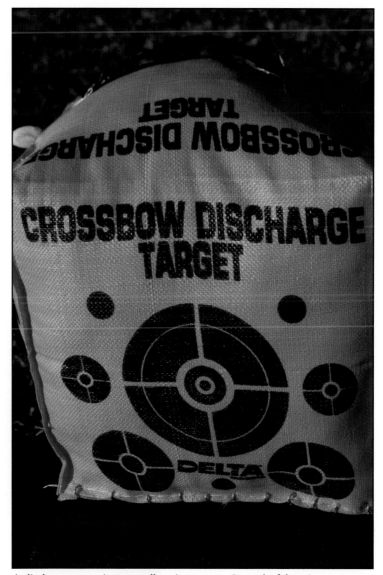

A discharge target is an excellent investment. Instead of shooting an arrow into the ground at the end of the hunt, this small target will serve that purpose.

to four. One of those I pulled from my quiver before I discovered the "coat cover" practice mentioned above. My discharge target was quite small and my scope was badly off target thanks to handling by the airlines. When shooting in the field, a crossbow miss often means a lost arrow, and that's exactly what happened. Luckily, I was only an hour from a competent pro shop where I bought more bolts and broadheads. But I still had to use them as backup for my normal gear. Some manufacturers make specialized discharge targets that are great for hunters who fly. But if you are driving to camp, pack a full size target, even if you have to tie it on top. You need to have confidence in your gear and a bull's-eye in the field goes a long way to bolstering that confidence.

DEAL WITH A LOCAL PRO SHOP

"The number one thing we see is people failing to use equipment consistently," says Doug Mongan of Keystone Sports. "They use an Easton bolt, a Carbon Express, and two different kinds of broadheads. We stress using the recommended nock: flat or moon, and even the recommended type of arrow." Buying gear on sale at various stores is a bad investment. Deal where you can get sage advice on your equipment and what works best, and get tips on improving performance. You may pay a little more for products than at a big box store, but the information you receive is priceless. Especially if you are a gun hunter, the advice you receive from an archery shop will be extremely important.

READ THE DIRECTIONS/WATCH THE VIDEO

I hate to read directions and often jump right into any minor assembly project, yet this is dangerous with crossbows. Unlike a compound bow that can slap you on the arm and leave a stinging, burning sensation, a crossbow can cut your thumb off if you handle it improperly. You won't read those exact words in the directions, yet ask any pro-shop owner about crossbow injuries and the answer will be graphic.

Fortunately, manufacturers have greatly reduced the probability of this happening by placing shields or large fore-ends on modern bows so that your thumb can't work itself into harm's way. Any time you work with a cocked crossbow, you want to be extremely careful.

Safety should begin before you open the box. Check out the safety features of your bow online as soon as you buy it, or before if the bow is ordered.

Most modern bows come with safety grips or shields to keep your fingers from the shooting rail. A bow can actually amputate your thumb if you handle the bow carelessly.

Most bows must be cocked in the "fire" position. The bow is then switched to "safe" after it is cocked. Make sure you know how this function works, and watch how the bow is cocked on an accompanying video. Or you can often go to YouTube and check for one. Some bows can be "un-cocked" using the cocking rope, but you must be extremely careful to follow the process correctly. Many bows store one hundred foot-pounds of energy or more, and you don't want that unleashed upon you.

COCK WITH CARE

Tree stands are one of the most dangerous elements of hunting, and we all know a deer hunter who has been crippled, injured, or worse from a tree stand fall. As if things aren't dicey enough in the tall timber, cocking your crossbow makes things extra dangerous.

Cock your crossbow in the best light possible. Ideally, do it in the hunting cabin in full light, and then carry the cocked bow to your stand. In some states, carrying a cocked bow in a vehicle may be illegal, so in this case park the rig and cock the bow in the headlights where you have good vision. Aside from being safer than cocking in the dark, you can be sure that the bow is cocked consistently to maintain accuracy.

Always carry the bow by the forend in a safe manner. Never put your fingers or hands on the shooting rail when the bow is cocked.

Once at your tree stand, cover the bow with your jacket and use a pull-up rope to raise the bow to the stand after you have your safety harness secured. Raise the bow stock-end first, so that you can handle it by the grip and not have your hands inside the tensioned limbs. I highly recommend a LifeLine, or similar device, that keeps you attached to a rope all the way up the tree. Once you are belted in, raise the bow carefully and make sure you can swing and sight the bow to your needs. Then load the bow and make sure the safety is on.

Crossbows sound so simple. You don't have to hold sixty pounds of draw force, a deer won't catch you pulling the arrow back and you can aim with a rifle stock and a scope. I mean, dude, what can go wrong?

If you will excuse the vernacular, even with all the advantages of today's high-tech equipment, "stuff" can still happen. After all, crossbows are machines with moving parts that hold and release a great deal of kinetic energy. The launch plane may be horizontal, but Murphy's Law still applies, and here are some prime examples:

TAKE THE RIGHT REST

A mature doe approached the elevated box stand from my right. That's a difficult shooting angle for me, because I'm right-handed. Several other deer were with the big doe, so I had to move very carefully. Eventually I was able to rest the forearm of the bow on the wooden rail of the stand. The rest was absolutely solid, and I had the crosshairs of the scope perfectly centered low on the deer's shoulder at thirty-one yards. When I released, the arrow seemed to fly high, and the deer didn't go down as expected. I found it a hundred yards away with a high, double-lung hit, and I instantly learned a lesson. Resting the bow against the stand made the vibration of release much louder, causing the deer to duck at the sound of the shot. From now on, I'll always rest the bow on my hand or something soft to help absorb vibration.

Shooting from a bench will enhance accuracy, yet your mind can wander with repetitive shots. Double-check that your hands are safe and that an arrow is loaded in the bow.

Chapter 6

How to Buy a Bow and Set It Up

Doug Mongon has fixed and set up hundreds of crossbows. A professional can diagnose a problem in a fraction of the time of the average shooter, and seeking their advice saves time and money.

Sports shows are great places to check out crossbows. Not only do manufacturers have knowledgeable staff to answer your questions, but you can often shoot the bow at their booth or on a range nearby. By this point in the book, you know that crossbows may look like rifles, but they don't shoot the same. And you know the various safety features and limitations of horizontal bows.

You met young Connor, who used a small bow modified by his dad to take down an African trophy antelope. Well now I'd like you to meet another father/son combination: Sawyer and his dad, Zane.

"Back in September Sawyer began asking for a crossbow for Christmas, and as the holidays grew nearer, he became more and more excited about the prospect," said Sawyer's father, Zane Rowe. Neither Sawyer nor Zane had shot a crossbow before, but the prospect looked like fun, and the bow could give the son a chance to hunt with his dad.

Excalibur had just introduced the Micro 335 model that was light, compact, and fit enough that even an elementary student could shoot it. Ten-year-old Sawyer made Santa's "nice list" and unwrapped the new bow on Christmas morning.

Over the next week, father and son shot each day, and the youngster soon demonstrated he was ready to hunt. Rowe had never shot a crossbow before, and seeing his son become proficient was really exciting. "We practiced on a 3-D target and he could put that bolt right behind the shoulder on every shot," said Dad.

The afternoon of January 2nd found father and son tucked away in a brushed-in blind, waiting for action. Half-an-hour before sunset, three does passed the blind, and

Though crossbows may look somewhat like rifles, their shooting capabilities are remarkably different.

Sawyer was about to take a shot when dad heard a grunting sound. "Hold on," he whispered. "I think I hear a buck."

Sawyer's eyes grew as big as saucers, as not just any antlered deer, but an eight-point buck came feeding along behind the does, twenty-five yards away. As the buck fed closer, Sawyer rested the Excalibur on a tripod shooting rest and concentrated on an exact spot. "Shoot when it looks good," whispered Dad, and within seconds an arrow launched.

The bolt flew so fast, they couldn't see the hit, so they decided to wait fifteen minutes before checking out the shot. They found blood and a trail that led toward an open field. Still, Dad suggested they go back home, get good lights, and return.

The double-lung hit left plenty of spore, and while Dad focused his attention on the blood trail, Sawyer's excitement ruled as he searched ahead with a beam of light. "There he is! There he is!" yelled the youngster excitedly, and he and his dad cautiously walked up on the deer, long since expired.

To bring the four-segmented whitetail season full circle, you only need to ask young Sawyer about his goal for next year. "I really want to take a buck while its horns are still in velvet," he says, showing quite some ambition for an eleven-year-old. Thus begins the last, and possibly the most exciting "period" of hunting. How many times will Sawyer relive that exciting hunt, talk about new stands for next fall, scour catalogs for the latest hunting gear, and dream of future hunts to come? The "touchdown" took four quarters, but a new hunter was born.

I love this story, because it illustrates how a crossbow can be a fast track to hunting for a youngster, and it shows how easy the transition can be. Zane stopped at a local sporting goods store, asked the clerk about a good bow for his young son and he and Santa made the purchase. Ironically, the same bow the archery shop

A crossbow can be shot safely by most youngsters with the proper supervision. Never allow a child to shoot a bow unsupervised.

recommended for this ten-year-old boy is the one I'm taking to Africa on safari. What a statement about the versatility of the sport!

MEET CHUCK MATASIC

I met Matasic, US Navy, (Retired) and President of Kodabow Crossbows, at the NRA Great American Outdoor Show in Harrisburg, Pennsylvania this past winter, and I found him to be very informative. I asked him specifically about steps a prospective buyer should take when selecting a bow, and he was eager to respond:

> We do a couple of things to help people select a bow. First, we suggest a recurve bow with no moving parts. Our bow appeals to folks who are into hunting and are looking for a couple of things. They want the ability to change their string in the field, and they want the ability to lower their bowstring after a hunt without firing the bow. Like if an outfitter is picking him up in an ATV. He doesn't want to shoot that arrow into the ground, and he will not talk the outfitter into bringing a heavy target with him. The hunter didn't shoot a bear, but he can let down the bow without shooting.
>
> A big question when you are buying a crossbow is, 'Does the bow have an anti-dry-fire device?' A better question is, 'Can you show me that the anti-dry fire is engaged?' When folks come by our booth, we change the string with them and show them how the anti-dry fire works by pulling the trigger on a fully cocked crossbow without an arrow.

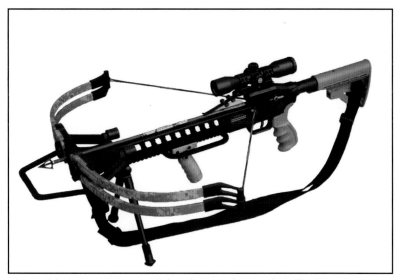

The Kodabow is a recurve model with many shooter-friendly characteristics.
Unlike most compound bows, the limbs can be relaxed without firing an arrow.

Right behind us is the picture of a fellow who shot a hippopotamus, about seven thousand pounds. Obviously he can choose any crossbow, but he picked a Kodabow. Even on dangerous game, we have an indicator that tells you the arrow is properly loaded. So you don't have to be putting your hand on the rail to make sure that the arrow is seated in the trigger group. If that hippo is coming toward you, you can look down and know that the bow is in a ready-to-go position.

One of the advantages of our bow and trigger group is we use a flat nock. The choices are flat nock and not flat. One of the advantages of the flat nock is that you can put it on the bow with three different orientations. If you look at our bow, you will see the arrows have three different colors: black, yellow, and orange. We tell the shooter to begin shooting black down and they will get a nice group. But there is often an arrow that doesn't join the group: a flier. Because you have a flat nock arrow, you are able to shoot in two other positions. And very often that arrow that didn't join the group does when you shoot it orange-down or yellow-down. This little feature is especially helpful if you are shooting fixed-blade broadheads, because they tend to go their own direction. Now you can tune that fixed blade broadhead, mark your vanes, and away you go.

We like a 3x scope on our bow. The 3x allows you to make a shot at fifty yards, which allows you to shoot out to fifty yards, where we draw the line. Ethically, you should have absolute confidence out to fifty yards. At the factory, we shoot every bow, and the individual gets the target with the bow. There are three shots with one arrow, and they should all be in the same hole. What we like to see new shooters do is use the same arrow, multiple times. They should put the arrow in the same hole. That tells us a couple of things. Number one, that they are cocking the bow properly. They are not putting more energy on one limb than the other, and the arrows are not moving left and right. Another thing we tell them: They are pulling the trigger correctly, not jumping on the trigger. Three or four arrows in the same hole give you a lot of confidence when you go hunting.

Tuning. There is lots of tuning on a compound bow. They start out new, and they move together. But as they wear or get dirt in them, one cam may move differently than the other, which will cause porpoising or fishtailing. On a recurve bow, when it's made well with the perfect till-ing, there is nothing you should do. Our bow only moves one way, and it will move that way the whole season. Next season, it will move the same. We have a recurve, but a split limb design so that when the string comes forward it doesn't hit anything. Solid limb bows, you hear a crack when the string hits the limbs.

The dampeners stop a lot of vibration. These decompress about 50 percent. I encourage everyone to read their instructional manuals, because every bow is built a little different.

POINTS OF CLARIFICATION

The purpose of this interview was to gain general points about selecting and setting up a crossbow. Matasic's remarks were very specific to Kodabow, however, which is under-standable since he is the president of the company. Still, a few of his recommendations contradict suggestions made in earlier chapters, and these need clarification. First, flat nocks are recommended by Kodabow and Excalibur, and they do provide the ability to rotate the shafts for more consistent arrow flight. The downside, however, is that the bowstring can slip under or over this type of nock, producing a misfire.

As part of my interview with Matasic, I asked to test one of his bows, but he was emphatic in his response. "If you want to test the bow, you should buy one." Unfortu-nately, buying dozens of crossbows was not an option in the course of writing of this book. I am most appreciative to the five manufacturers who loaned equipment for my hunts and tests.

Additionally, Matasic spoke to the ability to relax the draw of the Kodabow without discharging it. That certainly is a benefit of his bow, and he demonstrated it for me and other observers at the NRA show. Yes, it's easy if you do it often and correctly. However, the casual hunter or shooter can easily mix up the process and potentially unleash a lot of energy, possibly injuring him- or herself. That's why I shoot my bows at the end of each day, and like the ability to ensure that the bow is shooting on target and that there's no excessive noise or vibration.

I applaud the Kodabow stance on range. Fifty yards is about the maximum range for most crossbows. Not that an arrow launched farther won't kill an animal, but the force of gravity does ugly things to a heavy bolt, and critters just don't stand still very much. If an elk or deer takes half a step during launch, the arrow can move from the always-fatal zone to one that is very difficult to retrieve.

TEN POINTS TO CONSIDER

If you are considering the purchase of a first or newer crossbow, keep these ten points in mind. There is no one best bow, so the trick is to buy one that best fits your needs, dimensions, abilities, and goals. For sure, these are generalizations, but you need facts and, to some degree, my opinion on important factors. Here you go:

Both recurve and compound crossbows shoot well. Recurves are more difficult to cock, yet have fewer moving parts, which can make them more reliable in the field.

Recurve vs. Compound

I own each style of bow and took both kinds to Africa on safari. So one isn't necessarily superior over the other. Recurve limbs are simpler, may be easier to replace, and often can be relaxed with a cocking rope and the proper procedure. Recurve bows cock like a vertical recurve bow, such that the farther you pull the string back, the more force is required. If you are considering one, make sure you can cock it manually or purchase a cranking device. Recurve bows have fewer moving parts than

The cocking device of a bow is important. You must be able to cock your bow consistently for accuracy.

compounds and won't go out of tune, with one cam working differently than the other.

Compound crossbows, by contrast, are usually easier to cock since the cams reduce draw weight as the string reaches the cocking point. The Excalibur 365 is the maximum bow I can manually cock, while the Mission Micro, which shoots about the same speed, cocks easily. Compound bows can be more compact and store more energy, resulting in greater arrow speed from shorter limbs if speed is important to you.

Cocking Device

Crossbows cock differently—and with various devices—and this can be a deal breaker on some models. TenPoint has this process down to a science with their ACUdraw 50 and ACUdraw systems. The "50" uses a traditional cocking rope, yet the handles and the rope nest in the stock. In this way, you never have to wonder if you brought your cocking rope or where it is for a quick extra shot. Likewise, the crank handle for the ACUdraw system nests in the stock and is as easy as turning a crank.

Although easier to cock, the downside of a cranking system is failure. You need to follow the manufacturer's directions and realize that you are storing a lot of force in the process. And there is always a risk: Should the cranking system malfunction, how will you cock the bow?

Mission bows offer a standard cocking rope, yet they do not have a traditional cocking stirrup, which gives a much better cocking posture. I'm just 5'8" tall, and cocking a long bow with a stirrup forces me to pull the rope nearly to my chin, which is a poor mechanical advantage. Without the cocking stirrup, I can cock the Mission primarily with my leg muscles, and doing so is a breeze.

Anti-Dry-Fire Device

This feature is critical to safe shooting for you and your friends. At first blush, firing a crossbow without an arrow seems silly. Who would do that? Me, for one. While testing the bows in this book, on my second day, I dry fired a bow. I'm embarrassed to say that, yet I've done it twice in the past five years, and it only takes one dry fire to ruin a bow. Unless you are an extremely experienced shooter, purchasing a powerful bow without this feature may be a mistake.

All bows must be cocked with the safety in "fire" position. Most, but

Most modern compound crossbows have an anti-dry-fire device. Be sure you know how yours works and how to re-cock it after it engages.

not all, will audibly click from "fire" to "safe" when the bow reaches full cock. If your bow doesn't move to "safe" automatically, develop the habit of setting it there after every cock. Kodabows have a small device that tells the shooter the bolt is nocked correctly. It is one of the few models that have this feature.

The forend of a crossbow is a critical safety device. Make sure yours has a shield or opening to prevent hand trauma upon release.

Forend

Most modern bows have forends that prevent fingers and thumbs from getting accidentally caught in the bow string; however, older, used bows may not have these fore-ends. This is a critical safety issue. As you hold the bow, make sure you can't accidentally get your digits in harm's way. There can be no compromise on this.

Trigger Pull

Considering all of the factors of various bows, the one that consistently fails the Byers' test is trigger pull. If you are a rifle shooter, you know the importance of trigger pull. You want one that's crisp (about three pounds of pressure) and has no "creep" (trigger movement that you're able to feel). This varies not only from brand to brand, but from model to model within a brand. Here's where the importance of shooting the bow in the shop really comes through. On some of the most expensive bows I've tested, I can feel the trigger move and must continue the squeeze further before it releases. You want a trigger that's firm enough for safety, yet fires without feeling unnecessary movement.

TriggerTech is a manufacturer that makes custom triggers for crossbows. I've used them on two models, and love the result.

Scopes and Sights

Most crossbow models come as a package with accessories such as a quiver, cocking device, arrows, and a sight (usually a scope). The sight shouldn't be a deal breaker for a bow that you really like because you can replace the scope with another model or a red dot, as you'll see in the chapter on sights.

Crossbow scopes may not be interchangeable. The same brand of scope on a 310 crossbow will not shoot with accurate drop compensation for a bow that shoot 365 fps. Crossbow packages will come with a scope that meets the shooting specs of that specific crossbow and usually works satisfactorily.

If you are a fan of quality optics, you may want to check out the XB75 scope, engineered by Zeiss. This scope offers the

Bows come with a variety of scope and sight configurations. Use one that works well for you.

best in light transmission and adjusts to the speed of your arrow. Also, there is the Vortex Viper XBR that's specifically designed for long-range shooting. It offers a "tactical turret" that allows for dead hold on out to seventy yards.

Size

Just like a firearm, how well a crossbow fits your stature will impact your shooting consistency. The stock should fit your frame well, and you should be able to swing the bow without difficulty. Weight and size become important if you are very mobile or hunt from compact places such as ground blinds or tree stands. Does the bow come with standard sling studs? If so, you can carry the bow over your shoulder just like a rifle

The size of a crossbow should match your body. You can rest the bow for accuracy, but hunting conditions often dictate an offhand position.

Standard or Reverse Limbs

The Barnett Razr is an excellent example of the newer reverse-limb technology. By reversing the limbs, bows can create excellent arrow speed in a narrower profile. Usually, these bows require a special cocking device and can't be cocked by hand, so get a demonstration, and try it out before purchasing one. The slimmer profiles make them easier to transport, carry, and store.

Buy the best bow you can afford. Cheap bows don't wear well and will quickly lose their resale or trade-in value.

Assembly/Travel

If you test your new bow in a shop or at a range before buying, it has already been assembled. Even so, it's important to know how the bow disassembles, if that is allowed under warranty. Of the four bows I'm flying to Africa this year, all but one disassemble. For most readers, air travel isn't an issue, but I had one expensive western hunt where a crossbow cocking device failed due to tinkering by TSA, or the continual vibration of the airliner. If you travel extensively, and I hope you do, the assembly issue can be important.

Warranty/Price

Finally, the amount you'll pay for a crossbow is probably the biggest choice of all. Prices range from under $300 to nearly $2,000 for top-of-the-line bows. Usually, the more the bow costs, the better the warranty. But you should ask about the fine print, such as how the bow will be repaired. Do you need to mail it back to the factory, or can the shop fix it? Is the warranty transferable? Unlike compound bows, crossbows hold value well, and you may want to sell this model to a buddy when a new one catches your eye.

Ultimately, selecting a bow is a matter of choice. How much speed do I want or need? How will I cock the bow? Will it be for target shooting, hunting, or both? What kinds of sight do I like to use? And so on. If you can't decide, purchase a used bow, try it for a year, and after saving a few more bucks, you'll know exactly what you want.

Chapter 7

Bolts and Arrows: What's the Best Bolt for My Crossbow?

The arrow or bolt is the most tunable aspect of your crossbow gear. Using the right arrow can make a huge difference in accuracy.

Manufacturers often recommend specific arrows, but can an archer get more accuracy by experimenting with after-market shafts? Is carbon better than aluminum? Here's how to make sure your crossbow is launching its best bet.

"I always equate arrows to ammunition," says Rob Dykeman, president of Excalibur Crossbows. "There are a lot of great ammo companies out there, yet each rifle seems to like a particular load. The same can be true for crossbow bolts." He continues:

> Since crossbow companies want their bows to shoot as accurately and consistently as possible, most recommend specific arrow lengths and weights. Some will go as far as to state brand names. Dykeman cites the

specific example of the Excalibur line, which recommends their proprietary shaft, the Diablo. It weighs 250 grains and is eighteen inches in length, whereas most compound crossbows must shoot a minimum 300-grain arrow at twenty or twenty-two inches. Since Excalibur crossbows use recurve limbs for energy, they can shoot a lighter, shorter arrow than other manufacturers, whose cammed bows might be damaged with such a light shaft. Our recurve bow will shoot those heavier shafts, yet the arrow would lose 20–50 fps due to their heavier weight.

A PERFECT EXAMPLE

I received a phone call from a good friend while I was hunting in the West. My buddy was quite frustrated with the performance of his crossbow. "I just can't get good groups," he lamented. Since I was two thousand miles away, I recommended that he visit Keystone Sports, a local pro shop and let them have a look.

Variations in arrows are probably more important in archery than cartridges are in center-fire rifles. Always follow the manufacturer's specs.

Several days later, he called again and was excited to say that he was breaking arrows at fifty yards and couldn't believe the difference his new arrows made. The discovery of some new, magic equation would make a great read, but the owner of the archery shop simply looked up the manufacturer's recommended arrow for the bow. Previously, my friend had had two different types of arrows with different nocks. By using the suggested length and weight of arrow, his older model bow shot like it was brand-new.

"It's the number one nemesis to crossbow shooters, especially those new to archery," the owner told me later. "Guys come into the shop with six arrows of three different weights and configurations, and they wonder why the arrows don't group well."

THREE CRITICAL FACTORS

What makes a good arrow? Regardless of the brand name, Dykeman believes that arrows must have three ingredients for top performance: consistent weight, consistent spine straightness, and durability. "If you are shooting a 250-grain arrow, it must weigh 250

Arrows are made of various components, and the fit of each is very important.

grains, not 249 or 255 grains," he says. "A few grains may seem like a small difference, but it can make a ¾-inch difference at twenty yards and be considered a flier." Competitive shooters often buy a hundred arrows and weigh each one carefully. They may end up with only thirty that weigh exactly the same.

Straightness is the second important quality. The best way to test a shaft is to roll it on a table. Also, once inserts are installed, the arrow must spin perfectly, especially with a broadhead. Begin with a perfectly straight shaft and make sure the nock, insert, and point follow suit.

Finally, Dykeman is a firm believer in carbon over aluminum. They may both begin with the same straightness, yet he believes that aluminum shafts are vulnerable to slight bends when being extracted from foam targets. "Carbon will not bend, only break," he says. "Aluminum is a great arrow, but a dying breed."

DON'T FORGET FOC

A crossbow bolt may be perfectly straight, yet not fly consistently if the shaft is not balanced properly. "Crossbow bolts are very short arrows flying at high speed, and they can spiral or wobble like a football," Dykeman says. "Adding weight to the front of the shaft creates better and more consistent arrow flight, an element that Excalibur has been very successful with," he adds. "We had one of the first 150-grain broadheads and had to scramble to find field points that heavy. Now a number of manufacturers make 150-grain heads or use heavier brass inserts to add mass to the front of the shaft."

Arrows are made of aluminum, carbon, or a combination of both. Easton FMJ bolts offer excellent mass, straightness, and ease of target removal.

Career archer John Dudley speaks to the importance of FOC (Front-Of-Center weight) in his blog on the Easton Website:

> Up until a year ago I was a huge fan of the Axis, and also the FMJ (Full Metal Jacket). I was drawn to them first off because of their tolerances, but secondly because of the option to use the brass HIT (Hidden Insert Technology) inserts to increase the front weight of the arrow. I found that by using the brass inserts and increasing the FOC, it allowed me to shoot both mechanical and fixed blade heads with a much smaller variance between them. I also found that the higher FOC allowed me to shoot a shorter vane to control those broadheads, which has its benefits as well. The importance of that is a smaller fletching will have less ballistic drag, which helps a lot in longer shots, but it also creates less drag in a cross wind. Both of those factors are very common in western style hunting. The bottom line is the brass inserts not only increase my front weight, but they also help boost my overall arrow weight. Higher FOC allows me to shoot a more compact broadhead, which I find to fly best, and still maintain a high FOC. For example, most compact broadheads are usually 100 grains, but when combined with a 75-grain insert, you have some amazing front steering weight. My arrow configuration was a 300 spine with a 75-grain brass HIT and a 100-grain Shuttle T-LOK or Ulmer Edge broadhead. Overall arrow weight was over 520 grains.

KINETIC ENERGY VS. MOMENTUM

A general conclusion in the hunting community is that hunters should match the kinetic energy of their harvest gear (weapon) to the requirements of killing an animal ethically. Although these are approximations, many believe them to be accurate for tackle selection. Keep in mind that a sixty-pound compound bow, with a twenty-eight-inch draw length, shooting a 300-grain arrow, generates about 50 foot-pounds of kinetic energy. Using the chart posted on the Hunters Friend website (www.huntersfriend.com), the following benchmarks apply.

KINETIC ENERGY	
Hunting Usage	
< 25 ft. foot-pounds	Small Game (rabbit, groundhog, etc.)
25-41 ft. foot-pounds	Medium Game (deer, antelope, etc.)
42-65 ft. foot-pounds	Large Game (elk, black bear, wild boar, etc.)
> 65 ft. foot-pounds	Extra Large Game (brown bear, moose, and African Plains game)

Most crossbows shoot with kinetic energy of 100 foot-pounds or more, making them qualified hunting tools for almost any North American game. And by increasing the weight of your bolt, kinetic energy increases and bow vibration and associated wear and noise are reduced. To take this a step further, Ed Schlief, and now his son, Garrett, are strong proponents of momentum as a measure of an arrow's effectiveness, instead of kinetic energy. Without becoming too technical, suffice it to say that at comparable speed, the heavier the arrow, the greater the momentum and the better the penetration. Garrett will conduct a seminar at this year's Safari Club International Convention on bowhunting dangerous game. Momentum and his heavy GrizzlyStik arrows will be central to that discussion.

AFTERMARKET ARROWS: A LOT FOR A LITTLE

Some archers are like re-loaders of big game ammunition. Sure, there are great cartridges (or arrows) out there, but they'd rather do their own. Dykeman speaks to the traffic on the Excalibur website where some fans insist on building their own bolts. "Guys enjoy making custom arrows which cost a good bit more than our shafts, yet they get the

Like reloading custom ammunition, many archers enjoy building their own arrows.

satisfaction of creating their own arrows. It's a fun hobby, and they want things more personal, that comes from their creation."

There are a lot of good aftermarket arrows out there from Easton, Gold Tip, Carbon Express, and others that may tighten a group a fraction of an inch, but the precision depends upon your experimentation and consistency in production. Dykeman believes that as long as you stay with reputable brands, you will do well.

Here's a quick roundup of shafts available and their contact information. Some manufacturers make up to five different shafts, so check the website for the full product line:

Company	Material	Length	Weight	Straightness	Nock	Contact
Barnett	Carbon	18/20/22 in.	8.1 oz.	na	Moon	www.Barnett.com
Carbon Express	Aluminum	20/22 in.	367 gr.	na	Flat/Moon	www.CarbonExpress.com
Carbon Express	Carbon	20 in.	390 gr.	.00025	Flat/Moon	www.CarbonExpress.com
Easton Flatline	Carbon	20 in.	9 gpi	.003	Half Moon	www.Easton.com
Easton FMJ	Carbon/Aluminum	20 in.	13.7 gpi	.003	Half Moon	www.Easton.com
Easton BloodLine	Carbon	20 in.	10.5 gpi	.003	Half Moon	www.Easton.com
Excalibur Diablo	Carbon	18 in.	250 gr.	n/a	Flatback	www.Excaliburcrossbows.com
Gold Tip Laser II	Carbon	20/22 in.	7.3 gpi	n/a	Half Moon	www.Goldtip.com
Gold Tip Laser IV	Carbon	20 in.	278 gr.	n/a	Half Moon	www.Goldtip.com
Parker Red Hot	Carbon	20.5 in.	320 gr.	.004	Capture	www.Parkerbows.com
TenPoint Pro V22	Carbon	22 in.	420 gr.	.003	Omni Nock	www.Tenpointcrossbows.com

WHAT DO THE ARROW BUILDERS SAY?

Some call them arrows, some bolts, others "bullets," and the effectiveness of your crossbow depends on them. Easton's Gary Cornum has this to say on the subject of choosing your projectile:

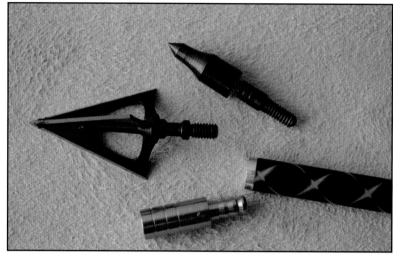

Are they arrows or bolts? It's all about FMJ.

> I like to let people know there are different attributes of carbon and aluminum. Aluminum is extremely consistent and a high precision material, and we can work it to specific specifications: spine, straightness, and weight, all of which contribute to accuracy. Carbon is lightweight and strong. When you marry them together you get the best of both: a very precise and lightweight product. It all works together.

The "marriage" that Cornum speaks of is the Easton Full Metal Jacket (FMJ), his personal favorite and a very popular bolt among crossbow hunters. Easton has been manufacturing aluminum-hybrid products for thirty years, and their effectiveness has been well-proven. The original A/C/C shafts were aluminum on the inside and carbon on the outside. Those are still very popular target arrows, yet the opposite layering works best for horizontal bows. Cornum believes the FMJ makes the perfect hunting arrow due to the tough carbon core and the precision of aluminum on the outside. Additionally, the polished, smooth finish makes FMJ bolts easier to remove from targets, which allows increased practice and thus improved shooter performance.

Easton is the leading producer of private-label crossbow bolts. If you buy the same brand of arrow as your bow, the shaft was probably made at the Easton plant. "Private labels sell them with the bow, and I think many consumers buy those arrows," Cornum says. "We do a lot of crossbow products, and that's our expertise. We do all-aluminum, all-carbon, and the hybrid (the best)."

Which ones should you shoot? "They are all good," says Cornum, who believes that lessons learned in developing arrows for the Olympics has filtered downstream to hunting shafts, just like space technology has helped us with daily life here on earth. "We've been making arrows here in the United States since 1922, and soon will have one hundred years of experience to build on."

Straightness is just one element of a bolt that can affect accuracy.

BOLTS THAT HUNT

A crossbow bolt may seem like a simple, individual object, yet its performance comes from the sum of its parts. A shaft that is perfectly straight may fly poorly if its nock, insert, or fletching are improperly installed. Additionally, several super-straight shafts with varying dynamic spines won't yield the group you'd expect.

Tim Gillingham is the manager of the Gold Tip shooting staff and shoots full time professionally, making him an arrow guru.

"Straightness seems to affect crossbow bolts more than other arrows," he says, and he recommends buying the best bolts you can afford. Gold Tip sells their Pro series to exacting standards, featuring .0005 straightness and a dozen shafts sorted to be within one gram of weight for the dozen. Since length can be an issue, shafts are sold in twenty-two-inch lengths so that consumers can cut them to length."

Like Cornum, Gillingham has his favorite arrow, and suggests the 500 Nitro (Pro series) for heavy hunting bows. "The Nitro is the heavyweight for high performance. It's more durable, and you get better fixed blade accuracy," he says. "There's a happy medium with speed and arrow performance, yet stiffer is always better with crossbow bolts."

TUNING YOUR CROSSBOW

Unlike vertical bows, crossbows come tuned right out of the box. Gillingham sets up both vertical and horizontal equipment and is quick to admit that there aren't many things to adjust on a crossbow. Basically, to tune the bow you must tune the arrow. He notes:

When tuning arrows, consider the balance or FOC of the shaft.

Front-of-center weight is very important. The reason Gold Tip bolts come with brass inserts is to put more weight at the tip. Nocks are a matter of choice, and premium arrows often come with moon and flat-back nocks.

I shoot every arrow through paper. All bolts are not created equal and you should get a bullet hole on paper just like a well-tuned vertical bow. If you get a flier, the spine of that arrow may be out of sync with the others. I rotate the nock to bring the spine into alignment, and usually the flier problem is solved. Tuning arrows is just like reloading ammunition. You are tuning a bullet to the gun.

Gillingham set up a crossbow for his wife and couldn't get it to shoot the bullet holes he's accustomed to. "I quickly saw that a stiffer bolt performed better," he said. "One way to achieve that was to shorten the bolt. The main thing is that all arrows react dynamically consistent."

Once target points fly well, the next step is to try your favorite broadhead, and Gillingham has had much experience in this arena. "If your broadheads do not spin perfectly, they will take off on you," he says. "A heavier insert helps with that [FOC], but the big issue is the tolerance of the ferrule to the insert. Both the insert and the nock must be in perfect alignment or accuracy suffers. I recommend mechanical broadheads, and there are so many good designs."

For in-depth information on arrow tuning, go to www.goldtip.com and click the "University" tab.

CROSSBOW BOLTS: WILL THE DIAMETER CHANGE?

Most crossbow bolts are $^{21}\!/_{64}$ of an inch in outside diameter. You'll often see them listed as 2117 or 2116, which means the outside diameter is $^{21}\!/_{64}$ of an inch, while the second number identifies the wall thickness. For example, a 2117 is slightly smaller in outside diameter (by $^{1}\!/_{64}$ of an inch) than a 2216, but the wall thickness of the 2117 is a smidge thicker, which makes the bolt stiffer than the "16." Ironically, they both weigh the same.

Crossbow bolts must have greater stiffness than arrows shot from most bows due the tremendous force created at launch. A thin, more limber arrow will bow like a piece of spaghetti and fly poorly. However, one arrow manufacturer believes he has the secret to a narrower arrow for crossbows, and is in the process of launching a crossbow arrow in the standard arrow format listed as a 2016.

Garrett Schlief is president and owner of Alaska Bowhunting Supply, which was recently renamed after their leading product, the GrizzlyStik arrow. Schlief is a staunch believer in momentum as a measure of an arrow's power, rather than the more traditional kinetic energy. His GrizzlyStik arrows, as the name implies, are built for dangerous game or for those archers who just want to shoot a heavy arrow. The GrizzlyStik has been used for almost every dangerous game animal on the planet, from elephants to Cape buffalo to Alaska brown bears. In a nutshell, these specialty arrows are heavy, stiff in spine, and tapered from the ferrule (point end) back. Once the broadhead makes its initial entry into an animal's skin, the taper of the shaft reduces friction on the arrow, and greater penetration is achieved.

The new arrow that Schlief is building may be a game changer for crossbows, although the finished product is still in development. The very stiff, all-carbon arrow will feature a thin diameter and a taper. This arrow will be parallel inside with an 11 percent taper from tip to tip. "It tapers point to nock. Once you clear the front end of the arrow, everything is a continuous taper behind that," says Schlief. "We want to do this to get over 30 percent FOC for a bolt that is point-heavy, which increases accuracy and consistency. With the taper and smaller shaft size, we think we will pick up 45–50 percent more penetration than traditional crossbow bolts and still build an arrow that is strong and durable."

Chapter 8

Sighting for Success: The Red-Dot Option

Red-dot scopes can make aiming much simpler. Sight your bow in at twenty-five yards and you are on target from fifteen to thirty yards.

Most crossbows are sold as kits with a scope attached. But factory optics may not be your best choice. Here's one year's experience with a red dot for whitetail deer and elk:

The bull bugled vehemently. Its vocalizations nearly shook the patch of saplings I hid behind. Too far to shoot and too close to stalk, I held my breath as the big New Mexican monarch turned and traveled a trail just twenty yards up the ridge. The tiny trunks that concealed me were as thick as pickets on a fence, and I knew I had to pick a narrow shooting lane and focus completely on it.

The beast bugled again, and my pulse pounded as the sound of its hooves came closer and closer. In seconds, the bull would be in easy range.

Then it happened. Maybe the sun glinted on its antlers or excitement ruled the moment, but I looked at the elk, lost my sight picture, and the bull passed by unscathed.

What a disappointment! Yet I learned a valuable lesson about aiming. Some time later, when a Wyoming archery elk tag arrived in the mail, that memory came rushing back with renewed determination. In anticipation of the hunt, I purchased a Mission MX320, which came with an effective Hawke multi-reticle scope. I knew that Hawke made quality optics, but would a different aiming system provide a better choice, especially in thick cover or, heaven forbid, another sapling jungle?

Using a single aiming point eliminates range confusion at the Moment of Truth, a time of great excitement when mistakes are often made.

THE RED-DOT OPTION

Simplicity is at the heart of a red-dot scope. At the Moment of Truth, when your heart pounds and your limbs tremble, concentration is paramount, and the single, glowing aim point allows you to focus on the shot, rather than the scope. When considering a red dot, your shooting history is important. If you are a longtime archer and familiar with multi-pin sights, then a scope with multiple aiming reticles will seem natural to you. However, if you come from the firearms side where scopes have one set of cross hairs, it's easy to get confused.

Red-dot scopes allow hunters to use one aiming point for multiple ranges, depending upon the trajectory of their bow.

Regardless of your experience, using a reticle in the middle of your aiming points can be complicated, especially at yardages such as twenty-six, thirty-three, or forty-seven. Often, an elk hunt can come down to a few seconds (perhaps even just one), and if you have to be calculating which reticle to use, opportunity can pass you by. For many shots, a range finder may be necessary, further complicating the shooting process.

Anticipating an exciting, anything-but-standing-at-twenty-yards-broadside shot, I tested an Aimpoint Hunter H34S sight on the MXB-320. Thinking back to that bull in the saplings that walked right past me, I believed I had the optimum aiming solution. The Hunter sight offered a single, precise dot on a target easily the size of a basketball, and it didn't matter if the broadhead penetrated the top, middle, or bottom of the lungs.

By testing the Mission, I learned that the Easton BloodLine carbon arrows and Hell-Razor broadheads dropped about six inches every twenty yards. This arrow trajectory allowed for a thirty-yard zero, such that my arrows were six inches high at twenty yards, dead on at thirty, and six inches low at forty yards. At fifty yards, I'd aim higher on the animal and still be in lethal territory. I knew my hunting area in Wyoming well and had planned to hunt several water holes and wallows that would provide the ability to pre-judge range. I had a system that "couldn't" miss.

INTO THE MOUNTAINS

Typically, the Southeastern section of Wyoming is very dry in fall, especially at higher altitudes. Any water source, even a small seep, often has regular visits from big game. Unfortunately, the 2015 season was a deluge with flooding that nearly washed away parts of Colorado and spilled into Wyoming. As a result, the first four days were uneventful, except for lightning, thunder, hail, and inches of rain.

The fifth morning my luck seemed to change when a bull came screaming down a mountain. The beast was traveling quickly, and I barely had a chance to duck

The author took the Mission MXB-320 into the mountains of Wyoming, and the bow performed perfectly.

behind a log beside the very trail it was traveling. At a hundred yards, the bull belted out a multi-tone bugle that nearly shook the forest. I sat motionless, waiting for the animal to come straight toward me. At twenty yards it would be toast.

However, it suddenly turned down the mountain and began to drink with the tops of its huge antlers piercing the sky. The range was too far, so I moved twenty yards closer and wished I had my range finder handy. It looked like a fifty- yard shot, but I wasn't sure. The animal was still, my rest was solid and the red dot steadied squarely behind the shoulder. But the bolt fell short. As if annoyed, the bull walked up the hill, stood broadside, and looked around while I tried to re-cock and reload to no avail. Because I had practiced the twenty- to fifty-yard scenarios so often, I didn't have a range finder in my breast pocket. That was pilot error that cost me success. The noise of the stream would have covered my approach, and the bull's vision was blocked. Sneaking to fifty yards would have taken mere seconds.

REPRIEVE ON WHITETAILS

Since whitetail hunting is often at closer range than elk hunting, I kept the red-dot setup and had a chance to try it out on a whitetail deer hunt. Not much moved on the warm October day, so several of us planned a deer sneak-drive, where two hunters still-hunt and two hunters post along likely escape routes. I knew the spot well and had seen deer mill around in a small patch of cedars before fleeing into open fields. If I could be there and the wind was right, I should get a close shot.

Slipping and sliding down a steep bank, I searched for a hiding place with the drive to begin any minute. Setting in front of a small bush, I had two shooting lanes and swung the bow to make sure there was no brush

The author forgot his range finder and needed it at a critical moment, a mistake that changed success into failure.

interference. Within a minute, I heard a stick snap and saw brown legs moving toward me. A dandy buck came to the edge of the cedars as I steadied for the fifteen-yard show. Thanks to the zero magnification of the scope, I could see the whole area clearly, including a heavy, white rack.

The buck paused a few seconds and then made a right turn where it would cross another shooting lane. I followed the buck's movements in the scope

The author muffed a shot on an elk in Wyoming, but made up for the mistake on this South Dakota whitetail.

as it stepped into the tiny opening and immediately spotted me. Too late! My arrow zipped through its chest cavity in an instant, and the buck burst up the ridge where it would soon be recovered.

CROSSHAIRS OR RED DOT?

Hopefully, my experiences (both good and bad) will help you make informed aiming decisions. The shot on the whitetail buck mentioned above was precisely what I had expected on the elk hunt, with the animal moving toward me at close range in dense cover.

One lesson learned, for sure, is the value of a range finder and how important it is to have it handy no matter what type of hunt or how good your system.

There are many fine crossbow scopes on the market, including those that come in kits, and I don't want to diminish their ability. However, for some

Most scopes come with a reticle scope standard. Switching to a red dot may be a good option.

people and in some situations, an aftermarket scope makes sense. I believe that my zero-to-forty-yard program has advantages in high-excitement situations. If I'm lucky enough to draw a license in Wyoming, I plan on giving it another try. And next time I'll have my range finder close by.

RED-DOT SCOPES

A red-dot scope follows the same principles as a single-pin compound sight, allowing the shooter to concentrate fully on the aiming point and eliminating the possibility of pin confusion. With no magnification, the shooter gets a full view of the animal and its surroundings. If this sounds appealing, keep these three things in mind when buying a red-dot scope:

Battery Life

A red-dot scope without power is worthless as a sight. If you purchase an inexpensive model, make sure you have spare batteries with you, and keep them in your pocket on cold hunts so they will last longer. My Aimpoint will stay lit in the "on" position for up to five years, and some scope require no batteries at all.

Durability

The price of red-dot scopes varies widely due to their construction. Models like Aimpoint and Trijicon are used by United States military branches and must function under incredible duress. Models costing less than $100 are designed for general hunting and although adequate, won't live up to the punishment of rugged use.

Parallax

Generally, the more you pay for a scope, the more parallax free it becomes. The point of impact on a parallax-free scope will not change no matter how you hold the scope. Whether you tilt it up, down, left, or right of center, the arrow will strike point-of-aim. This can be a huge benefit if you must shoot at an awkward angle from a ground blind window or tree stand. The effects of parallax can be diminished by always looking squarely into a scope such that the red dot is centered.

GEAR FOR ADVENTUROUS CROSSBOW HUNTS

Gear performance is important, but doubly so when you are away from home and high in the mountains, where a repair is difficult and a malfunction devastating. Here's a look at the products that made my hunt a joy, despite the cold, rainy weather.

Mission MXB-320

Weighing less than seven pounds, this bow was ideal for the constant walking and climbing that elk hunting required. It was maneuverable, remarkably quiet, and easy to cock. Because the bow does not have a cocking stirrup, a person of average build has greater leverage and can cock it more easily. www.missionarchery.com.

Aimpoint Hunter

The scope I used is identical to the ones our troops use in Afghanistan. It's built to take any kind of punishment and keep the dot on. Spot on. www.aimpoint.com.

Gear matters in all hunting, and quality products can help you have more fun and be more successful

Easton Carbon Arrows

For wilderness hunts, carbon arrows are preferable over aluminum because they will not bend. Crossbows must be discharged daily, and carbon allows for the occasional soft stump or dirt bank disarming shot without ruining an arrow. Also, in rugged terrain a hunter can slip or fall on his bow causing an unnoticeable bend in an aluminum shaft. www.eastonarchery.com.

HellRazor Broadheads

Elk are large, tough animals, and I wanted all the penetration I could get, which was the motivation for cut-on-contact heads. I found that 100-grain HellRazor heads impacted the same as target points, which made practicing simple. Also, I practice each day in the field if only by lantern at the end of the day. www.newarchery.com.

Test your bow and sight to see the amount of drop at various yardages.

LimbSaver Kodiak Sling

Once in elk country, I cocked the bow, slung it over my shoulder, and carried it like a rifle. The wide gripping-strap of the Kodiak sling allowed an easy carry, even with a backpack. LimbSaver lubes are a wise investment as well. www.limbsaver.com.

Under Armour Infrared

This material is designed to reflect heat back to your body, and I was amazed at how such a light, soft material could insulate so well. In fair weather it's a hunting shell, while in bitter cold or rainy conditions, it's ideal to carry in a pack and wear as an under layer. www.underarmour.com.

Browning Hell's Canyon

This jacket-and-pant raingear was my go-to outfit on this hunt and had just enough insulation with a base layer to be comfortable. Every seam is taped, making it completely waterproof. www.browning.com.

Zodi Hot Tap X-40 Portable Shower and Scent Killer

A hot shower at the end of the day, or during a midday break, helped to make hunting more effective and spirits soar. By using scent elimination products on clothes and bodies, we kept our scent at a minimum. www.zodi.com; www.wildlife.com.

Once you have the total package you will be ready for whitetail deer or larger game. Just don't forget your range finder.

Morrell Target

Having a quality practice target in camp greatly increases your odds of success. Bring one—or buy one if you fly—and transport it to camp. Wilderness hunts can be tough on gear, and you can maintain your shooting skills and test that all systems are go each day. www.morrelltargets.com.

Lost Camo

This versatile pattern blends in anywhere and uses variations in color instead of sticks and leaves. My set, made by Gamehide, was comfortable, insulated well, and water resistant enough for 95 percent of hunting situations. www.lostcamo.com.

Vortex Optics

Finally, quality optics make a tremendous difference in your effectiveness as a hunter. I used a pair of 8x42 Vortex binoculars and have never had a pair that was as bright, sharp, and easy to use. When stalking or glassing, the bright image was amazing. The Vortex range finder was in my pack when I needed it most, despite a pocket clip that makes it easy to keep handy in your front or vest pocket. www.vortexoptics.com.

The author used a variety of new gear on his elk trip. One way of packing through heavy timber was to zip a jacket over the bow during transport.

Chapter 9

Broadheads: Fixed or Expandable?

Broadheads are one of the most controversial topics in archery. Everyone has an opinion, and they can often back them up with anecdotal accounts of a particular head working wonders. Before exploring this topic in depth, I'd like to tell a story of a deer hunt in Texas that occurred in the late 1990s.

We were hunting with compound bows back then. And as we convened at the end of the second day, one archer said that he had shot a deer and trailed it for a short time, but then decided to wait and have the group help him. That turned out to be a wise

Broadhead selection is one of the most important decisions a hunter can make.

move. He shot a sixty-pound bow and used a large, two-blade expandable broadhead, and he believed that the shot was right on the shoulder.

Dogs can be used to trail deer in Texas, and we gathered at the blood trail with flashlights and the trailing dog. The going was slow, through very thick Lone Star bush, but we finally came upon the doe after a mile of trailing. Without the use of the dog, we'd never have found it.

"I can't believe how well this broadhead worked!" exclaimed the happy archer. "Wow! Look at the hole in its shoulder."

Personally, I was dumbfounded because the broadhead had performed very poorly. The cut was too large for the power of the bow, and we were lucky to retrieve the deer. I relate this tale not to speak negatively of two-blade heads, but to emphasize how subjective broadhead performance can be.

THE BEST BROADHEAD

The "best" broadhead is easy to define: It flies true to your practice arrows, cuts a large wound channel, and completely penetrates the animal so that it leaves parallel blood trails. Without mentioning brand names, let's look at these three elements individually.

The best broadhead is the one that performs best from your bow.

One of the greatest advantages of mechanical broadheads is their aerodynamic flight. In other words, they fly like target points. Of course, you can practice with a set of fixed-blade hunting broadheads and sight your bow in for them. However, this practice becomes quite expensive, and is often a detriment to practice since crossbow bolts can be difficult to pull from a foam target. Additionally, practicing with broadheads risks ruining the previous bolt by cutting fletching or busting the nock.

If your mechanical heads or fixed-blade heads fly like target points, you'll probably practice more and have more fun doing it. You can shoot a wide variety of targets at various ranges, and even if you miss, you can probably still use that bolt again. As Tim Gillingham stated earlier, you should be able to shoot a bolt into the same hole repeatedly from twenty yards if your arrows are properly tuned and matched.

DUE-DILIGENT DAMAGE

The size and design of the broadhead will determine the tissue damage of the animal you shoot. Smaller heads tend to fly more consistently than larger diameter heads or those with large blades. Although these differences may be small at close range, they amplify as shooting distance grows.

Expandable two-blade broadheads have become very popular because they cut a large entrance as well as exit hole, assuming the arrow goes all the way through. Since broadheads kill by hemorrhage, it makes sense that the more hemorrhaging that occurs, the quicker and more humane the kill becomes. The trick is to balance the power or kinetic energy of the shaft with the size of the broadhead, understanding that not every shot will strike the animal in the most vulnerable position.

I once hunted elk with a person who shot a bull elk squarely in the shoulder. The arrow hit with a solid *crack,* indicating that the bolt had struck the animal precisely on the large shoulder bones. We followed

Expandable broadheads have advantages over cut-on-contact heads.

the blood trail for four hundred yards, and riders on horseback searched for it the next day to no avail. Despite more than 100 foot-pounds of energy, the bolt struck the elk at an impenetrable spot and the animal survived; at least until the rifle season opened two weeks later.

If you will be hunting whitetail deer from ambush, tree stand, or ground blind, most crossbows will have ample energy to drive a large broadhead through a whitetail deer, especially if you concentrate on the lung area. A deer suffering a double-lung hit by an arrow rarely lives more than ten seconds and usually dies fifty to seventy-five yards from the spot. Additionally, this lung placement wastes very little venison, and the arrow can be easily retrieved on the far side of the deer.

COMPLETE PENETRATION

Of the three shooting elements, this one is somewhat controversial. If you use fixed broadheads you will encounter the argument that the arrow should remain inside the animal because the cutting blades will continue to cause damage as the beast runs

Cut-on-contact heads can be resharpened and used for deer or turkeys.

away. Since there are myriad factors involved, from the physical location of the broadhead to the organs involved to the penetration of the arrows, this will remain conjecture.

Complete-penetration advocates suggest that a broadhead should pass completely through an animal and leave a blood trail on each side of the animal as it runs away. The two-hole advocates believe that the animal will lose more blood, hemorrhage more profusely, and thus expire more quickly. Once again, this argument is based primarily on anecdotal evidence and hunter opinion.

One of my last bucks, taken with a crossbow, might help shed light on this situation. I was hunting in South Dakota from a bluff that overlooked a stream bed and a frequent deer trail. A buck passed below the bluff at twenty yards, and I aimed for the

Mature bucks have great stamina, so you want a combination of an effective broadhead and proper shot placement.

middle of the shoulder. I *urped* with my voice, the buck stopped, and the bolt released. You read this earlier, but here are more details.

The animal whirled and ran, and I slowly moved to pick up the trail with the assistance of six inches of snow. I found a small amount of blood on the snow, as well as the animal's tracks. After following them for about twenty yards, I decided to get help with the recovery rather than push the deer after sundown. Four friends and I returned and followed the spore for two hundred yards, to the point that I began to question whether we'd recover it.

Finally, our patience and patient persistence paid off, and I came upon the 140-class eight point, dead as a stone. After bringing the buck back to camp, I learned that the arrow had hit perfectly. It entered slightly above center on the near shoulder and exited low on the far side, catching both lungs. I shot a Mission MXB-320 with plenty of power, a 400-grain arrow, and a Grim Reaper expandable broadhead. The mechanical head had performed as expected, yet the arrow barely exited the far side. Virtually all of the hemorrhage occurred inside the body cavity without flowing from the entrance wound due to its height up the shoulder. Had the broadhead exited completely on the far side, I believe that the animal would have expired more quickly and the blood trail would have been easier to follow.

This was a three-and-a-half-year old prairie buck, and they are known for their stamina. When you select a broadhead-and-bolt combination, plan for the worst-case scenario and maximize kinetic energy and broadhead tissue damage. As long as your setup meets the three goals mentioned above, you will give yourself the best chance for quick, humane kills and hunting success.

EXPANDABLE VS. FIXED BLADE: A CLOSER LOOK

Jon Syverson is executive vice president of Rage Broadheads, one of America's most popular brands, and one that has changed the industry in the past five years. Syverson represents the Rage and Muzzy brands, two companies that typify the two theories of broadhead use discussed above. "Crossbows are becoming more popular every year, and we make a fixed blade and an expandable," Syverson says. "You

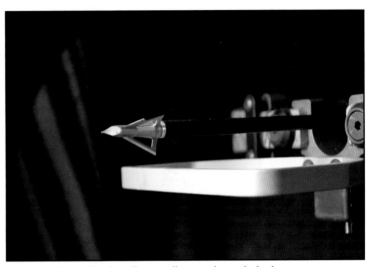

Mechanical broadheads will generally cut a larger hole than cut-on-contact heads.

generally get better arrow flight with a mechanical design, which simplifies the process between hunting and practice, allowing archers to switch from field points to broadheads and maintain accuracy."

A lot of guys prefer the dependability of a fixed-blade broadhead, a time-proven design that offers a no-fail situation. "For a guy who doesn't want moving parts, we make several types of fixed-blade broadhead," he says. "The Trocar CrossBow has angled blades that will fly like a field point. A guy can shoot fixed blade with field-point accuracy. The Trocar is 1-3⁄16 inches in diameter with a cutting point; it is a really solid, dependable design.

Crossbows produce a lot of energy, since you want to cut as big a hole as you can. A Rage broadhead does that. The slip cam opens from the rear, so its blades cut a hole up to two inches wide. All Muzzy or Rage crossbow heads are designed for crossbows with larger bolts, $^{22}/_{64}$, which helps them align perfectly. And all crossbow-specific heads feature the same collar, along with a shock collar for better broadhead alignment with larger shafts. Using Rage or Muzzy is a personal choice for a crossbow hunter. Some like the dependability of the fixed blade, while others want mechanicals for the accuracy.

Economy is frequently an issue, and Muzzy makes one of the most economical broadhead packages on the market. The 100- and 125-grain broadheads come in a six-pack that you can assemble yourself. Some archers prefer this option, and the system is both economical and effective. The standard four-blade head is still extremely popular in many archery circles, especially among those who believe, "if it ain't broke, don't fix it." This is evident if you spend time researching various broadheads online. I wrote a review of popular heads a few years ago, and found that the Muzzy four-blade had the most loyal fans, with most users giving them five stars in performance tests.

WHAT LIES AHEAD

Syverson is setting up a crossbow for his grandson, taking advantage of one of the great aspects of crossbows: their versatility. They come in all shapes and sizes, and many can be adapted for various shooter sizes. He sees the crossbow market increasing due to its inclusiveness and the changeover of rifle hunters to the archery world.

"With the legalization of crossbows in archery seasons, the expansion adds more time to that gun hunter's season. That's one of the main attractants," he says. "Like archery as a whole, you get a longer season, you are a lot closer to the animal, and you enjoy a better experience," said Syverson. He has seen archery dealers that now only sell and service crossbows who are doing well.

Lighted nocks are another popular option that can help hunters in the field. Crossbows launch arrows at such great speeds that seeing the bolt in flight is very difficult, even for the youngest eyes and those with the keenest vision. A lighted nock gives a visual string during flight and helps with seeing the exact arrow placement upon impact. It can also be helpful for finding it in the leaves or grass after a shot. If trailing an animal after dark, the nock can show the location of the carcass and help assure a quick recovery.

"We make a lighted nock and use a bolt, the Predator, under the Nockturnal brand," Syverson says. It comes in twenty and twenty-two inches with the nock installed, either a flat back or half moon. That nock takes the blow as the string comes forward, depresses the switch, and turns the nock on. Once it's on, there are two holes on each side. You just flip the LED back up to turn it off. We also sell the Nockturnal tool that helps with installation and turns off the nock.

TUNING BOLTS FOR BEST PERFORMANCE

At this point, you've read several tips about tuning bolts for more consistent flight from your crossbow. Tim Gillingham, manager of Gold Tip's shooting team and a professional target shooter, advises paper-tuning your crossbow just like a vertical bow. With a compound vertical bow, if the arrow doesn't fly properly, the solution lies in adjusting the bow, most often by moving the rest in or out from the riser. Or for high and low shots, one can adjust the nocking point.

Crossbows do not have these adjustments, so you need to tune the bolt to the bow. One of the easiest methods is to experiment with various arrow lengths and spines until you find one that flies well from the bow, tearing what is termed a "bullet hole." This singular tear in paper is made when the arrow strikes the paper in a perfectly perpendicular fashion, with the point and nock in perfect alignments. When the arrow flies in this manner, it is more stable and tends to fly consistently, striking the target where aimed.

If you are new to archery or crossbow hunting, the best way to find that perfect tune is at a pro shop, where you can get expert advice. I was launching arrows before the Beatles were a rock band, yet I still take my equipment to Keystone Sporting Goods, where Tim Gordon or Doug Mongan works his magic. A pro shop has the specific tools,

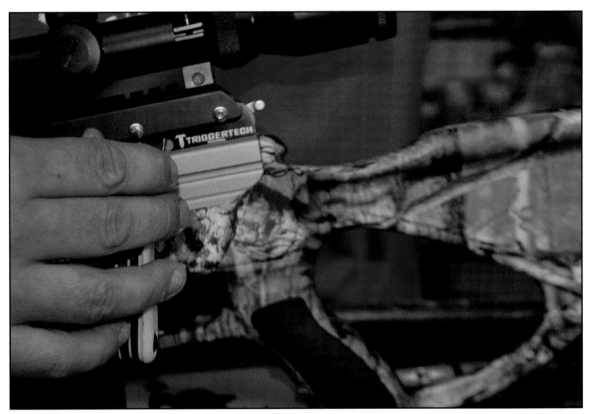

If you are new to archery, seek out the advice of a pro at a local archery shop.

and more importantly, the knowledge and skill to solve just about any problem. Plus, they will diagnose your problem quickly, offer solutions, and fix them, often while you watch. Additionally, if the same problem arises, you can go back to the shop for a different solution.

When buying or building bolts, always begin with the manufacturer's recommendations whether, you are purchasing completed arrows or building bolts on your own. They have tested their equipment extensively, and the arrows were probably built by Easton in the United States, making them of quality and good reliability.

A.S.D. TOOL BY G5

If you enjoy building or refurbishing arrows, then you must have an Arrow Square Device (A.S.D.) tool by G5. Just like square corners are important when a carpenter builds a house, building arrows that fly and perform consistently requires that both ends of the shaft be "square." But you can leave that large bubble device in the garage, as it won't work on arrow shafts.

The A.S.D. Tool by G5 is a mandatory device for anyone building his or her own arrows.

If you are building arrows, begin by weighing the batch, and only fletch the ones that weigh the same. Next, cut the raw shaft to the proper length. This is best done with a high-speed arrow saw that cuts the shaft cleanly, with few burrs. After this step, use a rasp to ensure that the inside of the cut is smooth. Then place each end of the tube onto the A.S.D. tool. Rotating it several turns will file the end until the shaft is perfectly square, which means the ferrule and nock will fit exactly against the arrow without any cant that would affect accuracy.

Once finished, spin the arrow with a field point and then again at the nock end. The shaft should spin without any wobble. If not, the end of the shaft is probably off-square, or either the insert or nock has been installed improperly.

If you still get inconsistent flight, rotate the cock feather, but only when using flat nocks. With moon nocks, you must rotate the nock as well or you risk the concave edge of the nock severing the string.

Chapter 10

Targets and Practice Techniques

A quality target makes shooting much more fun for everyone. However, match the type of target to your purpose.

The targets used in practice are important pieces of gear and will have a direct bearing on your success. The better and more user-friendly the targets, the more likely you are to practice and thus succeed in the field. Targets fall into three basic categories: bag, block, and 3-D, with the latter being a direct offshoot from companies that built taxidermy forms.

James McGovern is vice president of Rinehart, a company that has taken 3-D targets to the extreme. Way beyond bucks and bulls, shooting a full line of their targets is like a trip to Jurassic World. Son-in-law of company founder John Rinehart, McGovern had this to say about their entrance into the world of targets:

A Rinehart eighteen-sided 3-D target.

> My wife and I began working here with taxidermy forms. Rinehart went hunting in Africa and needed targets for practice back in 1997. He bought two or three 3-D and was disappointed. Since he had molding equipment, he decided to do it better, and the target line was born.
>
> Our first target was a Jurassic Park critter. There was a pile of deer targets on the market, and when consumers shot those targets, they remembered that dinosaur. It was a very smart marketing move to get the grass roots business going, and the entire business went straight to archery clubs. They became our customers due to the quality and durability of the targets.

My wife and I signed up for eight dollars an hour to work with Rinehart. We marketed the R100 3-D program and ran it during the summer. Unknown to us, Mr. Rinehart was sixty-four and had it in his mind to retire at sixty-five. We showed up to work one day and he was scraping his name off the door. 'I've retired and you will run the target company,' he said.

Barb and I took over and transitioned it into what it is today: A company with hat-high focus on 3-D archery clubs, and with increased emphasis on the dealer side, the retail side, and international sales. We bought the company in 2010, and now we own it.

WHAT'S AHEAD IN CROSSBOW TARGETS?

I'm seeing a growing demand for crossbow targets. Standard bowhunting is going to a higher velocity and smaller target shaft. Our foam was designed for aluminum shafts; now it's mostly carbon. Both sides have gotten harder and more complicated. Crossbows have increased speed, so are just as fast as heavier compounds. Also, crossbow shooters don't shoot as much and don't need as big a target. It allows me to focus all of the efforts into one product.

Archery target people have two needs: face size and pattern. Meet the face size the customer wants. Do they want fourteen to twenty-four inch? But whatever the face size, they are still going to focus on the middle. Even if you put ten dots on there, the center one is the most used. With the crossbow, we focus just on the middle. They don't need a twenty-four-inch target because crossbows are so accurate. I have one dedicated target in my line, the 14 x 14 x 14 made from our high density foam.

A Rinehart tom turkey target.

The 18-1 eighteen-sided target can be shot with broadheads and field points, and has a one-year broad warranty. It's one of our best targets, and a lot of those targets go for crossbows. Aluminum arrows pull much easier from targets than carbon, and all targets would function better if we had a technological arrow coating.

I would suggest two things, both types of practice. You need to practice with a dot, where you have a defined aiming point to make sure the bolt is going where you intend it to go. From a hunting standpoint, it's more important to be able to make that shot in that split second; you find the spot and shoot. Secondly, you need a good, realistic 3-D target so that you can concentrate on that lung shot.

R100: THE BIG SHOOT

The R100 is designed for vertical archers, but some clubs allow crossbows to be used. "In reality, we lease the targets to the club. If the host will allow it, we will allow it. It goes back to John, when he saw that competitive archery tournaments were not all inclusive. They could not include families, even though there were kid's classes. Mom, dad, and kids all shot different tournaments. We decided to include everyone. Is it more important to shoot competitively or together? We think the latter, and now it's great for everyone. If one person is a competitive shooter and the other is a casual shooter, that national level becomes fun. They can shoot targets like

Targets are a good investment. The more you shoot, the more accurate you will become.

rhino, buffalo, life-size elephant, world-record Cape buffalo, giraffe, and very unique entertaining aspects. It's one hundred targets, the Hole in the Horn buck, and the Johnson buck. Imagine being able to draw back on those deer. We have lots of door prizes and do a small novelty shoot, dirty dozen, and two-man teams for ten bucks a guy with a $^{50}\!/_{50}$ split at the end to satisfy those archers who must have competition. Otherwise, it's great archery fun."

REALISTIC AND FUN

The house next door to ours went up for sale recently, and one of the prospective buyers had a teenage daughter. The folks liked the house, and on the second visit, the daughter brought her camera to take a picture of the deer standing in my back yard. She was a bit embarrassed to learn that it was a target, yet the realism of the foam deer speaks to how realistic targets can be.

The manufacturers of the GlenDel buck learned years ago that targets sell better if they have large antlers, and my target has plenty of white mass above its ears; extra motivation to get out there and practice.

Quality crossbow targets take a bit of an investment, but like exercise, you want the experience to be fun and not something you will tire of. The fun of practice rises exponentially with multiple shooters, be they family or hunting buddies. Because targets are often mobile, you can set them up in realistic situations where you need to shoot from a deck or ladder, or between trees. Just be careful that you have a clear background, and make sure that everyone shoots safely as excitement builds. Keep celebratory beverages on tap until after practice.

As the season draws near, practice while wearing your full hunting gear.

Since crossbow targets absorb so much energy, buy targets that facilitate arrow removal. Bag targets are ideal for daily shooting with target points. These arrow grabbers work amazingly, and arrow removal is usually a matter of two fingers. Unfortunately, you cannot use broadheads with this type of target.

Foam targets can handle any type of point, and some cube targets have sides made for broadheads and another for target points. When just practicing, use target points since they tend to make it possible to shoot in higher quantities. However, never go hunting without trying at least one of your broadheads to ensure accuracy.

Chapter 11

World Class Adventure: Alaska Bulls to Illinois Big Bucks

The Aleutian Islands of Alaska are a barren, windy, and crossbow–unfriendly location for a hunt.

To this point, most of this book has been about gear and how to select it and use it safely and effectively. Now, let's go hunting! Gregg Ritz has trained with the US Olympic Shooting Team and headed a firearm program for years. But the crossbow challenge was calling. And he went for it: all in.

Siberian caribou, *Rangifer tarandus,* were imported to the Aleutian Islands from Russia in the early 1900s by the US Coast Guard as a winter food source for the Inuit. Natives could fish during summer months, but there were no other big game species living on these remote, desolate islands. Today, that small, initial introduction has grown into a herd of thousands, enough to sustain sport hunting and provide a means of income for local tribes. What's more, mature bulls often sport antlers that score up to five hundred inches and can be eligible for the Safari Club International Record Book.

Gregg Ritz is President of Wild-Comm, a public relations company that handles such popular TV shows as *The Crush with Lee & Tiffany*, *Pigman*, and *Hunt Masters*, along with thirteen others. Additionally, he has hosted numerous hunting shows on television, and he wanted to renew an old relationship with archery. "Tagging one of those huge caribou with a crossbow sounded like a great challenge and a really cool Native American hunt," said Ritz, who worked through the local units to gain the proper paperwork for the hunt.

Ritz wanted challenge, yet was aghast at the terrain when he touched down in the Aleutians. "When I landed, I could see one Charlie-Brown-type tree on the entire island. One!" he said, calculating his chances in wide-open country. "You figure this is a volcanic chain of mountains,

Call them caribou or reindeer, these animals were a challenge.

really steep terrain with rolling green landscapes, but *nothing* to hide behind. When I landed I was clearly wondering, *how will I pull this off?* Stepping from the plane, Ritz was immediately buffeted by the Bering Sea winds that routinely blow at thirty miles per hour and gust to sixty miles per hour, a severe complication to arrow flight.

Ritz had hunted around the world, and immediately took steps to prepare and adapt to this unique environment. He had the natives locate a large eight-foot-long roll of foam as a target. "They put an orange dot in the center, and I moved back from twenty yards to gauge how wind affected the arrow over thirty, forty, and fifty yards," he said. "Wind drift was significant."

TO THE HUNT

Once Ritz felt comfortable shooting with a crosswind, he, his guide, and a camera operator moved into the field. Spot-and-stalk was the only available option. But the terrain was vast, and some herds contained forty sets of eyes. On the positive side, the lack of vegetation helped locate game, since they had to use terrain features to hide. On the down side, these animals were hunted for subsistence, which meant that the sight of a human, or vehicle, or the sound of a vehicle, caused immediate panic.

Ritz and his guide hunted for two full days, glassing extensively, yet never found a trophy bull in a stalkable situation. Either the bulls were surrounded by cows, or they bedded in wide open terrain, giving Ritz no chance to sneak into range. Finally, on the third day, they spotted two big bulls in a deep depression. By moving out of the animals' sight, they closed to just under a hundred yards. "With a rifle or muzzleloader, the hunt would have ended right here," remembers Ritz. With no way of stalking closer, though, they stayed with the small herd, "roosting" them in a sense, and planned to return the following morning.

Like with most big-game hunting, Alaska requires a lot of glassing and stalking.

FINALLY, A SHOT

"These are elk-sized animals, and I imposed a range of forty to fifty yards maximum," said Ritz. "We came back the next day and began a grueling stalk, belly crawling in six inches of grass. Not crouched; commando style. Amazingly, we got within forty-five yards of the entire bedded herd, thanks to the howling wind that concealed noise and kept our scent at bay. It took hours to crawl into position. Finally, a big bull stood up. I got to my knees, shot, and the wind blew the arrow three feet in front of it."

Fortunately, the herd wasn't too badly spooked, and Ritz watched it go over the next rise and the next. The herd bedded in a narrow bowl, with the two bulls off to one side to get out of the wind. "We slithered down the top of the hillside within thirty yards. I got another shot, and the wind blew my arrow again. Now I was completely frustrated, and as the wind howled it dawned on me, *unless I'm under thirty yards, it's not going to happen."*

The herd spooked again, yet without the usual report of a rifle, animals begin to mill around and found a bedding spot out of the wind. "Four hours later, we found the two bulls bedded for the third time, and we moved around the mountain, where we located a possible stalking route," Ritz said. "Water had eroded a little creek bed that drained into the ravine. We had some terrain relief, maybe two feet, but not so much that we could walk. We slid down the mountain face-first in this tiny, two-foot-wide crevice and closed to twenty-five yards. I peeked out with my range finder and believed, like on a mule deer hunt, I'd have a split second to rise up and shoot. The plan worked perfectly, and the big bull went down at thirty yards. Wow, what a giant learning curve and thrilling hunt! I wanted challenge and got a full measure."

The wind and wide open terrain were two very challenging elements of the hunt.

BUSINESS, THEN PLEASURE

Despite a career in the firearms industry, Ritz was no stranger to a crossbow. The Siberian caribou was his grandest adventure, yet he grew up in Hillsboro, Ohio, where his dad owned a small farm. Ohio legalized crossbows for the general archery season back in 1976, at which point the horizontal option was available to him. "When I was going to college, I couldn't go shoot on campus, so I opted for a crossbow to hunt on weekends and took several deer with that method."

In 2015 Ritz attended the Archery Trade Association show in Indianapolis over the first weekend of January, with just enough time to squeeze in a late-season whitetail hunt in Illinois. An Arctic cold front swept down from Canada, and the prospects looked promising.

Ritz had a full week to hunt, but knew he couldn't just jump into the property without doing some homework. He spent the first two days running cameras and figuring out deer movements to formulate a plan. These bucks had been chased for months with bows and shotguns, so they wouldn't allow many mistakes. He knew of a small, hidden food plot, what he called a "kill plot," that contained an acre of Krunch N Munch with turnips and six inches of snow. Scouting showed that deer had pawed up and eaten the turnips, and camera images found a great ten-point, 145-inch, six-and-a-half-year-old buck.

The weather stayed bitterly cold, dropping below zero at night, and after imaging the big ten-point in the field on consecutive afternoons, Ritz believed he'd found a pattern. Could he play the wind and get a shot? Taking no chances, he climbed into his stand just past noon, doing his best to stay warm and still. Around 2:30, several does filtered into the small food plot, followed by a three-year-old buck. A nice deer, but not the big ten Ritz knew was nearby. Shortly thereafter, the hunter's patience paid off as the buck with high, heavy antlers stepped into the field.

Ritz smiles behind his great reindeer bull. The animal didn't come easily. Numerous stalks were required.

"After the buck began to feed, I ranged it at thirty-one yards," Ritz said and felt he'd prepared well for a shot at this range. "I like two things to help accuracy: the Nikon scope with the BDS reticle and HHA Optimizer between the scope and base. I had all the time in the world and a solid rest, and I twelve-ringed the 250-pound deer with a Wasp broadhead."

Walking up to the downed buck, memories from similar success back in college flooded his memory. "The frigid conditions had made this a fabulous hunt and accented one of the advantages of a crossbow. In late season, tucked in a tree stand with all of those clothes, you can bundle yourself up and insulate, with an EZ Hanger right there, and shoot from the seated position. It makes for a great late-season weapon."

IS A CROSSBOW FOR YOU?

Ritz believes that the majority of crossbow hunters are guys who are gun hunters and want to enter bowhunting. He cites research that 70 percent of crossbow hunters also use firearms. When the casual gun hunter thinks of preparing for hunting season, he

If whitetail deer are your thing, consider an out-of-state hunt to learn new skills and see different country.

If you become successful at whitetail hunting, you may want to give another species a try.

grabs his rifle and ammo, fires a few rounds to check zero, throws in his boots and coat, and he's done.

The crossbow hunter will have much more on his plate, such as camouflage, scent control, and how to get closer than ever before. The typical center-fire shot is fifty to a hundred yards, but the gun hunter has to learn to be a bowhunter and get shots from twenty to thirty yards, which is not easy.

When guys first start out they don't think of the preparation it takes to get close. They don't think about taking extra strings and cables. One bad trip through a briar patch can shred a cable, and Ritz carries extras on all of his hunts, even for whitetail. He says:

> I take extras strings and cables because they don't weigh anything. With a Mission crossbow, I can back out the limb bolts, and change my string and cable without going to a pro shop. I make sure I have enough arrows and broadheads. I have a three-arrow quiver and a tube of another dozen in my camp or on my four-wheeler. Also, I keep half a dozen decocking arrows to safely release the tension on my bow. The safest way to do this is to shoot the bow, and the heavy shafts with heavy points are ideal.

> Obviously, if you are a bowhunter, having a range finder is like wearing your baseball cap. You must know the distance. A shaft goes 300–400 fps, so you must know your trajectory. You can't use your twenty-yard crosshair on a forty-yard shot. Whether you use a scope, an Optimizer, or one pin, you must know the exact distance. From a tree stand or steep mountain slope, angles come into the picture, and today's modern range finders can help with this. Scent elimination is extremely important and requires attention to detail.

> You'll obviously want to practice shooting effectively, but gear, strategies, and techniques are equally important to success. Whether you travel to Alaska or challenge a big buck in your back yard, crossbow hunting will introduce you to a whole new world of exciting, close-up action.

CROSSBOWS CAN BUILD CENTER-FIRE ACCURACY

Ritz lives in New Hampshire with his wife and children, each of whom is excited about hunting. Interestingly, he taught his children to shoot in his back yard without a formal shooting range. Here's his story in his own words:

I have three girls, eight, ten, and twelve years old. My oldest daughter took a great buck at a hundred yards with a muzzleloader last year and really did well. In fact, all of my girls are great shots. If you look at their form you may wonder how they shoot so well. All my girls began with a crossbow, where they learned the fundamentals of gun safety, gun handling, and shooting just like you would with a .22 rifle. They learn where to put their cheek on the stock and how to allow eye relief. And we get a lot of practice in the back yard. There is no noise or recoil with a crossbow, and the added fun factor of recovering their ammo helps with shooting skills. I can watch and diagnose how they pulled the trigger, followed through, and looked through the scope, so we can improve their skills. By pulling the arrows, they can visually see success. From those skills, we went to the .22, and then to a muzzleloader, because she learned the proper skills starting with a crossbow. It was a personal experience. If you are a gun hunter looking for more time in the field and alternative opportunities, seriously consider adopting crossbow hunting.

Gregg Ritz taught his daughter to shoot in their back yard with a crossbow. She learned skills that allowed her to make a great shot with a muzzleloader.

Chapter 12

Know Your Crossbow: A Pictionary of Terms

Crossbows, like this Mission MXB, seem like simple devices, yet there are many parts making up each bow. It helps to know what each part is called.

Crossbows are fairly simple devices. One internet site shows how to make one from pencils, string, and a ruler. But we will be going way beyond that simplicity in our quest for effective hunting gear. Just like a physician can't practice medicine until he knows the human anatomy, a crossbow hunter needs to know all about his weapon, and that's what this chapter is about. Using diagrams and a brief description of terms, you'll end up with a knowledge of the bow and have a handy reference for the chapters ahead.

RECURVE CROSSBOWS

Since all bows are slightly different, let's look at one with recurve limbs, like the Excalibur models. Beginning at the front and working backward, you'll find these parts:

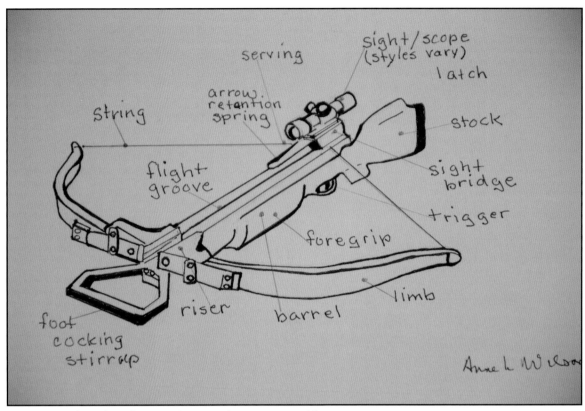

Recurve crossbows have fewer moving parts than a compound bow.

Cocking Stirrup

Most bows other than Mission have them. The loop is designed to provide an anchor when cocking the bow. If you have a big foot, make sure your stirrup fits.

Limbs

Similar to the limbs of a recurve or compound bow. They bend and store energy.

Barrel

The section of the bow that contains the flight groove and rail and extends to the riser.

Rail

The top of the barrel where the hen feathers touch.

Riser

The front section of the bow that holds the limb pockets.

Foregrip

Like the fore-end of a gun, the bow is gripped here. Most new bows have safety shields or cut-outs for hand and finger protection.

Flight Groove

The groove atop the barrel that guides the arrow upon release. The cock feather of the arrow slides into this groove.

Arrow-Retention Spring

This spring holds the arrow in the flight groove. TenPoint uses a brush instead of a spring to eliminate vibration.

There is not a quiz at the Moment of Truth, but knowing the technical parts of your bow will help establish your success.

String

The twisted string that connects the two limbs.

Serving

The reinforced wrapping at the center of the bowstring to guard against string wear. Compound bows may have servings in other areas.

Sight Bridge

The section that attaches to the rear of the barrel and holds the sight.

Picatinny Rail

The grooved rail that attaches to the sight bridge and forms the base for mounting a scope.

Stock

The rigid base section of the bow that provides shoulder aiming and support of other systems. May be adjustable.

Latch

The metal protrusion that holds the string. Pulling the trigger disengages the latch and launches the arrow.

Anti-Dry-Fire Device

A safety latch that will not allow the bow to be shot without an arrow nocked. Dry firing a bow releases all stored energy into the bow and may destroy parts of it. Misfiring occurs when the string slides under or over an arrow, launching the arrow, yet causing energy to be absorbed by the bow.

COMPOUND CROSSBOWS

The most popular bows today employ the same technology as the vertical compound bow. A cam at the end of each limb reduces draw weight dramatically as the bow reaches full cock. This principle reduces the physical strength needed to cock the bow, and an average person can easily cock a bow with 150–175 pounds of draw weight. Also, like compound vertical bows, upon release, this brief valley of reduced weight quickly

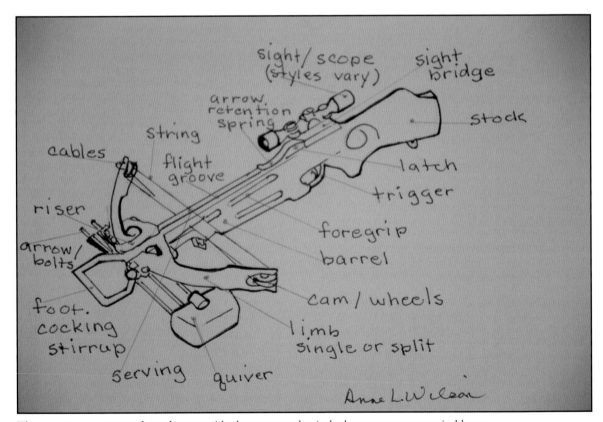

The cams on a compound crossbow provide the same mechanical advantage as on a vertical bow.

gives way to the full power of the limbs, generating significant speed.

Many of the parts of the compound bow are similar to recurve crossbows, with these exceptions:

Cams

The circular or oval wheels at the end of the limb which generate a reduced draw weight near full cock.

Cables

The cams operate using a cable system to store energy. Sometimes cables are contained in the barrel of the bow by a cable guide that helps prevent wear on the cables and allows them to move with less friction.

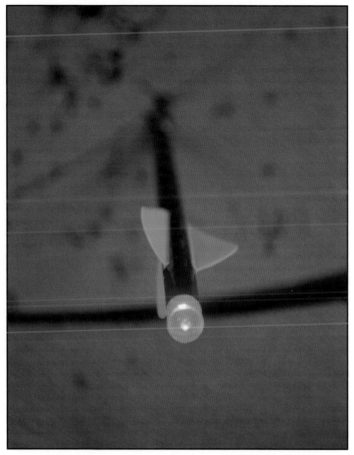

Once you have all the elements of an arrow together, it should fly directly to the target.

Limb Pockets

The section attached to the riser where the limbs fit and are bolted down.

Reverse Draw Limbs

Bows such as the Barnett Vengeance and BC Raptor have the riser directly under the foregrip. These bows are quite narrow and excellent for ground blinds and tree stands.

ARROWS AND BOLTS

The crossbow industry uses the word "bolt" to describe their "arrows" for safety reasons. Just as the muzzle-loading industry emphasizes the word "blackpowder" to be sure that consumers don't use smokeless powder in rifles, the crossbow folks cling to bolt so that archers don't try to use regular vertical bow arrows which are too light and limber to be shot safely.

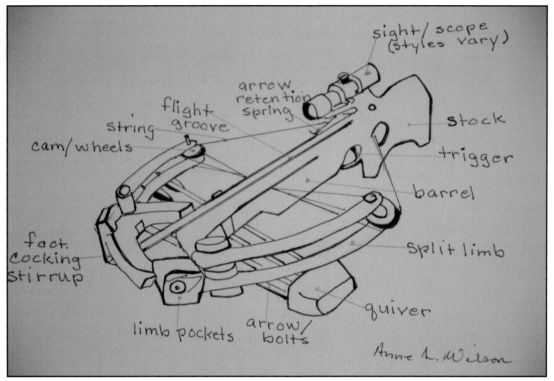

Knowing the parts of your bow will help you analyze shot performance and problem solve when needed.

For today's high performance crossbows, the terms "arrows" and "bolts" can be used interchangeably, but realize that a crossbow arrow is much thicker, heavier, and stiffer than most arrows designed for vertical compound bows. That said, let's begin at the rear of the arrow.

Nock

Nocks come in three basic forms: flat, concave (often called moon), and TenPoint's Omni nock. Some bows are designed to shoot flat nocks, while others require the use of a concave or Omni to maintain their warranties. Some nocks are illuminated such that when the arrow is released, the nock glows, making the flight of the bolt easier to follow and greatly facilitating recovery. The fit of the nock against the rear of the shaft is critical to accuracy. The end of the shaft is sanded and squared for a precise nock fit.

Fletching

The "feathers" of the bolt are mostly plastic and come in various lengths. The longer the vane, the more drag they impose on the shaft, which slows arrow flight. Two-inch vanes have become popular because they have little wind resistance, and still impart guidance and stability to the shaft. Bolts nocked with concave nocks must have the "cock feather" in the down position where the fletch slides in the flight groove. Arrows with flat nocks

A proper insert will allow you to switch off between field tips and broadheads.

may not have a designated cock feather, which is always a different color than the "hen" feathers.

Dynamic Spine

Although you cannot see this feature of the arrow, carbon, aluminum, and wooden arrows have a strength pattern along the plane of the shaft that determines how the shaft bends under pressure. Primitive archers used to build arrows from wooden staves, and then match the ones that had similar spines because they shot more consistently. Flat nocks allow the arrow to be rotated so that spines are similar. Doing this with a concave nock risks cutting the bowstring and is very dangerous.

Insert

This threaded cylinder allows various tips to be screwed into the business end of the shaft, and provides additional strength upon impact. Inserts can be permanently glued into a shaft or installed with heat performance glue so that they can be reheated and removed. Proper alignment is a very critical element for hunting arrows. If the insert has more glue on one side than the other, the insert will not align precisely with the shaft. Archers check for the malady by spinning the shaft on its point. If the point wobbles, the insert is improperly installed.

The stiffness of a bolt or arrow has much to do with how well it shoots from a particular bow.

Chapter 13

Maximizing the Moment of Truth

Bill Jordan is an icon of the hunting world. He and his family have hunted around the world, and here's his advice for MOT.

Releasing a bolt at live game can be so traumatic that your knees wobble, arms shake, and shooting skills self-destruct. Six top archers tell how they tame the Moment of Truth. Other than drawing the bow, compound and crossbow hunters face the same challenge of estimating range, picking a spot, and launching an accurate arrow. Whether with vertical or horizontal gear, buck fever does not discriminate.

"When I release an arrow, my adrenaline soars, and I shake like a quaking aspen in a hurricane," says Dan Evans, elk archer and owner of Trophy Taker products. "Excitement is why we are here, and if there is none, you should be knitting, playing golf, painting watercolors, or a whole bunch of other things."

Ironically, Evans gets more nervous when a big doe approaches his tree stand than a set of antlers, because does seem to be more wary and careful than "a big, stupid buck in the rut."

Evans readily admits to getting nervous and says he has blown shots. "That's part of hunting," he says. To help control the innate excitement of the Moment of Truth (MOT), he tries not to look at the rack, particularly with the world-class elk that he takes annually. "The more I look at the rack, the more frazzled I become, so focusing on the shot location has worked well for me. The toughest instance I face

Never look at a buck's antlers or body size; the key to staying calm and making a good shot is to focus solely on the shot.

is when I have to let down because an animal turns its head or moves behind cover. The drama of what will happen next really pumps my adrenaline."

Evans believes practice is the best way to mentally and physically prepare for MOT. First, make sure your equipment performs well, and then increase your practice distance. "If you practice at thirty to forty yards, you'll find that a twenty-yard shot becomes a piece of cake. The more you practice at longer distances, the better you will shoot on game close in." Evans takes a practice target on each of his hunting trips so he can stay in tune daily.

POSITIVE SHOOTING STYLE: CHUCK ADAMS

Chuck Adams, the iconic archer, has developed a positive shooting style that has become nearly automatic. "I follow good basics of shooting," he says. "I use an open stance about forty-five degrees toward the target with my feet. Then I aim and release, a process that takes about three seconds.

If Adams has a problem with shooting, it is usually his follow-through. If he does not keep the pin on the target until arrow impact, his accuracy suffers. "I have to have a little talk with myself every once in a while," he says, flashing that famous smile.

Adams often target shoots in leagues in the off-season, a process that emphasizes the importance of hitting a spot. "I pretend there is a bull's-eye on every animal I shoot. I imagine the heart and lungs behind the hide and aim at the center of it." Adams believes 3-D targets are the best practice for big game, especially the GlenDel Buck, which shows the vitals from a variety of angles, including a tree stand shot.

If you can visualize the shot beforehand, you'll have a much better chance of making the shot count.

BE A TURTLE IN A TREE

"As the Moment of Truth comes, you want to act fast, and things seem to be happening faster than they really are," says Bruce Barrie, of Rocky Mountain Broadheads. "You need to slow that down and keep control."

Barrie believes that many archers make the mistake of shooting arrows just to shoot arrows, launching forty to fifty shafts in a session. My practice session is to shoot five or six good arrows," he says. "Obviously you need to develop muscle tone, but what you want to do is to make that first shot good every time. It's a big thing to make sure the first arrow of the day is your best. So control the shot. Don't get quick."

Barrie suggests practicing in mental shooting situations, since exercising control in practice which will improve your chances on deer and elk. Practice and make sure they are great shots. Mentally practice as well. "When you are sitting on a stand without seeing game, get mentally ready. Imagine where the deer will come from and visualize the shot."

Barrie cites the experience of professional golfers who can visualize the shot before they make a swing. He takes a similar approach from a tree stand. "When you have nothing to do but sit and think, you can visualize that shot ahead of time. When the time happens, it may not work out that way, but sometimes it does. Being ready is 90 percent of the game."

Mentally and physically slowing the shooting process can help handle pressure.

THE FOCUS FACTOR

"I compare archers to other athletes," says Will Primos, President of Primos Hunting.

Will Primos uses organization to reduce the stress of the shot.

> Any athlete, football player, basketball player, or those who are consistently good are extremely focused. In the early days, being extremely organized helped me. I knew where everything was in my bow vest. If I needed a call or range finder, I had a pocket for each piece of gear. I could get the range with a range finder and never take my eyes off the deer. The same for my calls. That's why I put the Buck Roar call on my arm and the Can caller in a special pocket.

Your focus needs to be on distance, picking the right sight, and follow-through. You have to program that, and if something distracts you, if your stand squeaks, your mind gets fried. If a guy is about to take a three-point shot and bumps an elbow, his mind is taken off what he has to do. The Moment of Truth is all about being organized and being able to follow through with what you have to do.

Primos also believes that many archers forget to pick a spot, referring to his introduction into archery and practicing on the infamous "pie plate." As a result, he cut out the silhouette of a deer from a sheet of cardboard and began aiming with greater precision. In addition, Primos believes that many archers fold at the Moment of Truth due to self-imposed pressure.

By knowing where gear is and that all is well, Primos shoots with confidence.

They feel like, 'Here comes my chance, and it's going to be my only chance. I have to shoot.' That's not the way to think. Relax and enjoy the beautiful animal that you called in or outsmarted by scouting. Wait for the opportune moment to shoot and make a quartering away or broadside shot. Other angled shots are the beginning of horror stories, and it's no fun. Fun to me is shooting a deer and watching it pile up within fifty yards. For the Moment of Truth, be organized and keep focused.

3-D SIMULATION

"When I pull the bow back, the shot is natural, so that all I have to think about is when that deer steps into a lane," says Denny Steiner, an Illinois archer with a host of big deer to his credit. "I don't have to think of anything but the sight. I don't shoot at the deer; I pick a spot. I watch their leg go forward and let it go."

Early in Steiner's career he kept a checklist: bow ready, yardage, deer angle, pull back, anchor, check pin, deer in lane, pull trigger. If his form wasn't right, he started over. As the years went by, that list became instinctive so that he now follows the steps, but no longer consciously thinks of them.

Stiner visualizes an "X" behind a deer's shoulder.

I called in a buck last Fall from 286 yards with a Woods Wise Breeding Bellows, and the deer came running across an open field. As the deer approached, I ranged in a thirty-yard spot and got ready. At our 3-D club we have a moving target, and I practice on it a lot. The buck kept moving, and I considered trying to stop it by grunting. But sometimes that spooks a deer. Instead, I put the pin in front of his nose at the right height, swung with the movement and killed that buck.

Steiner shoots and practices often, visualizing the deer and the shot in his mind. On the target field he visualizes an "X" behind a deer's shoulder and practices at forty, fifty, and sixty yards. "If you can shoot eighty yards comfortably, then when that twenty-yard deer comes out, it's nothing," Steiner says.

Denny Stiner uses his 3-D skills when hunting, both to judge distance and to keep cool.

AVOID A MENTAL MELTDOWN

"If you are prepared and shoot well, the only reason you will miss those ten-to-thirty-yard shots is because you mentally failed," says Michael Waddell of *Road Trips* fame. "To me, when I miss, I am so let down because I know that I failed myself mentally. I have confidence in my gear, and if I miss, it's because I had a mental meltdown. I shot too quickly or didn't focus."

When practicing, Waddell shoots every practice arrow pretending there is something riding on it. Whether competing with friends or on his GlenDel buck, he looks at the rack and psyches himself up.

Even if a big buck is staring right at you, preparation and concentration will allow you to take a calm, steady shot, according to Waddell.

Every arrow I shoot, I follow that thought process. The mental process of picking a spot, taking my time, and releasing any mental obstacles that you can overcome. At the Moment of Truth, when I feel those nerves getting to the point of overcoming me, I try to think of anything but the outcome–like my kids playing T-ball. There's not a deer I shoot that I don't have to battle that desire to just pull and fling an arrow, and not even aim. Trying to focus on the other things to keep me cool, and not to focus on the rack is my solution.

Also, beyond putting the pin exactly on the spot, Waddell tries to keep the pin on the target one or two more seconds.

Emotionally, it gives you two seconds when you know you are ready. I do a lot of fist-pumping; it's an emotional flood of everything I have tried to control before the shot. Hunting is so much more emotional. It's a mind deal. The Moment of Truth is not hanging a stand in a great spot, or whether you are shooting a doe or a monster buck. It's the emotional

Waddell believes that staying focused is the key to success.

control to put that pin exactly on the target, resulting in a deer in the back of your truck.

Finally, Waddell always aims for the heart. "Watch an acorn fall near a deer sometime," he says. "That deer will duck three to five inches. I have never held on what I thought was a straight lung shot. Instead, I always aim for the top of the heart. No doubt the Moment of Truth is the defining moment of why we hunt and prepare," concludes Waddell. "It's why we experience that one juiced-up feeling, whether we release or let down."

HOW BILL JORDAN DOES IT

A stick snaps. Leaves crunch in a slow, steady rhythm, the unmistakable cadence of approaching game. The sound grows louder as you scan the brush, searching for the first glimpse of movement. Suddenly, antlers appear through a tiny opening and your heart races. The animal stops and seconds pass like hours. As your bow-hand begins to tremble, the beast steps forward and the shot seems imminent. By now you can feel the physical pounding in your chest.

Jordan practices by simulating hunting situations, shooting at different distances and even from tree stands.

Bill Jordan thrills to this sensation year after year and takes deliberate steps to handle the pressure. "The hardest thing a bowhunter has to do is to make that final shot," says the president of Realtree camouflage, and a major influence in the outdoor industry for nearly three decades. "Call it buck fever or whatever, but you have to control your nerves and emotions to face that animal. At times, an approaching deer doesn't bother me, while at others, my emotions try to gain the upper hand. I have had many hunting experiences and try to eliminate as many mistakes as I can. Releasing that arrow is critical to a bow hunter's success."

Jordan practices simulated hunting situations such as shooting at unknown distances, becoming well acquainted with his hunting gear, and shooting from tree stands. Once on the stand, he follows a mental practice regimen that boosts confidence.

Bill Jordan plays "what if?" when practicing. It is mental practice that pays off at times of great excitement.

I play 'what if' long before a deer comes into view. I make sure I know the range to likely travel spots, and I have the hunt planned out in my mind. Of course, deer don't always do as I plan; yet I try to be ready for any circumstance. I take the bow from the hook, come to full draw at shooting lanes, and concentrate on picking a spot and putting the arrow where I want it to go.

When game approaches, I'm mentally ready and not caught off guard. When I settle that pin behind the shoulder, I'm looking at one spot on that animal, whether it is broadside or quartering away. I try to control my emotions before the animal comes into view, and pre-play the hunt in my mind.

In order to reach the Moment of Truth, a hunter must predict the travel path of a game animal, especially the whitetail deer. "I'm fortunate enough to hunt some great places around the country," says Jordan, who puts up fifty to a hundred tree stands a year, sometimes fifteen to twenty in a single week.

I like to hang my own stands, and thoroughly enjoy hanging stands for others. Before picking a site, I look for food sources and transitions between food and bedding areas. Always keep the wind direction in mind, especially prevailing winds. In a really good spot, I may hang two or three stands to accommodate changing scent conditions.

Jordan anticipates shooting problems, avoiding a situation where a morning or evening sun will be directly in his eyes. He frequently sets a stand for a day or two and then changes it at midday, especially at times when the rut and food sources work together. "I like to hunt places frequented by does, since a female presence usually draws a big buck's attention," he says, then adds enthusiastically:

I hunt in my mind twenty-four hours a day. I lay in bed at night thinking about the consequences of doing this or doing that, reasoning why deer are where they are, and what their next move will be. I get the biggest joy out of hunting. It's not as much shooting at game as tactics and strategies, like playing a chess game. I have been so blessed by so many things. I sit on a tree stand and just love it.

BOB FOULKROD: RELEASING THE ARROW

"Almost every article or video that's out there tells you how to get deer in to you, but doesn't discuss the Moment of Truth, which is controlling your heartbeat and making the shot," says Bob Foulkrod, TV personality and one of America's most experienced bowhunters.

Part of making the shot is learning to do it correctly through practice, and an effective routine makes the pin stay on the target. Most archers, when the bow goes off the pin, will follow their arm and not maintain proper form.

When you first spot a deer and it begins to approach, your brain needs to say, 'I'm going to take this deer.' Go through a series of steps in your mind, constantly asking a series of mental questions that, hopefully, will keep you relaxed. When you stop thinking about wind direction, movement options for the deer, distance, etc., your heart rate will go up. When you don't know the distance of the deer, your heart rate goes up. Especially, don't admire the size of the buck's rack or be thinking of the cell

Bob Foulkrod is one of the nation's most experienced hunters. He operated his own bow school in Pennsylvania.

number of your taxidermist. You're going to get buck fever. Have confidence in your preparation and do small things, just like in practice. A feather or thread wind detector on the front of the bow will allow you to monitor your scent stream and determine when to shoot.

I don't wait for a deer's head to go behind a tree to shoot. When I make up my mind to draw, I come completely back, no matter what happens, whether the deer is looking at me or not. If a deer spots you, don't let the bow down. That takes just as much movement as drawing it back. Be positive and stay with the shot, keeping this next point in mind.

Keep the pin on the target until after the shot. Remember the acronym A.I.M.: *Always In the Middle.* Make sure the pin stays on the target. Don't drop your pin into the target or raise up from below. Put the pin into the middle of the kill zone and draw back. Many folks can't do that because they are over-bowed. They must raise the bow above their head or use body English to muscle the string to full draw. That adds movement. It's like starting a racecar driver with a flag. If you draw the bow correctly, the only movement is your elbow coming back. At the time of the shot, when your knees are wobbly and your palms sweaty, let the bow act as a shock absorber, which will allow the pin to stay in the middle of the kill zone. *Always In the Middle.* Before, during, and after.

Finally, the confidence level in your tree stand is critical. Become a deer hunter before you become a trophy hunter. How do you do that? Take advantage of the liberal doe seasons that many areas offer. Start out with small bucks, and try to get larger and larger. Eventually that trophy of a lifetime will come along. And you'll be ready.

Chapter 14

Turkey Hunting

The author used blind tactics to take this gobbler on opening day.

The MOT idea applies equally to wild turkeys as it does to whitetail deer. Plus, deer don't have fluffy feathers to hide their kill zone. Nonetheless, bagging a wily spring gobbler may be easier than you think. Follow these tips, and you'll have Thanksgiving dinner for Easter.

Opening morning was filled with gobbling, vocalizing from nearly every direction. By eight o'clock, I'd heard eight gun shots, a challenge to my patience, yet I believed that this setup would pay off. Suddenly, a pair of longbeards stepped from the tree line seventy yards away. Breaking from full strut, the duo eyed the jake decoy near the blind and came directly for it.

I picked up the crossbow, slid the safety off, and waited for the birds to strut into my shooting window. The range

A gobbler decoy was more than this jake could resist.

was about twelve yards, and in seconds the pair of mature gobblers surrounded the jake decoy, purring and doing their best to intimidate it. I was anxious to take my first bird with a crossbow, and as soon as one tom turned toward me, I aimed above its beard and squeezed, launching the bird briefly into the air. I could tell it was mortally wounded, yet it flew another twenty yards into the trees and disappeared.

Following up a turkey shot is not like hunting deer or elk, since there will be no blood trail. And as I searched for the bolt in the low grass, I was amazed to find no cut feathers. The expandable head I used has a 2-¼-inch cutting diameter, and I had to believe that at least some feathers would have been lost. Excited about the prospect of the turkey harvest, yet unsettled about the arrow's impact, I began to search for spring's roaring thunder.

SUCCESSFUL SETUPS FOR SPRING GOBBLERS

A pop-up blind is one of the most important pieces of gear for consistent spring gobbler success with a crossbow or vertical bow. If you hunt an area of sparse bird populations and must travel to find them, the small, deploy-in-the-air models work well, because they are so light and transportable, and easy to set up in seconds. I hunt a small farm that has a good wild turkey population, so I opted for a Browning hub blind that's roomy and comfortable for two people.

Turkeys have incredible eyesight, and can detect even a slight movement from dozens of yards away. One way to beat that is to set up in a blind.

Wild turkeys, unlike whitetail deer, are notoriously stupid about blinds. You can deploy one in the middle of a field, and turkeys usually pay little attention to it. A hunting guide told me once that he only brushed in his blinds to please the hunters, but turkeys didn't know the difference. Because whitetail deer and turkeys frequent the same habitat, I try to make my blinds as camouflaged as possible so that a pregnant doe doesn't spot it and began a snorting tirade just as turkeys approach.

A jake decoy is ideal for getting gobblers close to your blind.

Although turkeys often ignore the silhouette of a blind, movement in it will be quickly noticed. If possible, place the blind with the shooting window to the north or west so that rays from the rising sun won't reflect from your face or equipment, or amplify movement. Although some blinds offer a 360-degree view, this usually means that lots of light enters the blind as well. Personally, I like one open shooting window to the decoys and "peek holes" to see birds approach.

This spring I used Hunters Specialties Snood decoys, a jake and a hen, which come in a package. The artwork on the decoys and the body language they communicated worked perfectly. Three jakes tried to rough up the bogus bird and the two toms came with zero hesitation. Gobblers will usually approach the decoy from the rear and often parade around it. Put the decoy ten yards from the blind and make sure your bow is zeroed exactly for that distance.

Blind hunting takes patience, and you'll hear gobblers sounding off in the distance. If your blind is in a turkey travel corridor where you've found dropping and scratching, the toms will show up with a bit of enticement.

To succeed with turkey calling, "give what you get."

CALLING: GIVE WHAT YOU GET

The farm I hunt gets a fair amount of hunting pressure, and I'll never forget one opening morning when the woods seemed alive with gobbles. Using run-and-gun tactics, I slipped within seventy-five yards of a tree full of gobbling turkeys, sat down, and gave my best tree call on a slate caller. Suddenly, silence roared, and the turkeys never gobbled again. They flew down and vanished without another sound.

Turkeys that encounter hunter calling and decoys can become shy of both, so the best way to evaluate calling quantity is to "give what you get." Some flocks are noisy on the roost, while others are fairly quiet. If you hear a hen fly down and give a long series of yelps (the assembly call), try to emulate the pitch and cadence of her calls. She will call the entire flock together, so if you can lure her to your setup, a gobbler will surely tag along. Other times, a hen may make only a few yelps after flying down. In this case, call accordingly, emulating her sounds as best you can.

You can gauge a gobbler's interest by its response as well. If a gobbler answers your calls every time, keep it interested. But if the gobbler sounds off intermittently, change callers and try again. If the tom flies from the roost and stops gobbling, be especially vigilant as it may be approaching. The most exciting hunts occur when a tom approaches strutting and gobbling. But they often approach silently, and you need to be on your toes.

My favorite callers from a blind are pot (slate or glass), box, and diaphragm. Because the blind will cover your movement, using a slate caller is easy and very effective. Box callers also are easy to use, and the movement won't be detected. Mastering a diaphragm caller takes some work, but it is immensely beneficial, especially if you want a gobbler to stand erect for that perfect base-of-the-neck shot.

The blind setup allows you to lay out your callers, and make sure they are scuffed and chalked while waiting for action. This is also a good time to practice aiming your crossbow, using your jake decoy as a sight picture.

A good decoy, when well placed, can draw in even henned-up gobblers.

BROADHEADS AND SHOT PLACEMENT

The heart and lung area of a turkey is about the size of a tennis ball, so it's a very small target. Of even greater lethality is the spinal cord that's the diameter of a pencil and runs up the bird's back to its head. Any separation of this neuron center will instantly immobilize the bird, and drop it where it stands. Personally, this is my favorite shot.

Hitting a gobbler is easy. Killing it quickly takes practice and precision.

Broadheads for turkeys are different than for deer and other big game. The body of a turkey is fairly soft, and high poundage is not needed for penetration. In fact, some hunters actually reduce the draw weight of their compounds for added accuracy at full draw at a time when their shooting muscles may not be tuned. Generally, for turkeys, the larger the broadhead the better, since increased cutting diameter increases the probability of lethality.

Cut-on-contact heads cut on entry, while special turkey expandable heads give a greater cutting diameter and usually fly like target points. Because accuracy is so critical, practice is a must until you can hit that "tennis ball" every time. So your practice regimen may determine which head is best for you. The razor sharpness of traditional heads isn't necessary for turkeys, and I often practice a shot or two on a foam target to make sure my shaft and head fly exactly where aimed. You can use target points for more practice as long as they fly like your expandable heads.

Killing a turkey with an arrow takes practice and self-discipline. At ten yards that big, puffed-up bird looks like a barn door, and it's easy to just shoot. But remember the small size of the bird's vitals. Luckily, a strutting turkey is often stationary, whether it's approaching your call or attempting to intimidate a gobbler decoy. The best shot placements on a gobbler are at the base of the neck, just above the beard if it is facing you directly, and the wing-butt and the middle of the back if facing away. I tried the just-above-the-beard shot on the gobbler at the beginning of the chapter, but the tom wasn't facing me directly. I found the dead bird a hundred yards away, yet should have been more patient to wait for the perfect shot.

STAYING PUT, STAYING ALERT

I learned this strategy on a hunt in Mississippi many years ago. I was hunting with a guide who knew of a great roosting tree in a Mississippi swamp. We were able to sneak in silently, and we listened as the toms heralded the morning on the limb and on the ground. The problem was the swamp was so thick that getting a shot was nearly impossible.

These turkeys usually worked their way to a power line right-of-way where they strutted and gobbled until midday. "Let's set up there and just wait for them to show up," was my guide's advice. The next morning, we put a decoy along the power line opening and set up nearby. As usual, the toms gobbled and gobbled as we waited, most impatiently, several hundred yards away. My patience was in shambles, yet little by little, the gobblers grew closer. Finally, a mature longbeard came right to the decoy, hours after fly down.

Waiting patiently in a blind takes will power, yet the sit is immensely easier if you have confidence that birds are in the area. Drive back roads, and use binoculars to see where turkeys are feeding during the day. My usual spot is a small, two-acre field between woodlots where turkeys routinely cross the opening as they roam throughout the day. Even in early season, hens come to the field to feed, and a gobbler is usually close behind.

Blind hunting can become boring. It's important to stay put and alert.

Physical scouting works well too. You may find feathers, droppings, and evidence of scratching. If you are hunting Rio Grande or Merriam's turkeys, you can use scouting cameras or perhaps a spotting scope to capture the feeding route of flocks. These two species can travel miles during a day, so knowing their habits is a huge help.

Just like blowing a grunt tube from a tree strand, giving a few yelps or clucks every twenty minutes or so helps pass the time and won't diminish success. Once hens move to nests, gobblers begin to roam about, looking for more action, and those enticing calls may bring them right to you.

PUTTING IT ALL TOGETHER

The opening day success was a thrill, yet I wasn't pleased with the shot. Benjamin Franklin and I could have hunted together, so experience should have kept my shooting skills under control. I vowed to do better the next time.

Two days later I was in the same blind, where a gobbler hammered from a tree two hundred yards away. An hour after daylight, the tom was still sounding off, but he would not answer my calls. However, I enticed a hen that came and fed in the field near my decoys for half an hour. Suddenly I saw movement, and a big tom with a ten-inch beard was staring down my jake. Aiming carefully at the base of the bird's neck, I squeezed off the shot, and the bird dropped in its tracks. The HellRazor was spot-on. The plan laid out above worked perfectly, and my prize would make a great feast with no worry about shotgun pellets in the meat.

GEAR FOR SPRING GOBBLERS

Mission MXB-320

This compact, easy-to-cock crossbow has all the power you need for a turkey or ostrich. The pistol-grip stock design makes the bow ideal for accurate, offhand shots. www.missionarchery.com.

NAP HellRazor

I love these heads because they fly so accurately and remain sharp on foam targets. I notice no deterioration of sharpness after one shot, and the head design is a good mix of cutting diameter and aerodynamics. www.newarchery.com.

Spitfire/Rocket

The NAP Spitfire Gobbler Getter (1-¾) and Trophy Ridge Tom O Hawk (2-¾) mechanical heads have large cutting diameter and are devastating on turkeys. www.newarchery.com and www.trophyridge.com.

Easton BloodLine Carbon Shafts

I'm convinced that carbon bolts are the bomb for crossbows. Certainly aluminum shafts are just as straight, yet today's crossbows bury them so deeply into targets that bending on removal is an issue. www.eastonarchery.com.

Primos Power Crystal

I've used this caller for decades, and it provides extremely authentic sounds. Pot callers are ideal for clucks, purrs, and soft turkey sounds. www.primos.com.

ElimiTick Clothing

Using a blind camo pattern isn't as important, yet these new duds from Gamehide actually repel ticks, a source of Lyme disease. Like a safety harness for deer hunters, it's important protection. www.gamehide.com.

Jake and Suzie Snood Decoys

This pair of decoys from H.S. Strut is very lifelike. It poses the young gobbler in a semi-strut posture that brought gobblers directly to it. The hen is so well done that it didn't spook other hens feeding nearby. www.hunterspec.com.

LimbSaver Crossbow Sling

Turkey hunting is "digitally intensive," and carrying your bow over your shoulder keeps your hand free. This Kodiak sling is designed to keep your bow comfortably on your shoulder. www.limbsaver.com.

Chapter 15

The Ethics and Technique of Bowhunting Turkeys

Turkey broadheads are the most specialized of all. You can kill a turkey with a head meant for deer, but there may be a better way.

Wild turkeys are a large bird with a kill zone the size of a small apple. Here's a look at specialized broadheads designed for a clean, ethical kill.

Specialized turkey broadheads were all the rage at 2015's Archery Trade Association show, where more models were available than ever before. Mostly, turkey broadheads are larger than big game heads, often with twice the cutting diameter of a standard head. Sure, a Bear Razorhead will kill a turkey the same as it has deer for decades, yet the larger heads allow archers to aim for the bird's most vulnerable area: its neck.

A few years ago, I hunted the Gould's subspecies of wild turkey in Mexico. I took two broadheads: the Rocket Tom O Hawk and the Gobbler Guillotine. Interestingly, these two heads represent the two schools of thought for gobblers: very large expandables and fixed heads with large diameter blades.

The main strategy was to spot and stalk or ambush from thickets, so I opted for the expandable, which provided a kill range out to forty yards. I experimented with the Guillotine, and it flew well at twenty yards. But I only had a few, and there wasn't a Walmart nearby to resupply.

My chance came on the second day when I noticed several hens walking along a fence line, followed by a gobbler a few minutes later. I wasn't sure why birds were traveling the fence, but with

Shot placement is absolutely critical on wild turkeys.

the sun on the horizon, I figured another would probably come along. I moved into a small tree, and removed several branches so that I had a shooting tunnel to the fence just twenty yards out.

Barely five minutes passed before I saw a monster gobbler paralleling the fence and heading right toward me. It had a long, swinging beard, and I tried to keep my cool and aim carefully. As the bird entered the shooting portal, I made a *pucking* sound, which caused the gobbler to stop and raise its head. I aimed at the base of the neck and squeezed, launching an arrow that immobilized the tom immediately. The gobbler was large and its plumage gorgeous. It was one of the best trophies of my life, and I was as excited about the quality of the shot as the turkey fajitas that would follow.

LETHAL HITS ON WILD TURKEYS

To visualize the kill zone of a wild turkey, imagine if you could only shoot a deer in its heart, an organ twice the size of the small vitals of a turkey. Unlike deer, turkey gobblers disguise their body's silhouette by strutting. Plus, a turkey can fly away after being hit, leaving no possibility of trailing them. For these reasons, oversize heads are a good idea, as they increase the probability of a quick recovery.

Where to shoot wild turkeys is easily a full article in itself, so if you are new to the quest, research the topic carefully. In short, aim for the wing-butt on a broadside shot, the vent on a facing-away shot, and the beard for a frontal shot. Complicating this process is a gobbler's ability to tilt its fan so that it is not perpendicular to the plane of its body.

A number of successful turkey hunters have advised aiming at the top of the drumstick. Since the gobbler's legs are visible, a large broadhead in this area will cause massive bleeding and prevent the bird from springing into flight.

OFF WITH THEIR HEADS

Wide, fixed-blade heads have the potential for decapitating a turkey, and the internet has lots of examples in which a broadhead completely severs a turkey's head. As mentioned above, I'm a big fan of the neck shot, even though the target is very small, but not of decapitation. To me, this shows disrespect to the bird we chase and chase and chase. I find

The vitals of a wild turkey are very small and often camouflaged by feathers.

a wild turkey to be among the world's most beautiful birds, and I often spend a substantial amount of time admiring their beautiful plumage and thanking my Maker for the harvest. Photos are also important, and I revel at capturing the luster of the plumage, the length of the beard, and those dastardly spurs which often do battle for dominance.

I will experiment with the wide, fixed-blade heads this spring, but I plan to shoot where the feathers meet the neck. The wider blade diameter provides a larger margin for error and should still sever the spine for an instant kill. A gobbler or hen decoy is critically important in making a lethal shot, since gobblers almost always strut near a hen or adversarial gobbler. They tuck their neck and head into that apple-size ball and stand motionless, which is your signal for bolts-away.

SPECIALTY BROADHEADS

Turkey specialty broadheads come in two categories and a hybrid. Here are the pros and cons of each:

Large Expandables

Since a crossbow has plenty of kinetic energy, complete penetration is nearly guaranteed with the largest expandable heads, and increased diameter creates a larger margin for error. If you shoot a large-diameter, fixed-blade head and it flies well, there's no advantage to switching to an expandable head. However, practice and precision become extremely important, giving mechanical heads that fly-like target points the edge. In addition, if a tom stops and struts dead still at thirty yards, you can maintain your pinpoint accuracy.

Trophy Ridge Meat Seeker

This is a three-blade expandable with a two-inch diameter cut, weighing 100 grains. This head opens from the rear and requires no O ring. www.rocketbroadheads.com.

Practice on a realistic, 3-D target for best results.

Rage Crossbow X

This two-inch diameter head weighs 125 grains and offers the penetration and wound channel Rage is known for. www.ragebroadheads.com.

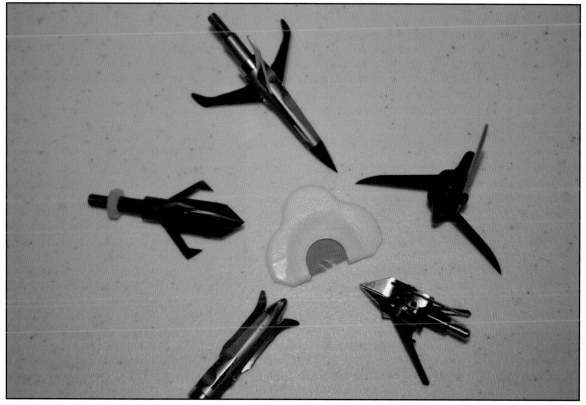

A variety of specialized broadheads give large cutting surfaces for quick, sometimes instant, kills.

Rage Krossbow Kore

This broadhead has a 1.6-inch diameter cut in a three blade model. These 100-grain heads have a compact ferrule for optimum weight distribution. www.ragebroadheads.com.

NAP Spitfire Maxx and Gobbler Getter

This expandable weighs 125 grains with a cutting diameter of 1-¾ inches. The Spitfire Gobbler Getter has the same size cutting diameter, but with a blunter head to provide greater penetration control. www.newarchery.com.

Wasp Jak-Hammer

This large mechanical opens up to 1-¾ inches and weighs 100 grains. Blades are replaceable once they become dull. www.wasparchery.com.

The right gear can make the difference between turkey success and failure. More than with deer hunting, calls and broadheads are specialized.

Oversize Fixed Blade

These heads are designed specifically for wild turkeys and to be shot at the head and neck area. A hit with this shot provides instant results, with either an instant kill or a miss. Since a gobbler's head is a small target and these wily birds move quickly, this may seem like a sport for optimists, however, a gobbler nearing a hen or gobbler decoy will often stand motionless with its head and neck tucked into an apple-size ball. A successful shot at this point will kill it instantly, possibly decapitating the tom.

Be sure to practice at a realistic range with the head, since the large blade surfaces can cause erratic flight. Also, before purchasing this type of head, make sure it will clear the cocking stirrup of your bow, if it has one. (Mission does not.) You may need to shoot a longer bolt than your manufacturer recommends, which will require some trial and error. Finally, if you plan to hunt from a ground blind, you'll need to double-check window clearance, as it's easy to get excited and crease the blind portal, ruining accuracy and potentially becoming dangerous to the shooter.

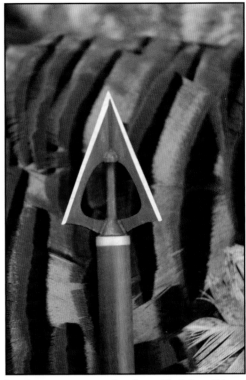

Large, cut-on-contact heads are ideal for wild turkeys.

Gobbler Guillotine

This four-blade head has a four-inch cutting diameter from a head that weighs 125 grains. A special archery quiver facilitates carrying the arrows with the heads mounted. www.arrowds.com/guillotine/guillotine.htm.

Magnus Bullhead

This three-blade design comes in 100- and 125-grain options with cutting diameters of 2-¾ and 3-¾ inches. www.magnusbroadheads.com.

BloodSport Archery Wraith Turkey Lopper

This fixed-blade head comes in two sizes made specifically for wild turkeys, although they should work for small game as well. The Lopper weighs 125 grains with a cutting diameter of 2-⅜ inches. The smaller size is 100 grains and 1-⅛-inch diameter. wwwbloodsportarchery.com.

Hybrid

Muzzy MORE

This unique head can be used with fixed blades in a one-inch-diameter configuration, or you can lock the blades open, at which point it becomes a three-inch-diameter, four-blade cutting machine. www.muzzy.com.

Wild turkey hunting out of state is lots of fun, as it was with this big Merriam's gobbler.

Chapter 16

Ground Blinds and Ground-Zero Tactics

Ground blinds are an exciting way to hunt deer and turkeys. Two hunters celebrating a kill using a blind.

Will innovations in portable blinds make tree stands a thing of the past? For spring turkeys or deer, here's how to get in on the ground floor of today's most exciting bowhunting tactic.

Brooks Johnson intensely watched a big eight-pointer and two lesser bucks chase a doe down a fencerow. Collapsing his ground blind, he tucked the concealing device under his arm, crossed the fencerow, and set up along the trail just traversed by the rutting trio. "I was in the blind perhaps four minutes when I saw the biggest buck returning," remembers Johnson, smiling about his plan coming together. "The eight-pointer came directly toward the blind, passed at fifteen yards, and stopped at thirty, offering the quartering-away angle I wanted. From setup to blood trail was less than five minutes."

Ground blinds aren't new. Native American hunters used them effectively; they are a staple in Africa, where they are called hides; and they are inherently safer than tree stands since you can't fall from them. However, until now, ground blinds have been immobile, heavy, or easily identified by game. Fortunately, a new wave of pop-up technology is changing the camouflage landscape. Ground blinds, including a comfortable folding chair, weigh less than many tree stands, and go up and down in less time. You can drop your release repeatedly with no problem, and it's even possible to purify the wind of scent. Here's the lowdown on this latest hunting strategy.

GOING FOR GOBBLERS

Whether you are an experienced turkey hunter or just a curious beginner, now is the time to get portable and blindside a tom. Regardless of the subspecies, the American wild turkey is one of bow hunting's greatest challenges. Blessed with incredible eyesight, a gobbler can practically spot a bowstring coming to full draw two counties away. Savvy hunters have figured out the best calling strategies, effective camouflage, and setup techniques, but other than using 99 percent let-off, the motion of the bow arm reaching anchor has always been a stumbling block.

Spring gobblers pay little attention to a ground blind, even in a wide-open field.

Fortunately, you can move as much as needed in an enclosed blind. Brooks Johnson spends about sixty days a year hunting, and he does things undreamed of in the open woods. "For deer hunting, we usually clear all the leaves under the blind for quietness," he says. "For turkeys, we do just the opposite. We intentionally leave the leaves and make scratching sounds as the gobbler approaches. These are precisely the natural sounds that draw the bird close; ones even a perfectly camouflaged hunter could not perform in the open." Not only do blinds conceal the movement of the bow, they can provide total concealment. "We offer a special mesh that archers can shoot through and maintain accuracy, he says. "In this way you have total concealment."

Despite the ultra-sensing eyes of a wild turkey, spring gobblers pay virtually no attention to blinds. Erect a brown blind in the middle of a green field, place a few decoys next to it, and the turkeys will walk right up as long as the blind isn't blowing in the wind or making an unnatural sound. An experienced turkey guide in South Dakota, who specializes in hunting from blinds, told me confidentially, "We camouflage the blinds more for the hunter than the turkeys. Gobblers really don't care what it looks like, but good camo helps the client become more confident."

ANATOMY OF THE CHALLENGE

Choosing to hunt spring gobblers takes commitment. Of course, that should be the rule for all hunting, yet the wild turkey requires an extra level of dedication. Deer hunters have had success with pie-plate accuracy, putting half a dozen arrows into the circumference from twenty-five yards. However, with turkeys, you must hit a tennis ball in most cases, and you can't whistle or grunt to make the bird stop. A turkey is a big target, yet the kill zone is very small, requiring sufficient patience to make just the right shot.

Ground blinds help this process immensely. You can literally watch the bird come into range, and raise the bow just as the best shot presents itself. From a side or frontal view, aiming for the head will dispatch the gobbler instantly. And it's easier to hit than most think. When a tom struts, it often pulls its head and neck into a tight ball that's a bright blue and white color. Put your shaft here and it's as good as on the table.

Mechanical broadheads may be controversial with deer, yet they are ideal for gobblers, since many archers want the arrow to stay in the turkey to help prevent flight. In most cases, the bigger the cutting edge the better. New Archery Products makes a special turkey head called the Spitfire Gobbler Getter.

Why not accept the challenge of spring gobbler hunting? A pop-up blind makes it much easier.

SETTING UP FOR SUCCESS

Spring gobblers prefer open areas where they can use their incredible eyesight for protection. The portable blind changes this strength to a weakness. Since they can't see a hunter, the birds act naturally and are more responsive to decoys and calling.

If you know an area well, select a location where gobblers go to strut and mate. Typically, these are open sections of hardwoods or open fields. Place the blind so that you have a twenty-yard shot in all directions or toward more focused shooting lanes if you believe the gobbler will approach from a given direction.

Place a decoy or decoys at ten yards, facing the blind. Gobblers often strut in front of hens, and this tendency will put the tom closer to the blind. Your decoy also acts as a distance marker, allowing you to be sure the tom is in range.

If you are hunting a new property, tuck the blind, decoys, and folding stool inside the carrying case and locate toms in the usual fashion. Once you hear a bird gobbling, set up a hundred yards or so from the roost, and you are in business. From the concealment of the blind, you can make soft tree sounds. Call softly once the bird is in sight (ordinarily taboo because of hand movements). Scratch in the leaves (an alluring sound that even pressured birds will respond to). Then draw the bow undetected at the Moment of Truth.

Once you become experienced at setting up and taking down the blind, the process will occur with amazing speed. Each blind takes a little practice, but once mastered, up and down become second nature.

The prospect and proximity of other hunters is a safety concern. When placing decoys, especially jakes, you must exercise great care, since an excited hunter could fire at the decoy. Placing blaze orange behind the blind will alert other hunters to your presence. Also, check your state regulations carefully. Hunting spring gobblers from blinds is not legal in a few states.

THE EYE OF EXPERIENCE

Ray Eye is a household word in turkey circles, and he has used blinds to become one of the most successful turkey outfitters in the country. "I have forty-one blinds spread over twenty-five hundred acres, and the success is tremendous," he says, pulling no punches. "Last season we experienced 100 percent success."

Ironically, Eye hunts properties that many traditional hunters would pass up. "The farms are very open with fields, crops, and some wood lots," says Eye. "This is country where a gobbler will spot you more than a quarter mile away. The turkey densities are heavy, and moving to set up on one gobbler you'll often spook several others."

Eye points out an often-overlooked aspect of blind hunting: reduction of hunting pressure. We have a three-week season here in Missouri. On my neighbor's property, intense hunting pressure and human presence causes the birds to stop gobbling after the third or fourth day. On my leases, toms gobble the full three weeks."

Scouting, pursuing wild turkeys on foot ("run and gun"), and driving through likely terrain are traditional pre-season hunting activities. But not for Eye. He uses binoculars and glasses to scout strutting grounds and travel corridors from afar. Once he locates a hot strutting ground, he deploys a blind in the location and hunts it as soon as the season opens. If food sources change, he may use a pop-up blind, using darkness to get into a good location. When selecting a blind location, he looks for an unobtrusive entrance such as a ravine, wood line, or thick draw. In this way, hunters can move to and from the blind without disturbing the normal wildlife patterns.

Eye discourages walking in the open, driving to blinds, and other types of disturbances. Typically, hunters are in a blind forty-five minutes before daylight and stay there until late in the morning, or until they get their bird. "At first this may sound boring," says Eye, "but you'll see things you've never encountered before. You will see turkeys in an undisturbed state. Like a nature show on TV. Birds will do all the things they do in the wild because they are not pressured, and they get so close it's not uncommon for them to brush against the blind."

Use binoculars, even when in a blind, to detect any incoming turkeys.

He recommends blinds for small properties too. A farm with 150 acres can be overrun with hunting pressure in just a few days. By using blinds, the birds act naturally and are pattern-able.

Finally, Eye displays decoys in a flock of five or six. When hens are nesting and gobblers are on the prowl, the dekes have the best magnetic affect. Jakes (one-year-old gobblers) bring out the beast in longbeards, who won't tolerate an upstart in their territory and make a beeline to kick butt. Thanks to the concealing nature of the blind, you can bank on a close shot if your nerves can handle the pressure.

GROUND BLINDS FOR ALL GAME

I had the chance to deer hunt with whitetail expert Dennis Steiner, near Springfield, Illinois. Although we only spent an hour in his Double Bull blind, the process greatly impressed me. One minute we were walking across a cornfield; the next we were peering from inside a blind with total camouflage concealment. I was comfortable, warm, and able to use a range finder and raise my bow without worry of detection.

Portable blinds are ideal for spring gobblers and other game. Steiner took two coyotes in the same evening from his blind. After arrowing the first, its mate came by for a double dose of Double Bull. Field reports indicate that elk, mule deer, bears, predators, and other game pay little attention to a blind. The one exception is the whitetail. "The roof line is critical for deer," says Brooks Johnson. "Whenever possible, we try to set up so that the top of the blind doesn't present a horizontal line. We also "brush-up" the blind, disguising the outline by adding natural foliage and branches. To see how close hunters can get to game, buy or rent the video "Another Year on the Ground."

Constructing a natural ground blind can also be effective.

Blinds are great for getting kids involved in hunting – even the young ones!

MINI BUYERS GUIDE FOR PORTABLE BLINDS

Ameristep Under Armour Carnage Blind

I used this blind in 2015 because it camouflaged well, and it was advertised that it would deploy in sixty seconds. I didn't use a watch, but I'm sure I had seconds to spare. The blind was very roomy with lots of openings from top to bottom. Gobblers walked right to me as if the blind didn't exist. www.ameristep.com.

Browning Powerhouse

The ability to move is one of the greatest hunting gifts any blind can provide and the Powerhouse is extra tall, so all but NBA players can stand up, stretch, and aim. The blind has a skirt to keep the sides down and boost interior darkness. I've killed several gobblers from them. www.browningcamping.com.

Cabela's Gun/Bow Blind

This blind sets up in less than ten seconds. Made from brushed cotton, it is disguised in all-purpose camo, an excellent balance of quiet and conceal-ment. www.cabelas.com.

Cutting Edge Blinds

This very portable blind is easy and fast to set up. It weighs only fifteen pounds and has no loose parts to lose or assemble incorrectly. A stor-age/carrying bag with dual backpack straps is included. The blind stands 6'6" tall. A waterproof dome sheds water and snow. Custom-made "leafy blinds" are available by order.

Primos Double Bull Archery

Produced from a blend of cotton and polyester, these blinds pro-vide much more light-blocking ability than department-store nylon blinds. They also offer a lined model with a thin coating of black rub-ber on the inside. One is super quiet; one is super dark. These are very roomy blinds for two people. They are available in Predator Deception, the first camo designed specifically for blinds. They go up and down in under ten seconds. "A Year on the Ground" video is a must. www.primos.com.

Big bucks can be fooled by a blind. Just take care to set it up in advance and cover it with natural camouflage.

WWW.RAYEYE.COM

Special thanks to Ray Eye for his savvy turkey input. Check out his hunts and products at this web address or phone (636) 944-3981.

Chapter 17

The Big Date: Opening Day for Whitetail Deer

Opening day is a big date no matter your gender or age. It has all the excitement and ambiance of a romantic encounter.

The biggest bucks of the year follow a predictable routine in early season. Whether it's for a "beau" or with a "bow," the right game plan can put this much-anticipated encounter right in your lap.

Preparing for opening day is like going on an important date. You want everything to be perfect. You've waited anxiously, prepared well, and anticipated an exciting interaction. Will it progress like many others, from a situation that seemed promising but only ends in disappointment? Or will your plans and preparation come together for a lifetime memory?

Montana's Milk River region is one of North America's best deer areas. Bill Jordan hunts there. So do Gene and Barry Wensel and Jack Nicklaus (the other Tiger). Excited to walk in the footsteps of such legends, I arrived early, got my gear together, and was anxious to get started. Despite a gung-ho attitude, I found success by cooling my heels.

"We spent the first evening scouting, looking for the best stands," said an experienced cameraman for Realtree Outdoors, the host for this exciting adventure. Up at 5:00 the next morning, the same pattern continued. "We don't want to bust well established patterns," he said. "Keep looking and we'll be ready to hunt this evening." On this five-day outing, I'd get to hunt four evenings, a scouting-to-stand ratio of about 2:1. For every hour hunting, I'd spend two scouting.

As Monday afternoon finally arrived, I showered in preparation for this much-awaited, early-season encounter. I couldn't help reminiscing, looking back more years than I care to mention, just like going on a big date. The excitement, preparation, and

Once you have that special spot, just wait for the magic to happen.

anticipation were tremendous. It was a blind date maybe, but I had a definite rendezvous in mind. I'd be "dressed to kill" and have a half-dozen fletched roses of sorts. I hadn't felt this pumped since the prom. The plan was to score on opening day and make the most of each heart-pounding moment.

PICK JUST THE RIGHT SPOT

Opening day will not be successful unless you scout an exact location for a stand. In the East, finding this special place usually means careful and odorless searching for trails and other deer sign at midday. Milk River taught me another way. This area's high deer population and diverse age structure made deer easy to disturb. Alfalfa fields and bedding areas adjoined, such that deer rarely traveled very far. If you bust deer from their favorite sleeping sites, the routine is destroyed.

Patience is a virtue on that first date. If you have done your homework, good things will happen.

A buck's antlers are fully formed by the end of July, and watching favorite travel patterns in August and early September can zero in the best places for the big date. I spent three hours the first evening, and the same time in early morning, watching how deer entered fields, where they fed, and how they left, carefully noting wind direction. Quality binoculars and/or a spotting scope were required tools of this trade.

After six hours of intense glassing, my observations matched those of Mike McKinsey, who had observed the same field several days earlier. Two Pope and Young bucks consistently entered an alfalfa field through a gate or by jumping the fence next to a large cottonwood tree. As we discussed with the landowner how to cover both trails, he came up with the perfect solution. "Why don't you close the gate?" Voila!

Scouting, rather than just hunting outright, was difficult, but I quickly saw the merit of the plan. Like taking out that special someone, once you know where they want to go, a good time is practically assured.

THINK CLEAN THOUGHTS

On a date, the aroma of perfume or cologne can add to your allure. For hunters, the best scent for the big date is no smell at all. When Monday evening finally arrived, my preparation began well before hunting time, taking a shower, using scent-eliminating soap on skin and hair, and paying careful attention to scent on clothing. Before leaving for this trip, I carefully washed my regular camo clothes in scent-eliminating soap. Also, I activated my ScentBlocker Plus outerwear by placing it in a dryer, on hot, for thirty minutes. My cameraman and I sprayed down all surfaces that regularly have human contact, such as my bow, arrows, backpack, binoculars, release strap, and boot bottoms. I wore a new pair of Rocky Gore-Tex Supprescent boots and found them comfortable, waterproof, and odor absorbent. Unfortunately, my cameraman's regular clothes were lost by an airline and hadn't arrived. He used black tape to cover his white sneaks and borrowed other camo clothing.

Perhaps smelling like an alfalfa sprout could have attracted a buck, however, the best bet for early season is to be scent-free. You want your targeted deer to behave in the same way it has in the past and have no reason to change its routine.

Makeup is a good idea regardless of gender.

By scouting from a distance with binoculars, we left no chance of human scent in its environment.

DRESS TO KILL

Scott Shultz, President of Robinson Outdoors, the makers of ScentBlocker, was my roommate and hunting buddy at Milk River. During meals and bull sessions, I learned a great deal about the Scent Blocker Plus products, how they work and were developed. "The scent-absorbing liner is the same material used by our troops in Operation Desert Storm," explained Shultz. "It was developed to protect troops from bacterial and biological warfare agents with one exception: they used the carbon and odor absorbing material on the outside. We reversed the material and use it as a liner."

The outside of the suit was a soft, quiet material, water resistant, and imprinted with the Advantage Timber pattern. "Remember, there's nothing magic about the outer layer,"

When on a stand, keep an eye on all approaches, not just what's in front of you.

Shultz cautioned. "You have to keep it free from odor like any other article of clothing. You can't come home and hang it in the kitchen and expect deer not to smell you."

The ScentBlocker Plus suite came with a scent-absorbing bag that helped ensure scentlessness. Offered by a number of companies, these "scent containers" help ensure that odors on the outside of clothing are absorbed. Even with plain camo cotton, whatever scents have embedded in the fabrics will be absorbed by the container. This isn't a cure-all, yet every little bit helps.

PRACTICE HEAD GAMES

In college, I dated Timmy Troth, a drop-dead brunette who was about the best looking gal on campus. I met her with a cheerful greeting, yet we barely spoke the rest of the evening. It was actually two dates in one: the first and the last. I was so nervous that I choked up in the same way that hunters freeze up when a big buck pops into view. You've dreamed about taking aim at that big ten-pointer, yet when it appears, excitement rules.

Head games should be part of any pre-season preparation. First, you must maintain the discipline to scout carefully to learn the travel routes of deer. Does that buck pass

Dress to kill. Wear clean clothes and use your best scent-absorbing gear.

through a bottleneck? Stop by a salt lick? Or cross a fence or stream at a particular place? Next, mentally visualize the proper steps to control your scent, approach a stand quietly, and stay focused when the Moment of Truth arrives. Imagine the presence of that big buck. Simulate the pressure as you prepare and practice.

Many effective hunters develop an unspoken phrase to ward off buck fever. They silently ask, "Is the pin on the animal?" Instead of ogling at antlers, they control their mind and muscles. Instinctive shooters can focus on the crease behind the front shoulder, trying to hit an exact hair. If your game is frequently hunted from tree stands or seems nervous, aim lower than usual. Spooky deer often drop at the sound of the bowstring.

MY BIG DATE

Big bucks had repeatedly entered the alfalfa field about an hour before dark. Taking no chances, we were in place by early afternoon to avoid spooking does that usually arrived earlier. Since this was a working ranch, the landowner drove us to the stand in his old pickup, eliminating the possibility of an entrance trail. I closed the gate using a clean glove, and the table was set. I was dressed to the nines and had five "long-stems" in my quiver.

Whether it's a deer or turkey hunt, the opening date can really be a date.

Shortly after we arrived, a storm blew up. The wind howled initially, but settled down as does jumped the fence in front of us. At 5:45, like a doorbell ringing, I caught a glimpse of deer approaching. Three eight-points and a six walked and fed toward the gate, the smallest in the lead. Glancing at the closed gate, it changed course and jumped the fence. When the biggest buck followed suit, I gave a loud *baaa,* stopping it at twenty yards.

My arrow whizzed through its chest just behind the heart. Although the animal had enough energy to jump back across the fence, it bedded down in plain view. The wide ten-pointer scored just under 140 and displayed a heavy, chocolate-colored rack. Was I happy!

The Milk River hunt was a learning experience for me, despite having bowhunted whitetails for thirty years. Even the biggest, wariest bucks have exploitable weaknesses, if you have the patience and persistence to learn and exploit them. Don't take the scouting process lightly. It is a serious investment and may occur at the cost of hunting time. Like the big date, you have to prepare both mentally and physically, pick the right location, be flexible, and follow through. Implement this plan and I believe you'll score. Will it help your love life? I haven't a clue.

Chapter 18

Elk During the Rut: The Grandest of Adventures

Elk hunting during the rut is one of the grandest adventures in North America. Archers can do well when they find water.

Hunting bugling elk is every archer's dream. But how about a crossbow on a rugged, high-altitude hunt? Join the author, two miles up, on a classic wilderness adventure.

"The bull's just ahead, slightly down hill," whispered Toby Shaw, my hunting buddy, on this third day of a six-day elk hunt in Wyoming's Bridger-Teton National Forest. Our foursome had spent the first three hours of daylight climbing to timberline, and had located a bull in a deep gorge. The bull bugled regularly, so we split up and worked our way toward it using stealth and silence instead of calling, often a gamble on public land. With a little luck, the rutting beast would work our way.

In fact, the bull was incoming, and my down-slope friends frantically hand signaled, "I see it, and its coming our way." My TenPoint was already steadied on shooting sticks, and I'd ranged several snags and rocks. In two previous years, I'd taken good bulls with compound bows, and my heart pounded with the prospect of a high-mountain hat-trick.

Better yet, with the crossbow, I didn't have to worry about the bull seeing the movement to full draw.

Expecting to see the bull at any second, I searched intently for the tiniest movement, trying to remain calm. Seconds turned to minutes, yet no target emerged. Shaw signaled downhill, but they saw nothing. Five minutes led to ten, ten to fifteen, when suddenly the bull bugled on the far side of the canyon.

Weather is uncertain in the mountains, and a hunter must be prepared. Good binoculars are a must.

The wind was right and we were well hidden, but lady luck, maybe in the form of a hot cow, turned the bull's course and kept it from harm's way.

SWITCHING FROM IDAHO TO WYOMING

Ken Byers and Toby Shaw had operated a wilderness elk camp in Idaho for their friends and business associates. But recent years had brought minimal success, and elk seemed to bugle less each year, perhaps as a result of the increasing wolf population. Daunted but determined, Byers and Shaw moved their camp to Wyoming and encouraged "the gang" to apply for tags. Most drew, with the exception of Byers and Shaw in an ironic twist of fate.

I was one of the lucky tag guys and helped set up camp along one of the many Forest Service roads. I then went about exploring the huge expanse of public land south of Jackson Hole. Whereas Idaho elk were frequently found in the deepest, steepest canyons, most Wyoming elk were in remote regions near timberline. This observation proved golden the third day of the hunt, when Andrew McKean, executive editor of *Outdoor Life,* proved his hunting mettle by taking a respectable 4x4 bull after bivouacking overnight, high on the mountain. Elk bugled vigorously before daylight, and McKean sneaked into position just as the eastern sky paled. Stalking a bull in sparse terrain, he cow-called, and the bull turned and came to forty yards. One bolt was plenty. Kudos to McKean for his hunting stamina as he packed the bull off the mountain over the next day and a half, a three-hour climb each time.

My partner on the trip was Barb Terry, a retired United States Army Captain and media-relations person for TenPoint Crossbows. This was my first crossbow adventure in the backcountry, and I was excited to have a product expert for shooting and performance tips. While Byers and the boys hiked the mountaintops, Terry and I explored the medium altitudes, looking for pockets of elk activity. Our first day was magical as we drove to eight thousand feet, parked our rig, and hiked a long, gradual ridge. Since every inch of country was new to us, we moved slowly, bugled occasionally, and glassed often. We returned the next morning well before daylight, hoping to catch elk in distant meadows at dawn, but we saw none.

As noon approached we headed back to the rig for new territory, and we drove past a sheepherder near the roadway. "Let's ask him if he's seen any elk," suggested Terry. "Maybe what we need is more intel," she added with a laugh.

"I haven't seen many elk lately, but there was a bull bugling up a storm right behind our camp this morning," said the friendly rancher, who willingly gave us detailed directions.

WELCOME TO THE WILDERNESS

With a lead on a hot bull, we found the camp, just where our benefactor had indicated. We grabbed our gear and hiked into the mountains. Sheep had made well-used trails, yet we

Practice in full hunting gear to get ready for this challenge.

Sleeping in tents allows hunters to remain close to game, and the entire hunt can be on foot.

found fresh elk tracks and droppings as well. Not wanting to move too invasively, we cowcalled at the first opening, but got no response. This was Terry's first elk hunt. It was also my first mountain crossbow hunt, making each of us rookies of a sort.

The afternoon began in bluebird conditions with barely a cloud in the sky, yet as we worked our way up the mountain, dark clouds built in the West. We located active elk trails where it appeared animals were moving from high-mountain bedding to lowland feeding, and we agreed to watch separate trails until dark.

Within an hour, lightning flashed in the distance, and we were bombarded with marble-size hailstones and a howling wind. I carried a Montana elk decoy and used it as a shield, like in some gladiator movie, fighting arrows from above. The storm ended with an inch or more of hail on the ground, making travel treacherous. We chose to hunt until the last minute, which meant navigating the many deadfalls and steep terrain in complete darkness with no visible landmarks. Crossing one log, my feet flew into the air, and I landed so hard that my bulb elk call squeaked, a humorous moment that could have been a disaster.

Arriving at the rig, I breathed a silent prayer of thankfulness, yet I learned how easily a crossbow can be carried even in thick, dark timber. I'd chosen to cradle it under my arm rather than over my shoulder, but I had little trouble navigating. And occasionally

A motionless hunter has a good chance of elk approaching within range.

I'd use the cocking stirrup as a staff for extra balance when crossing logs and slippery ground.

HOW IT'S SUPPOSED TO BE

Although neither Terry nor I had killed an elk with a crossbow, Chuck Jordan, Director of Business Development at TenPoint, raved about his experience, and the exciting story was a motivator when grades became steep. "I wished I had a video camera on the hunt," said Jordan.

> The rut was at a peak, and bulls were bugling and almost constantly on the move with cows. I hunted from a pop-up blind that overlooked a watering hole large enough for bulls to wallow in, and the excitement was off the charts. I actually passed up two small bulls as they came to drink, which was a difficult decision when the huge animals were only twenty yards away.
>
> Luckily, after a brief hiatus from activity I heard a deep, coarse bugle in the distance, and the ever-increasing sound indicated the bull was

coming closer. Cow after cow came to drink, with the bull bugling just out of sight and my heart beating like a drum. Tension reigned as the big bull stepped into view. Unfortunately, it drank while facing me, not offering the broadside shot I wanted. Several times, the bull raised its head to bugle, slobbers bubbling from its mouth. Such incredible action just twenty yards away!

Finally, the bull turned to leave and horned at a cow, presenting the shot angle I sought. My bolt zipped right through it, and the bull went right down. I was using NAP's Spitfire three-blade heads, and the results were incredible. I'd heard that elk can be tough to kill, so I aimed carefully and shot a second arrow. This time the bull jumped up,

Stalking also works, since elk are normally noisy animals in the mountains.

but went barely fifty yards before tipping over. This hunt was incredibly exciting and one I'll never forget.

HERD BULL, HONEY HOLE

Terry and I explored the sheep-camp area further, locating a secluded water hole where fresh tracks indicated that our bugling bull visited regularly. Since this was a one-person ambush, she watched that spot while I headed for the high country. Bugles had been heard near a huge shale slide, a great landmark and a boundary of sorts that kept elk in the timber.

The final morning I located another secluded, hula-hoop-sized water hole where rutting elk had freshly ripped limbs from trees. I watched the spot all afternoon that final day and heard elk bugle in the distance, constantly raising the question, "Should I go after them, or wait for them to come to me?" Actually, logistics gave a key element to the answer. We had to break camp in the morning, which would require a downed animal to be packed out overnight, and the water hole ambush held the highest probability for that perfect double-lung shot.

An hour before dark, bugling suddenly grew closer, and then a herd bull gave a horrific roar directly up the mountain, not more than three hundred yards away. Ohhh, the indecision! Wait, or stalk? The bull screamed again,

Bagging a trophy bull takes effective practice and knowing the exact range when shooting.

even closer. Was it coming to drink? Cow calls became evident. Was the whole herd coming to drink, or was this just a water cooler for big bulls? Tension was off the charts.

There were thirty minutes of daylight left. What to do? Cow calling had been the kiss of death to most elk interactions, and I held the diaphragm in my lips. Light was fading fast, so I gave my most aggressive cow call. The herd bull bugled back. Heart pounding, again I called. And again the bull returned fire.

Then . . . silence . . . followed by darkness. Once again I had a long descent through dark timber to reach camp, and with every step I wished for just ten more minutes of daylight. However, that hula hoop of hope will be there another year, and next time I'll be ready. On opening morning. I'm not sure I will pass up two bulls like Chuck Jones, but once inside forty yards, that high-mountain bull will experience a bolt above the clouds, and I don't mean lightning.

Stalking bugles is especially exciting. Savvy hunters locate a hot bull, and then sneak in silently for the shot.

A buddy system works well for elk. One person calls while the other moves downwind to ambush incoming game.

PLAN NOW, MENTALLY AND PHYSICALLY

Preparing for a high-mountain elk hunt is similar whether you are toting a bow, cross-bow, or center-fire magnum rifle. First, you need to bump up your cardiovascular conditioning to tone muscles and help increase your lung power. Of course, if you have any medical issues, you should see your doctor first and follow those directions to the letter.

Secondly, don't forget your feet. You'll need a good pair of breathable, waterproof boots that are well broken-in to avoid blisters in the field. Socks are equally important, and carrying an extra pair in your daypack is always a good idea. Additionally, exercise with your daypack and twenty pounds of gear during the final weeks before the hunt.

Practice shooting as well. Although today's crossbows are very accurate, especially when mounted with a scope, you want to practice as realistically as possible. Personally, I like to climb the stairs on my back deck until my heart begins to pound and then make a quick, offhand shot. Likewise, I shoot from both kneeling and standing positions. I believe the greatest shooting variable on a crossbow, like on a rifle, is the trigger, and you need to be comfortable with the pull until you can squeeze quickly without jerking the trigger. Rick Wilson, a good friend and lifelong archer offered a suggestion that has proved invaluable over the years. As you fine-tune your practice regimen, take a single

Plan to cover lots of ground. "First find the elk" is the cardinal rule.

bolt and step outside for a single shot in a realistic condition, say, thirty yards offhand. If you can put that bolt where you aim, your confidence will soar. If you miss, you must wait until the next morning before shooting again. This two-minute practice routine will help tremendously at the Moment of Truth, because the pressure is on, and you will only get one shot.

If there is a 3-D archery range near you, take at least one session where you can practice on a life-size target. A large deer 3-D target will work in your back yard, yet nothing replaces the size and mass of the real deal. Also, you can shoot your deer target in the shoulder, yet that arrow placement is a disaster on an elk. Even with today's high foot-pounds of kinetic energy, an arrow on the shoulder of an elk will rarely penetrate the vitals and be fatal. Your arrow must strike behind the shoulder to catch the lungs.

In fact, you should also consider the frontal shot. Despite what you may have heard, an elk at close range is very vulnerable when it faces you directly. I hunted with Idaho guide Darwin Vander Esch, and before we packed into camp, he led a mule into our midst and stated emphatically, "Do not pass up a frontal shot. This area [*pointing to the mule's chest*] just below the brisket is the size of a basketball and is extremely accessible. An arrow in this spot will kill a bull elk quickly, because there are no leg muscles or ribs for protection." Ironically, the first bull shot in camp approached to fifteen yards, took a direct frontal hit, and went down in less than thirty yards.

MOUNTAIN GEAR THAT MATTERS

Crossbow

My TenPoint Maverick HP shot a very accurate, powerful arrow (461-grains at 314 fps) and was surprisingly easy to handle in the mountains. A standard rifle sling worked well, and I carried the bow over my shoulder much of the time. It also disassembled easily and fit in a standard bow case, making it easy to fly.

Broadheads

I chose NAP HellRazor 100-grain broadheads for their cut-on-contact feature, yet expandable heads from a crossbow would also be a good choice. Bolts from modern crossbows often generate over 100 footpounds of energy, offering excellent penetration.

The author took this good bull while watching a water hole.

Shower

Hygiene is a necessity in outdoor hunting, and the twelve-volt, 40,000 Btu Zodi shower was perfect for our base camp. After a hard day spent climbing and sweating, a hot shower was uplifting. It was also a key to eliminating chafing and other hygiene problems. We hooked it up to a car and were good to go.

Boots

I opted for six-inch Irish Setters, which were easy to break in, waterproof, and lighter than eight or ten-inch models. Comfort and ankle support are critical in a high-country boot.

Bolts

Easton's FMJ bolts were sturdy and massive, resulting in high kinetic energy (100.97 foot-pounds). I chose the flat nocks as TenPoint recommends, realizing that for loading in the dark in a moment of great excitement, flat would be foolproof.

Get in shape. You will cover many miles and thousands of feet of elevation change on an archery elk hunt.

Optics

Nikon's PROSTAFF 10x42 binoculars were bright, lightweight, camouflaged, and a perfect partner to the Archer's Choice MAX range finder. Despite the flat shooting abilities of today's modern crossbows, every game animal requires an accurate range reading, and this Nikon model illuminates the range reading in low light, which is the most critical time.

Headlamp

A quality LCD headlamp is critical for wilderness travel, since it allows hands-free navigation, field dressing of game after dark, and fire building. My Brunton battery pack had plenty of candlepower and battery backup.

Chapter 19

Black Bear Adventure

A crossbow provides the exact shot placement needed for a quick dispatch of a bear.

Every so often I run into a hunting story that is truly extraordinary. I recently conducted an interview with Daniel James Hendricks, publisher of *Horizontal Bowhunter* magazine and a veteran archer with sixteen bruins to his credit. That interview will be covered in the next chapter. After the interview, however, he mentioned that he had written up the hunt and had it published. The teaser is that Hendricks resolved not to be outsmarted by a particularly intelligent bear that had outfoxed every hunter in the previous five years. Here's his account of how he scored by going way more than the extra mile, and ending with a shot that was literally life-or-death.

"SHOWDOWN AT DAWN"

Story and Photos by Daniel James Hendricks

The darkness was beginning to lose its grip on the night. As the sun approached from the far side of the northeastern horizon, the blackness was quickly losing its depth. Atop an eight-foot ladder stand, I sat with my body securely lashed to a spindly jack pine as I waited for daylight and the arrival of a large black bear that I had been hunting for the past five days.

This was my third trip to northern Manitoba to hunt black bears; my first with a crossbow. During the past week I had been trying to outwit an animal that always seemed to be just one step ahead of me. The glimpses I had gotten of the elusive bruin confirmed that it was a big one. The beast fascinated me because it did not have the roly-poly, round shape that one usually associates with black bears. Instead, its shape resembled that of a polar bear. It had a lean, muscular body with legs that seemed far too long for its well-muscled trunk.

On one of the two nights the big boar had allowed itself to be seen, it came in to the bait, just at dark. I marveled at the size and grace of the animal and the way it used the surrounding trees and bait-barrel to cover its presence.

The big bruin had watched me from the trees that surrounded its feeding area as it moved alongside the fifty-five-gallon drum. Crouching behind the barrel, the hungry bear reached one paw around and hooked a bag of fresh suckers. It clamped its jaws around the fish and then bolted into the heavy cover, never providing me a clean shot. At that point in the hunt, I knew that this bear was not going to be easy to outsmart.

Our TrailTimer was providing "intel." With this device we were able to tell when bears were at the bait and usually for how long. One night the unit had been torn from the tree, but it's durable, weather-resistant case had protected it from any serious damage which may have been inflicted by the angry bear. The bear was there every night. By the number of events and the duration, we suspected that we were probably hunting over a multiple-bear bait. The unit was tripped all night long and well into the morning at very regular intervals.

The first three nights in the stand provided only glimpses of the animal we pursued. On one of those nights, just at dark, a second bear had come in to the bait, while our target bear hid in the fringes. The second animal was also a big one, as evidenced by its small ears and low-hanging belly.

I watched through the thick jack pines as the bear we hunted growled and then furiously attacked the trespasser that had its head inside the barrel, innocently checking out the menu. One stout blow from a huge, clawed paw sent the intruder fleeing for the safety of the deep woods. The show of absolute power was impressive! This creature was indeed the king of the walk in this part of the Canadian bush!

Since the TrailTimer told us that the bear was at the bait well after daylight, I decided to go to the stand at 5:00 a.m. on the fifth day of the hunt. Lee, my guide, and I arrived at the bait to find the bear there. As I attempted to stalk in for a ground shot, the black bruin slowly moved off into the heavy cover, just out of reach of my crossbow.

I crawled into the stand and sat there for the next four hours without seeing a single black hair. As I sat on the stand that evening, I decided that I would come back to the stand a full hour before sunrise the following day.

Our host for this hunt was Russ Bettschen of Lynn Lake Fly-In Outpost Camps. Russ and his head guide Lee Nolan were, as usual, extra accommodating. They yielded to my arduous requests because they knew how badly I wanted this particular bear. For that I was both grateful and appreciative. This kind of devotion to their clients' needs keeps us going back to hunt with Russ and Lee year after year.

Being among the finest of outfitters, both men were there to get me settled into my stand on the last morning of my hunt. It was a full hour before sunrise and the bright beams of their flashlights failed to reveal any bears at the bait when we arrived.

Mature black bears learn that baits are available after dark and seldom show themselves in daylight.

As I nestled in, I decided to go one step further than the usual safety belt that I wear in the treestand. On this morning I strapped myself snugly to the trunk of the tree with a single safety strap. I had been getting very little sleep during the past few days. As the end of the hunt drew near, I had been devoting more hours to the treestand.

On this cool morning I was concerned that I might nod off and fall to the ground. With my body lashed to the tree in a sitting position, I could still nod off, but I knew I would not fall from the tree. At my age, even an eight-foot fall could be fatal. I just don't bounce as well as I once did.

Once I had finished the chores required, my loyal guides bid me "good luck" and headed out of the woods, chasing the beams of their bright flashlights. When the sound of their retreating vehicle had faded into the stillness of the predawn silence, I settled in for what I hoped would be a short wait. As my eyes adjusted to the low-light conditions, I noticed that it was getting lighter with each passing minute. Several times I thought I heard the sound of cracking underbrush in the heavy bush to the northwest of the stand. I even thought that I caught a waft of bear odor but then convinced myself that it was just an overactive imagination on my part.

Black bear hunting is a game of patience. Sometimes they come in quickly; sometimes they watch a bait for hours and never approach.

Tree stands are effective tools for black bears, but the bears can climb trees as well.

Like with elk hunting, bear quests have their own specialized gear.

Half an hour after the guides had disappeared into the waning darkness, I decided to lower my head with the intention of taking a short nap to refresh my tired brain. As I slowly nodded forward, my still-open eyes came to rest on the huge form of a black bear as it moved past the very base of my ladder stand.

My heart stopped beating, lodged in my throat, and then started to beat again, pounding the cider out of my Adam's apple. As I swallowed hard, I watched the massive beast quickly pad to the trail that led away from the bait, out to the road.

Making good shots takes mental practice as well as physical prowess.

When it reached the exit path, it turned toward the road and stopped. For a full two minutes it stared down the trail searching for any sign of the recently departed guides. I could not believe that this monster had passed right under my ladder stand without looking up.

As I watched the big, black animal study the trail and the surrounding bush, I marveled at its form. It was standing broadside a mere twenty feet away from me, completely unaware that it was being studied by another predator. As I watched, the big bruin turned and slowly moved toward the bait barrel, muscles rippling under its heavy black winter coat. It was an incredible sight!

As the animal passed my stand and neared the bait, I made a major mistake. I reached for my crossbow, which was hanging on the tree next to my stand. In doing so, I made enough noise, movement, or both to alert the bear. The animal suddenly burst into motion and darted into the thick trees behind the bait barrel.

From its protected position, the alerted animal studied me while it decided what it would do next. Minutes the length of hours dragged by as the bear and I stared at one another in the early morning light, each wondering what would happen next.

Suddenly the bear moved out of the trees and stepped into the clearing in front of the bait barrel. It did not seem to be alarmed, as its beady black eyes stared at me with an intensity that made my insides squirm and my skin crawl. The tension and the excitement made it impossible for me to tell how long the stare-down lasted.

Dan Hendricks poses with his trophy black bear that required an "all-nighter" to bag.

Without warning, the big bruin turned and moved back behind the bait barrel. The animal continued moving as it made a wide arc around the edge of the clearing, stopping only when it was exactly downwind from my position.

I watched the bear's head lift into the air and work the gentle breeze with its sensitive nose. It was trying to find some trace of my odor within the wind currents that connected the dots of our positions. At this particular point in time, the ScentLok suit I was wearing was getting its toughest test of the hunt.

After several moments of serious sniffing, the bear turned and quickly padded its way back to the bait barrel. Once there, it turned and again locked eyes with me in another intense stare-down. A minute, possibly two, or five passed as I watched the black statue-like form of the big bruin eyeing my position.

Suddenly, the bear made its move. It headed straight for my stand in an easy, sure stride. I watched in fascination as the big beast rapidly chopped away at the twenty yards that separated us, one silent step at a time. I felt my skin begin to move beneath my hunting clothes as the hair sprang to attention on the back of my neck. The decisive moment had arrived. As the big, black, belligerent boar narrowed the distance that separated us, I raised my Horton Hunter Supreme crossbow to my shoulder and found the bear's approaching form in the scope. The motion of my response to its advance caused the animal to stop suddenly and turn broadside. As I looked over the top of the scope, I could only marvel at what I was seeing in the deep bush of the Canadian wilderness.

Bagging a mature black bear with a crossbow is a huge challenge. Deer always run away; bears don't.

As the morning light chased away even more darkness, I gazed down from my eight-foot perch at the most incredible bear I had ever seen alive and in the wild. Its large, trim body had the definition and muscle tone of a professional athlete. This fine specimen of a bruin stood just eight paces away, staring at me with those cold, little, black-marble eyes.

My body seemed unreasonably calm as I tried to figure out why the overdose of adrenaline that I knew was surging through my system was having no noticeable effect. Never, in thirty-five years of hunting, had I experienced such primeval intensity.

It lasted only a moment, although it seemed like many, eye to eye, man to beast. Each was waiting, like a gunfighter in the street, for the other to make the next move.

The bear moved first. It turned in my direction and began to pad toward me. As it started to turn, my right eye dropped to the scope. I lowered the crosshairs to the animal's turning shoulder and released the arrow, which buried deeply into the chest cavity of the huge animal. It spun without a sound and exploded into a frantic flurry of furry motion. Its long, muscular legs carried it crashing into the heavy Canadian bush.

I watched the string peeling away from the string tracker attached to my bow, as I listened to the racket made by the fleeing beast.

Suddenly, all was deathly still.

As I sat in total silence in the cool wilderness morning, I waited for and longed to hear the death moan of the huge animal. I needed some sure sign that this mighty, maimed monster was down for the final count.

It never came. As I waited for something to happen, my body rediscovered its lost adrenaline. I said a silent prayer of thanks that I was solidly strapped to the tree as convulsions rumbled through my body.

To put a short ending on a long story, I will say that my guide helped me track my big trophy with a loaded shotgun. It had run only seventy yards before dropping stone dead to the ground. The bear measured 7-½ feet from head to tail and its skull measured 19-⅜ inches. This bear was the first—and is the largest—bruin that I had ever shot with a crossbow. A very destructive lung shot had prevented the animal from making its final death moan.

I have replayed the events of that Canadian morning in my mind many times. I am still not sure whether the animal was being protective of its larder or if it was intent on eliminating the threat it thought I posed. It's very possible that the ScentLok suit I was wearing so completely eliminated my odor that the bear was unable to determine whether I was a human being or another bear violating the master's food cache. I can only speculate about the bear's reasoning. But I will never speculate about the thrill I received on that cool, spring morning.

Chapter 20

Black Bear How-To

BOWHUNTING "THE KING OF SPRING": 16 TIPS TO SCORE

Whether with vertical or horizontal gear, chasing a monster bruin from a tree stand or ground blind is a pure adrenaline rush. Hopefully, Hendricks's account of his hunt ignited a passion for a bruin pursuit. Here's how to make it happen:

"I hear you can kill a black bear with a gun, but I haven't tried it," Dan chuckled during our interview. "Black bears are a challenge, and sometimes you have to go the extra mile to bag one."

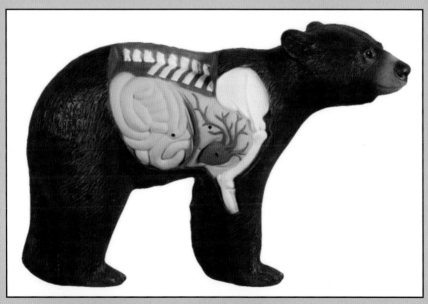

A black bear is the king of spring hunting. Shots on black bears are different than deer, and you must learn its anatomy.

MENTALLY PREPARE

More than any other game animal, bear hunting is a match of wits. Expect to experience every emotion from intense anticipation, to excitement, to moderate boredom. To prepare for this mental game, watch videos, visit bear-hunting forums, and read bow-hunting magazines on the subject, which will help put realism and excitement into your practice sessions. Understand that bears, especially in western Canada, often climb trees, but rarely actually attack.

Bring your A game to outsmart a big bruin. To help you prepare, keep these four categories and sixteen tips in mind:

Feel Safe

Bear hunting can be scary stuff. Carry a day pack with a bright flashlight, compass, snacks, and a mobile phone or portable radio. You'll probably spend five to ten hours daily waiting by a bait and checking in with a buddy or the outfitter every hour makes time seem to pass more quickly. Plus, you can enjoy the antics at other stands and share in the excitement. Sit on a comfortable pad and use a safety harness.

Pace for Success

You'll be excited and anxious to get on stand, but don't burnout the first day. It's better to watch a bait for three or four hours while sharp than to get restless and lackadaisical on a much longer stint. One Canadian outfitter makes his clients sit a stand without a bow the first night so that they become used to seeing bears and won't shoot the first one that shows up or take a hurried shot.

Trail cameras provide critical information about bear movement and are an essential part of most hunts.

GEARING UP

If you are already a deer hunter, most of your white-tail gear is adequate for black bears. In the hierarchy of game animals, many suggest that a black bear hunt is the next step up from whitetails. You will probably hunt from a tree stand and be required to make a carefully-aimed, downward-angle shot.

Being comfortable while still in a stand will boost patience and success.

Big and Bright

Use a heavy draw weight, heavy shaft, razor sharp broadhead, and a lighted nock. Trailing a bear is no picnic, and you want complete penetration for maximum spore. You may trail through cover so thick you can reach farther than you can see. Lighted nocks help you better see the location of impact, and assist in assessing blood on the arrow after a pass through. If you miss, the arrow is easier to find and offers assurance the animal was not wounded.

Use a Single Sight Pin

One bright pin helps focus your attention at the Moment of Truth. Consider a lighted pin or a red-dot crossbow scope. If you use a battery-powered sight, be sure to bring an extra battery and carry it when hunting.

Carbon Up

Today's scent elimination products are better than ever. Just like for whitetails, begin with a shower before the hunt, and pack your outer clothes if they could be contaminated by vehicle travel, buying gas, or food. Spray down before walking to the stand, including the soles of your boots. If you must use insect repellant, use the same brand as the outfitter, as bears become accustomed to the scents of those who freshen bait sites. An Ozonics unit can completely eliminate your human odor, whether in a tree stand or ground blind.

Bear Calls

Zig Ziggler has had excellent luck calling big boars with the Woods Wise Sow Moan. This call works particularly well on old boars that are often bait shy and only approach

Bears don't have good eyesight, yet they can see you move if your silhouette isn't concealed.

in darkness. This estrous bear call causes mating males to shed their inhibitions, like a buck deer in the rut.

PERFECT PRACTICE MAKES PERFECT

The number of arrows launched before the hunt is not nearly as important as the circumstances under which they fly. You want to condition your mind and body to draw, aim, and release consistently. Despite this close-range shooting, bears are very elusive and often "just appear."

Practice on a 3-D Bear Target in Hunting Gear

Shot placement on a black bear is very different than on a deer. Bears have plates of gristle to protect their vitals, so the arrow must hit behind the shoulder. As the hunt draws near, make sure you practice wearing your headnet, gloves, carbon clothes, etc. Organize your backpack so that you know where everything is to minimize movement.

Beat Bear Fever

One way to beat buck and bear fever is to use an aiming phrase. Bob Foulkrod, who had to kill one bear with a knife, uses the question, "Is the pin on the target?" By practicing this technique with each shot, aiming becomes the priority. Mentally, it forces your mind to focus on the pin, thereby increasing accuracy. This technique works with both bows and crossbows

TREE STAND SAVVY

A well-concealed stand will eliminate your silhouette and provide a shot at a relaxed animal. What you do and don't do in the stand can determine your success. Here are a few more tips to make the most of each situation:

Shoot a Big One

Judging a mature bear from a young one is easy . . . with lots of time, in broad daylight, and in wide open spaces. Hunters rarely have these luxuries. Three features most clearly help determine age. Young bears appear to have long, lanky legs, a narrow body, and a long stride. Their head looks like that of a German shepherd dog, with a narrow head and long nose. Finally, ears on a young bear are high and pointed. The ears of an old bear appear circular, like cookies. Some hunters and guides use a stick or marker near the bait to help them judge size. Essentially, that spot is saying, "Shoot if the bear is taller than this mark."

Pick the Right Tree

If you have the option of selecting a tree for stand placement, avoid any with claw marks. One evening a Quebec hunter returned to camp from a productive bait with little to say. The next afternoon he chose to stay in camp. Another hunter took the site, but he hunted from a different tree. In late afternoon, without warning, a bear rushed past the bait and hung on the trunk of the former stand tree. Apparently it had learned to intimidate hunters, and it worked.

Judging the size of a bear is difficult, especially in dim light. Use a mark on a tree or a reference object to help.

Keep a rock or two in your pocket to scare away smaller bears that can become pests.

Rock 'N Roll

Savvy bear hunters carry a couple of rocks in their pocket. If a young bear gets curious about your stand, you can *boink* him and shoo him away without alarming other bears. More often, a bear may feed at dark. By tossing a rock or two, you can scare it away without revealing your stand location.

Rise and Shine, Black Bears

Mature bears often learn the baiting routine. Either they return after dark or visit the bait early in the morning. On three different hunts I have hunted a total of three mornings and seen five bears. Morning bear hunting is effective (as Hendricks learned on his all-nighter), but it can often burn out guides and camp staff. Keep it as your ace-in-the-hole.

Work the Angles

No matter how close the bear, the angle of the arrow is critical. A shoulder shot on a mature bear inevitably ends in a long trail and a dubious recovery. *You must have a broadside or quartering-away shot.* The arrow needs to enter behind the shoulder to avoid the gristle plate on the shoulder.

Orient Express

Think about after-shot success. After you release, pay attention to every detail, especially where the bear was last seen. Take a compass bearing of the spot or a picture with your cell phone so that you can show the guide. Things will look different from the ground, especially in darkness. Listen for bear sounds. A double-lung hit on a black bear is lethal in ten seconds.

Picture Panoramic

The camaraderie of a bear camp is unforgettable. Yes, you want to bag a bear, yet don't miss the big picture of the hunt. Bears inhabit wild and wonderful habitat, the kind most outdoor enthusiasts dream of. The pace is easy and relaxing. Many archers fish in the morning, take a nap, double-check their gear, and then hunt until dark. Bear recoveries by flashlight and midnight campfires create memories to last a lifetime. If you have never hunted black bears, consider it an experience of high enjoyment and great adventure. Veterans of the woods understand the need to be at one's best. Mentally, physically, and mechanically, it deserves your best shot.

Finally, Consider a Ground Blind

Dan Hendricks bear hunts exclusively from ground blinds these days, and he loves the excitement of the experience. "I once heard something moving behind my blind and tensed for a shot at a bear," he remembers. "Suddenly a ground squirrel jumped on top of the blind. I'm still patching the hole in the top where my head poked through." He adds with a laugh, "Don't even ask about my undershorts." All kidding aside, he often takes handicapped hunters who operate from blinds because bears, like wild turkeys, don't pay much attention to them. And for bears, the blinds needn't be brushed in like for whitetail deer. "Just take them with you when you leave," Henderson advises. "Bears can trash them overnight."

Pay particular attention to the bear after the shot. Take a picture with your cell phone so that you can identify the spot of the shot.

You can hunt bears from the ground. It's extremely exciting!

Chapter 21

Anatomy of a Blood Trail

What you do after the shot can spell the difference between grief and grandeur. Prevention and execution are the keys to quick recoveries.

Leaves crunched and sticks snapped as two deer stopped directly below my stand. Rolling my eyes and rotating my head at the speed of a cold turtle, I saw a big whitetail buck come into focus. The buck was close, so I dared not move. Long moments of silence seemed like hours. Then the chase resumed. I reached for the bow, but our efforts ended in a tie. The doe had stopped. I gripped the bow, waiting to aim.

The buck stood at thirty yards, a high, heavy, seven-point with double brow tines. Its massive chest and neck looked like an Angus steer. Despite my full camo, I was in plain view. Suddenly, the doe took several jumps up the hill, pulling the buck behind her. The buck stopped, I squeezed off the shot, and the bolt sped to its mark. The deer made two

Learning to read blood trails is essential to all hunters, but especially those who hunt with bows and arrows.

Broadheads must be kept razor sharp, since a clean cut bleeds more than a jagged one.

bounds and stopped in a patch of saplings. Its shape was visible, yet I could not see where the arrow had hit. As a minute passed, I expected it to wobble and crash, yet the deer stood perfectly still. A full five minutes passed before it walked slowly uphill and out of sight. Had I missed?

Bowhunting has many dramatic moments, yet the most critical occur after the broadhead strikes. Exhilaration and excitement are tempered by the awesome responsibility of creating an ethical, clean demise. Did you follow your best shooting form? Did you pick an exact shot and wait for the proper angle? More importantly, what should you do next? Should you climb down, look for the arrow, and begin trailing? Or should you sit tight and wait at least half an hour (a nerve-racking task)?

Quick and dependable game recovery is one part preparation and two parts execution. First, to get close shots at calm game animals, you have to be as unobtrusive as possible. My day began with cold cereal to avoid the strong aroma of bacon and eggs. I took a shower, using an antibacterial soap, and dressed in warm layers. The outermost was a suit of Browning Scent Sorb to absorb odors that could cause deer to avoid my stand or even become alert. As things worked out, the buck and doe came from directly downwind. Also, I used doe-urine lure on my boots to cover my entrance trail.

Quickly readying to shoot is another proactive step. Getting caught off guard could result in an errant shot. After putting on your safety harness, load the bow and anticipate approach routes deer might use. I used a Bushnell range finder to log in several reference

Deer don't often die in the open, and your trailing skills will be needed to retrieve them.

trees and logs. My buck stopped five steps beyond a cedar tree that was exactly thirty yards away.

Close shots can be challenging, due to steep angles and the tendency to overshoot targets close to the stand. Be sure to practice shooting closer than ten yards as part of your hunt preparation. Lay a broadhead target flat on the ground, shoot at a designated spot to anticipate how your arrow strikes at close range. Always aim for the heart at short distances. It's a good habit that builds in an "aim-low" solution.

Responsible bowhunters must know their effective range with their hunting gear. I had practiced for months with broadheads and felt confident about the shot. It's also important to know when to say "when" as darkness falls. Legal shooting times vary from state to state, but remember to allow time for recovery. Returning in the morning to trail your deer is only an option in cold weather when the meat will not spoil. Additionally, with coyote populations booming around the country, there may not be much left.

Conditions during our hunt were taxing. Two inches of rain fell the first morning, followed by high winds and sub-freezing temperatures. Before leaving camp, I put on my full hunting attire and headed for the elevated practice stand behind the camp. My first arrow was exactly on target, but I wanted to experiment with a bulky glove on my bow hand. If you wear bulky gloves in cold weather, make sure you can work the safety and feel the trigger. If you lose the feel of the trigger, consider wearing a light cotton glove under an insulating one.

REPLAY THE SHOT

The instant you release an arrow, your mind should become a video camera mentally capturing every sight and sound. Where did the arrow strike? What was the angle of the deer? Did it bound away, hunch up, or race through the brush with reckless abandon?

When the arrow struck, did it make a solid sound (a muscle hit), a cracking noise (from hitting bone), or a soft, supple sound (suggesting a midsection hit)? Each of these observations will help make better trailing decisions in the minutes ahead.

Noting landmarks is particularly important. What object did the deer pass as it left your vision? What tree, rock, or other marker indicates the direction of the last sound? If you have a compass, take a bearing, because things will look very different when you climb down from the stand. Use your cell phone and take a picture of the escape route from the tree, noting landmarks in particular. Once on the ground, the escape route will look very different, and the image on your phone's camera can be of immense help. As I would learn, the age and size of the deer can make a difference too.

After allowing the longest thirty minutes of my life to pass, I climbed down from the stand, reasonably optimistic about what I would find. Although the big buck had been partially obscured, the arrow appeared to be on target. Heartland Lodge, my host, asked hunters not to trail deer unless certain that they are down for good. My intentions were to adhere to the camp policy. However, I figured I'd locate the arrow and get a general direction to "save time."

Being careful not to disturb the trail of the deer, I walked below the landmarks, scouring the leafy forest litter for blood. To my surprise, I found nothing. No arrow, no hair, no blood. Replaying that videotape in my mind, I was convinced the cedar tree hadn't moved and that the deer was hit.

I continued to circle the trail and was headed for camp when I came across an immense blood trail. Holy cow! Confused about the sudden sign, I back-trailed a dozen steps and located my arrow. The cut-on-contact head had completely penetrated the far side, yet the arrow had not exited. The snapping sound I had heard after the shot was the breaking of the arrow. Once dislodged, it uncorked a fountain of body fluids, and I felt confident the buck would be close by. My experience reminded me

The author took this buck, which left a meager blood trail. The buck showed signs of a liver hit and soon expired.

that even a boiler-room hit can leave little sign in the immediate vicinity, and this verified the importance of thoroughly searching the shot area. An arrow missing the mark can bury itself in the leaves or simply fail to cause immediate blood loss. Crossbow bolts fly at speeds such that recovering them is often impossible. Be sure to search at least a fifty-yard diameter, using your cell phone image to give you direction.

FOLLOW THE TRAIL CAREFULLY

Recovering the arrow was an important step. The fletching, shaft, and broadhead were all a crimson red. Arrow analysis, along with arrow strike and deer angle will help provide important clues. Pink, bubbly blood is the best sign, since it indicates a lung hit. Look on trees and underbrush to see if spore splattered as the deer ran away. Do you have one trail or two? I found bubbly blood in one trail and bright red running parallel in another. In the excitement of the moment, I failed to recognize the significance of this fact and proceeded onward.

Big bucks have exceptional stamina and may travel a hundred yards, even with a mortal wound.

When trailing a deer, always anticipate the need for a second shot. Hopefully, your trophy will be lying still in the leaves, yet caution must prevail. Use binoculars, if for no other reason than to slow your pace. I had left my range finder and binoculars in my pack, since I was "just going to see where the trail started."

Motivated by the abundant spore, I sneaked carefully ahead. The trail led prominently into a deeper ravine. Catching movement, I saw a doe's tail flash. I searched the area as best I could. Three other deer were feeding, and a large animal was bedded. It was my buck! I could see a red patch directly behind its shoulder on the exit-side. Despite what appeared to be a heart-shot, the animal was watching its back trail alertly.

HOW LONG AND HOW FAR?

"You began trailing the deer by yourself?" questioned chief guide L. J. "Matt" Matthews. "Don't you remember the Sunday orientation?"

Duly chastised, I recounted the events of the shot and the trail, and then I quickly received the lodge's experience with many such encounters. "Many hunters don't realize how big and hearty these Illinois bucks become," said Matthews.

> They are such powerful animals that we always exercise caution when trailing them. That's why we believe it's best to get help from the lodge. The last thing we want is to lose an animal.
>
> With a double-lung hit and bubbly, pink blood on both sides of the trail, we recommend you wait thirty minutes and trail cautiously. If you have dark-red blood, such as a high shoulder hit or other flesh wound, we recommend giving the animal at least a full hour before trailing. In your case, where you have at least one lung and the animal has gone more than a hundred yards, we need to wait at least three hours from the time of the shot.

Since all archery hunting depends on hemorrhage for retrieval, learning to trail various animals can be very helpful.

As we discussed the lodge's practices for retrieving deer, the yardage factor entered the picture. If a deer runs a short distance with red blood or signs of a stomach hit, it's imperative that it not be re-jumped. An arrow through the paunch leaves little sign and the animal is capable of traveling long distances.

A double-lung-hit deer, especially a big, Midwest buck, can go a hundred yards with a lethal hit. However, once the trail surpasses the century

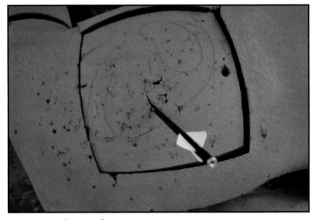

Practice makes perfect.

mark, trackers need to reevaluate the situation. Any number of things could have caused an on-target arrow to go awry. Heartland guides frequently retrieve deer that sustained hits other than what the client described. Releasing an arrow is such an emotion-laden event that cool heads and accurate observations are rarely quite so cool or accurate.

A seldom-discussed hit occurs when a broadhead penetrates the liver. This occurred on one of my 2014 deer, and an understanding of the prospect led to a quick recovery. An arrow through the liver leaves a dark red blood trail, often on both sides. Blood is steady, but not profuse. In the case of that 2014 deer, after the shot the buck bounded uphill a few yards and stopped in a patch of saplings. To me, the shot looked good, and I expected it to collapse any second.

However, a full five minutes passed before the deer casually walked uphill and out of sight. A double-lung hit would have dropped it in seconds, usually on the dead run. A gut-shot would have caused the buck to lay down in a few seconds. Reading the reactions of the deer caused me to believe the hit was through the liver, so I waited a full half hour before climbing down from the stand.

On such occasions, guessing time is impossible. I pulled out my cell phone and noted the time. It was agonizing to wait and not trail the deer, yet I knew it was the best course. I knew this area very well and hoped that the buck had gone a few yards out of my sight, lain down, and expired.

When that half hour passed, I began following the trail, and I was elated to find it stiff and stone-dead after traveling seventy-five yards. In 2013 I shot a bull elk in a similar fashion. It traveled about a hundred yards, and I watched it fall over as it followed several cows.

TRAILING TACTICS

After waiting three hours, Matt, James, Myrta, and I picked up the trail and followed it carefully. Matt commanded the "last-blood" position, a critical part of any trailing situation. He had a roll of toilet tissue and placed a small piece every so often. The trail led from the last sighting over a ridge and into a streambed. I had an arrow loaded and let James lead the trail. "You watch for sign; I'll watch for the deer," was our arrangement. The sign dropped to the edge of the stream, but did not cross. It progressed another twenty-five yards and then turned to ford the stream. After passing through the water, the sign disappeared.

We retraced our search back to Matt and the critical last sign. Making small circles, the spore was located again. It headed uphill toward a fence. If the buck had jumped this barrier, I knew we were in for the long haul. Fortunately, it turned and paralleled for another hundred yards. Then two positive signs emerged. Two does sprang from thick cover just ahead of the trail. And the path led into a thick patch of briars.

Trailing over leafy vegetation takes extra care. One person should mark last blood while the front person searches for more sign.

The best assurance for a short trail is an accurate, well-placed shot.

When a buck beds, especially a dominant breeder, it's not uncommon for does to join it and remain motionless, following the mature deer's example. Also, when a big buck feels the end is near, it will often seek thick cover, sometimes doubling back on its trail.

"HERE IT IS"

Next to "I love you," these are the sweetest words a hunter can hear. My big two-hundred-pound-plus Midwest monarch lay just beyond the briars. A quick look showed a heavy rack with ten points, including a double brow tine. As a trophy, it was a beauty. As a trailing lesson, it was textbook.

The razor-sharp broadhead had penetrated the shoulder on the near side, caught the lung, and then exited through the neck. Even on whitetail deer, you cannot have too much kinetic energy, and the more penetration the better.

Arriving back in camp, I helped recover another hunter's deer. Using the same techniques, his trail came to a happy end as well. Trailing a deer is part science and part detective work, requiring self-discipline and perseverance. Just remember, the hardest buck you'll ever trail . . . is yours.

Chapter 22

After the Shot: Wait Time and When to Follow

The hunt isn't *over* until you *stand over* your game. What happens between release and recovery spells the difference between success and failure.

A stream of animals walked eerily through the soft muskeg, their hooves making a distinct clicking noise, yet no other sound could be heard. Suddenly, among the flow of cows and calves stepped a tall, antlered caribou bull, the velvet on its antlers enough to carpet a living room wall-to-wall. Fortunately, it stopped to munch on a bush, and I closed thirty quick steps, aided by the soft tundra. In a flash the fletching zipped into the crease behind the shoulder, and the bull lunged forward. Seconds later it collapsed in plain view. A visual demise is the best trail of all.

The author trailed this big buck more than a hundred yards despite a double-lung hit.

The author retrieves an arrow gone awry.

Of course, every shot isn't like this. Even with a perfect double-lung hit, a deer, bear, or other game animal may race into thick cover, making recovery a challenge. Mortally-wounded game often bursts into a "death run" that may take them fifty to a hundred yards from the site of the shot. If this path includes water or open terrain, or if it occurs in darkness, retrieval will be more difficult. More challenging is an arrow gone awry. Perhaps an arrow brushed a twig or the animal moved at the last second. With marginal hits, extra care must be taken to ensure results, especially if you are alone.

LOOK AND LISTEN

Bob Barrie introduced the Rocky Mountain Razor nearly thirty years ago, and he and his son Bruce have encountered hundreds of trailing situations. I had the pleasure to hunt with Bruce one September, and our conversation naturally turned to broadheads and their effectiveness.

"Dad always taught me to *look* and *listen* at the Moment of Truth," said Bruce. "You want to see where the arrow hits and where the deer goes. Just as importantly, listen to the hit. Does it make a cracking sound like an arrow hitting bone? A soft sound as if it hits the paunch? Or the pumpkin sound of hitting the rib cage?" Barrie believes he can guess an arrow's hit by the sound, because he has heard it so many times.

After taking a shot, Barrie climbs down from his stand and retrieves the arrow, examining it carefully. "I begin with the broadhead," says Barrie. "Does it contain tissue, bone fragments, or hair? These are clues to the path of the arrow." If Barrie finds white hair, he knows that the arrow flew low or left of the cavity low. Remembering the angle of the shot determines if this is a good or bad sign. Next, Barrie smells the arrow for the

Gain as much information as possible about the shot before you begin trailing. The deer's reactions after the hit and sign on the arrow determine how long to wait.

fragrance of stomach material. Any sign of green or olive fluids on the shaft indicates a stomach hit or exit.

Blood on the arrow and fletching reveals important information. A double-lung hit usually saturates the arrow with blood. Lung blood is often pink and contains bubbles. Dark red blood often comes from muscles such as the leg, shoulder, brisket, or the meaty section above the lungs and below the spine. If the arrow stayed in the animal, you have much less information, which is one of the reasons looking and listening is so important.

DEER PHYSIOLOGY

Before continuing with experienced recovery advice, learning about the physiology of deer (in case you skipped that class in school) can help.

Dr. Robert Cody is a veterinarian with more than thirty years of experience in animal care. He's also an ardent bear and lion hunter who has taken an excellent specimen of each in the past two years. He hunts whitetails on his small farm and was happy to assist. Without becoming too technical, here's a brief summary:

- All mammals (deer, bear, caribou, etc.) have two lungs with three lobes on each side.
- Blood vessels are evenly disbursed. There is no concentration at the top or bottom of the lungs.
- Each lung is separate. An arrow through one lung will not collapse the other or cause it to fill with blood.

- The heart has its own protective membrane. Heart blood will not enter the lungs. (This is why a heart-shot animal can run so far.)
- Blood takes approximately sixty seconds to circulate through the body. If you shut off the blood supply, the brain is not immediately affected. Lung hits cause muscles to become weak through lack of oxygen (hypoxia). The animal will lie down. Death occurs when the animal's tissue receives no oxygen (anoxia).

Dr. Cody voiced a strong opinion about arrow penetration, lauding the merits of an arrow that remains in the chest cavity as opposed to passing completely through. "As the deer runs, the skin acts as a fulcrum," he said. "The broadhead is slashing like a knife in the chest. This process can tear the aorta, pulmonary vessels, and other blood-rich tissue. The thorax will fill with blood, taking blood away from the extremities."

FOULKROD ON FOLLOW-UP

Bob Foulkrod included a trailing session in the regular and advanced Bowhunting Schools he offered at his Troy, Pennsylvania home. As a guide, he has followed up hundreds of blood trails, mostly with happy endings. "The Game Tracker string taught me a great deal," admits the savvy archer. "When that string went through a section of cover, I made myself look for tiny clues

If you take a big buck like this, wait at least thirty minutes before taking up the trail.

of the animal's passage. Over the years, I have learned to pay close attention to the environment, what is disturbed and what is not."

Like Barrie, Foulkrod begins recovery before ever leaving the tree. He notes as much information as possible about where the animal went, then takes a compass reading of the course. "Things always look different once you are on the ground," he says. "The compass course will get you started in the right direction."

Before beginning any conversation on trailing, you can bet Foulkrod will raise the importance of a large broadhead, lauding the effectiveness of a big-diameter head and extra slash value. "It not only kills quickly, but you have a good blood trail to follow," says the Pennsylvania native.

HOW LONG TO WAIT

Foulkrod and Barrie recommend waiting twenty to thirty minutes on even the best of shots. Unless you actually see the animal fall, hear it crash, or are worried about darkness or impending bad weather, hurrying the recovery only risks losing the animal.

With bright pink or bubbly blood, the half-hour wait time is usually sufficient. If you have dark red muscle blood, you should wait an hour or more. If the arrow or spore contains stomach content, you are looking at six to eight hours.

Making a trail decision is like detective work. Combine all the clues for the best solution. What was the angle of the animal during the shot? Was it relaxed or tense? After the shot, did the beast ignore the arrow, walk away timidly, or race into cover?

I once double-lung hit an antelope at twenty yards, and the animal walked away as if nothing had happened. Then it suddenly burst into a break-neck run, crashing 125 yards away. An animal that walks away slowly with its back hunched up has probably suffered a stomach wound.

Animals that are "gut-shot" usually run less than a hundred yards and lie down. If left alone they will die in their bed or move toward water. In this situation, allow six to eight hours or leave the animal overnight. In the morning, if the animal has moved, look in a downhill location, especially along trails leading toward water.

BEGINNING THE TRAILING PROCESS

"The hardest deer to recover is my own," admits Bob Foulkrod. "I'm excited and impatient to retrieve the animal." Trailing is much more effective with company. First, you have more eyes to find spore. Secondly, you have a person to man the "last-blood" position. His responsibility is to stand beside—not on—the location of the last blood sign. If blood sign isn't immediately evident, Bruce Barrie climbs back into his stand and asks a friend to stand at the location of the shot. This reenactment can reorient the trailing process and get things started on the right foot.

A trail-marking material is important, especially if you are following a meager trail or dark blood. Small pieces of toilet paper attached to branches works well. So does orange flagging or other retrievable material. These markers establish a general-direction pattern that can save time and make spore location more successful. It's easy to lose the big picture of the trail while intensely focusing on the ground.

The first hundred yards are critical. Muscle wounds bleed profusely at first, and then begin to peter out at seventy-five to a hundred yards. Lung hits can begin as dark red muscle blood and then become pink blood as the trail progresses. Barrie always pays close attention to areas near hoof prints. "When the animal bounds, it often forces blood from its cavity, and that sign may be three or four feet away."

COLD TRAILING

Roger Kerr manages Heartland Outfitters in Versailles, Illinois. As a commercial hunting operation, Kerr gets plenty of practice following up big Midwestern bucks, and sometimes the trail dries up. "When the trail goes cold, I always check along streambeds and other sources of water. Wounded deer often seek out ravines and gullies. Also, when a deer has to exert extra effort to cross a ditch, you often find blood on the uphill side."

Glenn Garner from LaGrange, Georgia is a go-to guy when it comes to trailing. "I guess I've earned a reputation as a tracker," says Garner modestly. "When someone in the area can't find a deer, my telephone rings."

Garner believes the toughest place to trail a deer is in an open field. Without a flat leaf surface for blood to splatter on, it gets easily lost in standing vegetation. Garner also limits the trailing party if possible. He typically opts for three or less, reasoning that too many footsteps can trample critical signs.

He has had several big bucks pull vanishing acts as their retrieval seemed imminent. "I've had four or five blood trails suddenly dry up, and I have learned to back-trail and look for sign toward thick cover. When a big deer feels the end is near, it often back-tracks and jumps from the trail, bedding in really thick cover," he says.

Finally, where legal, a trailing dog is worth its weight in gold. Many southern lodges have a black lab or other breed that will follow a cold trail. Dogs and deer hunting pose a problem for some sportsmen. But once an animal has been wounded, I believe ethics dictate retrieving it by any legal means. It's every archer's responsibility to do all he or she can do to recover wounded game. Patience is important at first, then persistence and careful trailing will get the job done.

HAPPY TRAILS: SIX TIPS FOR QUICK RECOVERIES

1. Practice exact simulations. Wear full gear during final practice sessions. Practice regularly throughout the season.
2. Begin each day with one practice arrow. If you miss, wait until tomorrow to shoot again.
3. Shoot for the heart, especially on alert game.
4. Avoid steep angles. Even a fixed blade may deflect from the rib cage.
5. Hunt backward. Place your stand with your back toward approaching deer. They will see you less and offer the best vital-angled shots.
6. Pass every approaching shot. Even a slight onward angle will only catch the near lung. Let the deer pass and *baaa* like a sheep. That buck will stop every time.

Chapter 23

Hunting the Rut for the First Time

If you are new to archery, prepare for one of the greatest seasons of your life, because the rut radically changes the behavior of big bucks. As they cruise their habitat searching for does to breed, they suddenly "appear," and hunters see them perhaps for the first time all year. Not only do bucks become more visible, but they make rubs, scrapes, and other visible signs of their presence. These normally shy, elusive giants become mobile and visible during daylight.

A buck's urge to breed is more important to it than survival itself, and no clearer example has occurred to me than during a hunt last fall. I was visiting friends in South Dakota, and we were almost to the family lease where we planned to hunt for the day. As the predawn light set the eastern sky aglow, I asked my friend to stop the truck so that I could take a picture. I stepped from the vehicle and raised the camera, and two bucks stood up a hundred yards away. I wanted the picture, but hey, this was a deer hunt, and I quickly climbed back inside and closed the door as the two bucks stood and stared in our direction.

Then it happened. A third buck stood up, mere feet from the gravel road, and its antlers took our breath. This was a magazine-cover deer for sure, and now three bucks were right

If you've never hunted the rut, you are in for the outdoor adventure of a lifetime. The deer woods change dramatically as breeding begins.

in front of us. After a minute of stare down, the three bucks jumped the fence and ran across a wide-open field. We slowly moved ahead on the road, and the monster buck turned and came back to the same hay bale it had stood by. "There has to be an estrous doe bedded in the grass," I said, because the big deer would have been a sitting duck for a rifle. Suddenly, a doe appeared like a jack popping from a box, and the two raced away, now in full flight.

Without the estrous doe present, the mature buck would probably have lain in the grass and allowed us to pass, or burst from its bed and raced at full speed into the cover of a tree line two hundred yards away. Although this was private land, the deer had surely been hunted for numerous years, and yet it survived. It full well knew the danger that a pickup truck meant, yet it put the urge to breed above its own safety.

SCOUT NOW, SCORE LATER

Deer hunting has very defined dates, yet scouting for and engaging deer is a yearlong event for serious hunters. As you will learn in the following interview, some of the nation's most successful big-buck fanatics never take a season off. Many even embrace winter as a wonderland of information. A big buck's travel in late winter is an open book. During and just after trapping season, the country's most successful deer hunters scout exclusively in the off-season, gleaning information and clues that help them take monster bucks. Here's how they do it.

A good acorn crop can concentrate deer in an area.

"I'd been after this buck for three years," said Midwestern deer hunter Stan Potts, the excitement of the event still vividly detailed in his mind.

> The big buck was with a hot doe, and he actually bred her several times as I watched through binoculars. Then my big break came. The doe lay down. Eventually, the buck bedded beside her, and my window of opportunity flew open like a barn door.
>
> I was so excited I practically leaped from my stand and began a stalk, before suddenly realizing my bow was still in the tree. 'Calm down; be cool,' I thought to myself. 'This is your big chance. Don't blow it.'

A quarter mile away, the deer's huge antlers protruded just above the corn stubble on table-flat land. Despite the open terrain, Potts had several factors in his favor. First, another buck was chasing a doe at the far end of the field, activity that kept the big buck's attention. Also, a misty rain fell and winds gusted to thirty miles per hour, elements that gave a careful stalk at least a fighting chance.

Potts crawled on his belly for nearly an hour. At seventy-five yards, he rolled from one cornrow to another, careful to keep his gear intact. At thirty yards he wanted to shoot. But the angle was poor; he had to get closer. Finally, at eighteen yards, Potts raised his bow, rocked to his knees, and released. As the buck burst from its bed, only the nock was visible.

TELLTALE SIGNS

Potts's big deer scored 167 Pope and Young, a massive, impressive rack that is any hunter's buck of a lifetime. The Illinois resident credits late-season scouting for the success. Each year he relies on information garnered from January through early spring to bag big

An active scrape can mean just one thing: buck in the area.

deer. This buck was 6-½ years old. Potts had found its shed when it was 4-½, a sign that he was on the trail of a real trophy. He scouted thoroughly for the other side of the rack, ultimately concluding that another person probably found it, since much of the big deer's core-activity area was public land.

Potts also recorded the buck on videotape, giving him a chance to study its antlers and size up the trophy potential. Today, video cameras are moderately priced and come with zoom lenses up to 200X, giving operators the chance to look eyeball-to-brow-tine with a whitetail. The zoom of a video camera will allow you to see exactly which tree a deer walks by or which trail it takes. Knowing good doe trails can be productive as well, especially if you can pinpoint the exact entrance or exit from a food source.

"Many hunters fail to realize that after the season, everything from November and December is still perfectly visible," says Potts. "That means all the scrapes, rub lines, and trails." His favorite tactic is to go afield immediately after a fresh snow or heavy rain.

At first light, he locates a big track and follows it, noting exactly where it travels, until the deer is jumped. Then he follows the deer to learn its escape routes. In this way, he can pinpoint the exact trees a deer will walk under, learn where it beds, what it eats, and where it will go if bumped by a coyote or another hunter. All of this is incredibly valuable information for the next season's hunt.

SCOUT NOW, PREPARE NOW

Potts not only uses tracks and sign to locate productive stand sites, he also cuts shooting lanes, trims branches, and otherwise readies the site for next fall. January is too early to hang a stand, however, you can make sure you know the exact location of deer travel and ready the environment for arrow passage. Potts hunts on public land about 80 percent of the time

Scout now, prepare now. When you find a rub like this one, a big buck is in the area.

"Big deer make big tracks," says Stan Potts.

and adheres to public-use regulations carefully. Even picking up sheds on some public land is forbidden, so check the rules to be sure.

When Potts scouts, he's on the lookout for specific signs of a trophy deer. "Big deer make big tracks," says Potts, who tries to find a print that is at least four inches long. The size of a rub is usually commensurate with the size of the buck that made it. Deer rub telephone poles in some parts of the country. When you find this kind of sign, you know you are onto a monster.

"Scrapes are important, but I want a special kind of scrape," Potts says. "I don't pay attention to boundary scrapes (those made along fields and on transition routes). I want a primary scrape that's often visited by more than one buck." These larger-pool, table-size creations are usually near a bedding area and well into the woods. Since deer use these breeding sites year after year, finding one is a giant step. "When you find a big rub line that leads to a big scrape, salivate," says Potts enthusiastically. "You've hit pay dirt."

EARLY SPRING CAN WORK, TOO

World-champion turkey caller Eddie Salter is no novice in the deer woods, having bagged three bucks over 150 Pope and Young with stick and string in a single year. Living in Alabama, Salter combines scouting for deer with the early turkey seasons of the South, "killing two birds with one stone," if you will excuse the pun.

"I like late-season scouting because you can get into places that are really thick in summer and early fall," says Salter. "Inside pine plantations, cutovers, and swamps you

Big tracks mean big deer, often more than one.

often find a clearing or opening that is literally filled with deer sign." Once a deep-cover "island" is located, Salter goes through the preparation of establishing a stand, trimming and pruning as necessary. Cutting a small trail or corridor through very thick cover can actually produce a deer trail where one did not previously exist. If a deadfall blocks a trail, trimming the branches can assure that a deer will step exactly through the portal and enable the most effective ambush point for the hunter. Caution: As you prune, even in winter or early spring, wear gloves so that deer are not repelled by the scent from your hands.

During one deep-cover, late-winter scouting adventure, Salter discovered a shallow slough that led to an island of incredible deer activity. The rut usually occurred during the rainy season, and the slough formed a moat that big bucks used to ward off an army of Robin Hoods that pursued them. Salter foiled this plan by taking a canoe across the deep water and putting a stand in a prime location.

One huge buck traveled the trail within range of the stand, and Salter passed up two Pope and Young bucks, hoping for a shot at the real wall-hanger. One afternoon, the deer was headed straight for the stand when a hot doe crossed the trail and lured it away. A relative took the big deer the next evening after a short boat ride. Salter shared his good fortune with family.

Salter scouts for the travel habits of deer, selects ideal stand locations, and is alert for the best way to approach the stand. In level, damp areas of the South, human scent can be a big problem. The best stand in the woods won't be effective if your scent contaminates the environment on the way in. A canoe is certainly one way of solving the entrance-trail

Whether hunting or scouting, keeping human scent to a minimum will pay off.

odor problem. However, boats have rather limited application in most deer cover. Salter credits his Hunters Specialties scent-elimination products with much of his success this year. Whether hunting or scouting, keeping human scent to a minimum will pay off.

SHEDS ON THE SIDE

As winter winds down and spring arrives, we all need a cure for cabin fever. Spring scouting is the perfect remedy for this annual ailment, because it provides an incentive that can pay off now and in the fall. Like having your cake and eating it too, the sheds you find make interesting conversation and indicate that a quality buck will be even bigger in the fall. In the deer woods as in civics class, history tends to repeat itself.

Every whitetail deer loses its antlers in the late winter or early spring, and the sheds have become a popular and valuable collector's item. The North American Shed Hunter's Club, Inc. (NASHC) promotes collecting and hunting "calcium deposits" for sport and recreation. Founded in 1991 to improve and perpetuate the recognition and gathering of natural-shed antlers in North America, the organization publishes the "Shed Antler Records of North American Big Game," using standard Boone and Crockett scoring methods. Hunting sheds is kind of like a treasure hunt, because you never know what you'll find. In some cases, found shed antlers surpass the world record of animals taken in fair chase.

"Whitetail deer outfitters are beginning to book hunters for spring hunts," says Jeffrey LeBaron, founder and president of the NASHC. "Although the cost is much less, once clients find a huge shed, you can bet they'll book a hunt for the fall."

Whitetail deer shed their antlers annually, providing clues to deer that exist but may not have been seen by hunters.

Aside from the size of a deer's antlers, experience provides additional insight into the former owner. "The size and shape of the antlers are usually due to heredity," explains LeBaron. "But the mass of the antlers often depends on diet." Although the number of points on the rack is not an indication of age, the pedicle imprint (the base of the horn where it attaches to the skull) can reveal a buck's longevity. "After you have seen a few hundred antlers, you get pretty good at judging age," adds LeBaron.

Whether, you hunt sheds for fun, information, or both, finding large antlers is an invitation to an exciting one-on-one hunt for the fall. The clues are out there in late winter. Find them before they melt into thin air.

HUNT BACKWARDS

Stan Potts often hunts on public land in the Midwest, not far from his home in Illinois. Potts does much of his scouting in late winter, especially after a fresh snowfall. "I want to see where big bucks are traveling," he says. "They often use less-traveled trails, and a fresh landscape of white really tells the tale." If Potts jumps a buck, he pays close attention to its escape route, which indicates a probable movement pattern when the hunting season opens the next fall.

Once he locates a bottleneck or area of buck movement, he prepares a stand site, trims shooting lanes, and plans a silent ascent. "I always remove the brush from the area so a deer will not become suspicious," he says. "This also helps remove human scent."

Potts specializes in big bucks, critters that are warier than does. He wants a close shot at an undisturbed animal, and he uses a special technique to make this happen. "I like to stand behind the tree," says Potts. "Although I can't always predict the direction a buck will approach, placing the stand behind the trunk gives much greater camouflage and less chance of detection. I can wait for the animal to pass and get that perfect quartering-away angle."

This strategy greatly helps disguise your silhouette in a tree, but crossbow hunters must be very careful that the limb of the bow does not strike the tree upon release. This will not only ruin the accuracy of the shot, but it can knock you off balance and potentially out of the stand. Let the animal walk slightly past your position, giving you that perfectly angled shot.

"IS THE PIN ON THE TARGET?"

Realistic practice is one of the best ways to make precision shots on live game. Use a McKenzie or other life-size target to demonstrate the effectiveness of your arrows. Paper is excellent for early practice and tightening groups, but it falls far short of reality in hunting situations.

Bob Foulkrod offered a Bowhunting School for a decade, at which dozens of archers stretched the limits of their hunting skills. Foulkrod's target animals moved, made noise, and frequently stopped behind trees. "I try to give my 3-D critters as much realism as possible," says Foulkrod proudly. "Some are so challenging that few archers succeed."

Foulkrod is quick to espouse steps to improve success on game. "Know your equipment," says the Pennsylvania native. "Practice from elevated stands and on targets at various angles and ranges. Know how your bow and arrows perform."

To overcome buck fever, he suggests practicing a mental question for each time you shoot: "Ask, 'Is the pin on the target?' This sounds simple, but the question clears your mind and helps you deal with excitement. Finally, put the pin on the target and keep it there until the arrow arrives. Your form will not be effective unless you follow through."

Ask the question, "Is the pin on the target?" Regardless of what type of gear you use, this small question focuses your mind on the shot and not the antlers.

Foulkrod's school targeted vertical archers, yet his tips and suggestions work for cross-bows and even rifle hunters at the Moment of Truth. A pre-cocked bow is no shield against buck fever, and your hands and knees can tremble no matter what device you hold. Ask the question, "Is the pin/red dot/crosshair/reticle on the target?" The verbiage isn't important, but forcing your concentration on the shot makes a tremendous difference, regardless of what word you use. Also, follow-through is important in all sports, so hold the sight picture completely through the shot. With today's scopes, you will probably see the arrow strike, a factor that helps maintain form.

EASY AS ONE, TWO, THREE

Scott Schultz is a 3-D world champion, president of Robinson Outdoors, and an accomplished hunter who understands the mechanics of tackle and the variables of shooting form. He suggests three basic steps for tree-stand accuracy, a plan that deals with form and equipment function. First, understand gravity's effect on an arrow. "When I used to shoot in 3-D competition out to eighty yards, I had to adjust my sight for targets either

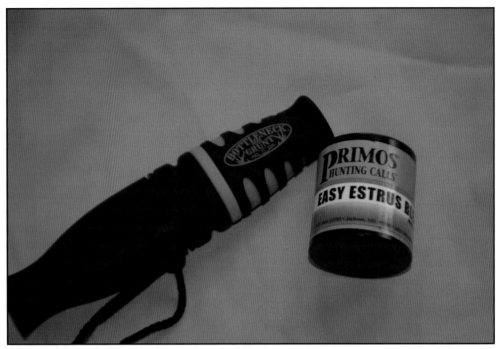

A can-call and a grunt tube should be in every deer hunter's coat pocket.

up or down hill. Instead of shooting at eighty, I'd have to drop back to seventy-five to be on target," explained Shultz. "Gravity affects arrows according to the horizontal distance regardless of the up or down angle. From a high perch in a tree stand, your range finder may read twenty yards, but the horizontal distance will be closer to seventeen. As a result, you may shoot high."

The second step deals with the emotions before the release. "As a hunter lowers the sight pin into the kill zone, the excitement of the moment can take over," says Shultz. "Once the sight pin crosses hair, he pulls the trigger." The solution is to maintain focus by picking an exact spot low in the chest, or by thinking "Is the pin on the animal?" as Foulkrod suggests.

A third preparation involves shooting form. "You should come to full draw and bend at the waist," says Shultz. "Muscle tension through your shoulders, back, and elbow should remain the same. The only thing that should move is your waist. Tip downward with the exact same form as shooting on the level.

"When I invite a person to go deer hunting, we start in my back yard," he said. "I have a ladder stand and a McKenzie target. I move the target around and ask my guest to shoot from various angles, while I add verbal pressure. Often their hands shake with the created

Tyler Durr, a medical student, found enough time from his studies to bag this great buck during the rut.

excitement. Invariably, the first couple of shots are high, and that target doesn't duck. Once they learn to control their form and aim for the heart, they improve dramatically."

Whether you are trying to outwit a wary doe or a foxy big buck, a tree stand can be an awesome ally. Just remember: Careful attention to shooting form and execution will spell the difference between enthusiastically retrieving a trophy and dejectedly pulling an arrow from the dirt.

A DOZEN STRAIGHT-SHOOTING TIPS

1.   Shoot at relaxed game by arriving early, quietly, and containing human scent.
2.   Practice on a 3-D target while wearing full hunting gear.
3.   Carry a practice arrow. Take a practice shot to test your aim from the stand.
4.   Practice at longer distances.
5.   Practice shooting offhand. You can use rest aides from a stand, but they can become a problem as the deer moves.
6.   Don't see the whites of their eyes. Take the first best shot.

7.   Be comfortable and still. Hang your bow within easy reach.
8.   Consider cover scents to hold a deer's attention to the ground.
9.   Practice shooting with broadheads.
10.   Expect does to be more alert than most bucks.
11.   Range in landmarks for quick distance decisions.
12.   Aim low in the chest. Think, "Is the pin on the target?", to stay calm.

Chapter 24

Crossbow Success in Firearm Seasons

The author took this buck during the South Dakota firearms season.

WEAR ORANGE, BUT THINK CAMO

Bowhunting during a rifle, shotgun, or muzzleloader season may seem unusual, because stand placements are so different. Generally, a firearm hunter wants to maximize his range and may select a clear-cut, field edge, or timbered area with extensive shooting lanes. Because a modern firearm will accurately shoot two hundred yards or farther, it only makes sense to tap this extensive range to cover more ground and conceivably see more deer.

Conversely, bowhunters have a maximum range of fifty yards and seek stand placements and ambush points where deer are lured or forced into close proximity, with shots of twenty to thirty yards more likely. Ideal places are bottlenecks, narrow timber lines,

You can share the woods with firearm hunters. Be sure to follow all blaze-orange laws for your safety.

Stand placement is critical for early-season cross-bow success. Put your stand where the deer move, and allow other hunters to push them toward you.

and distinct terrain features such as a ravine or water hole. In this case a narrow creek bottom paralleled the open prairie and deer had to move around and below the bluff to avoid climbing a steep hill.

I used this tactic in Maryland's early muzzle-loading season. In mid-October success on antlered deer is quite low despite the hundred-yard capability of most black-powder rifles. I believed that stand placement was much more of a success factor than effective shooting range, so I placed a stand along a well-used trail at the edge of an old clear-cut. I was in the stand at dawn and saw very few deer, which was typical for that time of year. Around 9:00 a buck fed along the trail, munching on freshly-fallen leaves. The range was right at twenty yards, and I was able to take the deer without it having a hint of my presence, even though I was wearing hunter orange

Don't stop scouting just before the season. Deer movements can change with a food source, and you want the latest information of what's happening.

JUMP THE GUN FOR ADDED SUCCESS

Many states have extended archery seasons in which the bow season is open on the eve of and during a firearm season. You've probably heard hunters express regret about seeing a huge buck during their scouting efforts or last-minute stand preparations and lament the bad timing.

As an archery hunter, you can and should continue scouting to find the latest scrapes and travel corridors. But you aren't just scouting, you are hunting. Likewise, with a tag in your pocket, you can have infinitely more patience to see how deer are moving and the quality of bucks in the area. Few rifle hunters will spend more than an hour or two on a stand without a gun in their hands.

Although some hunters will be mobile in the deer woods prior to opening day, you

Keep scouting, and listen to what other hunters say about game movements.

can still use most of your rut-season tricks, as deer will be carrying out their normal feeding and travel routines. Lay down a scent trail on your way to the stand. Rattle, grunt call, and doe bleat. These are tricks that will work until the guns begin to crack.

Be mobile. Many hunt clubs have designated or traditional areas where hunters post on opening morning. In some cases, these stands and areas don't change for generations, and a gun hunter will be most unwelcome once the season opens. In most cases archers are seen as a minimal threat to these territorial instincts, and you may be able to hunt places that you cannot or dare not with a firearm.

Keep an open mind and ear during the season. I belong to a hunt club with twenty-seven owner-members, and my hunting buddies rarely talk about the big deer they have seen prior to opening day. However, at the end of the opener, the brew and the truth come out. Wherever those hunters posted the first day, they will probably continue to cling to their stands while you can be more mobile. You might even use a climbing tree stand to put yourself into prime position.

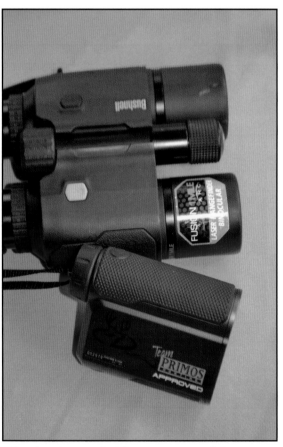

When hunting near bedding areas, you need the exact range for high-percentage shots. Get a rangefinder and use it.

THINK THICK AND CLOSE

If you have a rifle zeroed in at one hundred yards, why hunt a place where you can only see half that distance? Many firearm hunters think this way, but bucks don't. They seek out the thickest bedding and travel areas they can find. Posting in locations with limited visibility often allows you to see more deer.

When hunting dense bedding areas, you want to replicate a full page from the archer's playbook. Approach your stand with as little disturbance as possible. Since firearm hunters typically climb into stands in the dark, you may need to be extra early and allow their movements to bump deer toward you. Be sure your boots are scent-free, and pull a scent rag with estrous lure. Or put rutting scents directly onto your boots.

Keep your trail cameras up. Since you will be concentrating on a small corridor of movement, you may capture images of bucks that are seldom seen from distant stands.

Especially on opening day, rattle and use deer calls such as estrous bleats or grunts. These rarely spook deer, but can bring a buck to your exact location for the close shot you need. Finally, take extra scent precautions. I once hunted in a Texas deer camp where I was the only archer. Arriving for breakfast the first day, everyone was dressed in their full hunting gear, while I wore jeans and a flannel shirt. "Are you going out later?" one hunter asked curiously.

"No," I replied. "I'll dress in the field so that my clothes aren't scent contaminated."

After I'd bagged a very respectable ten-point, I noticed that fewer

If you hit a deer, watch its movements and pinpoint to the site where it went out of sight.

hunters were fully dressed at breakfast. One fellow commented, "There must be something to this scent-elimination business."

MAINTAIN YOUR ETHICS

Bagging a buck with archery gear in a firearm season is thrilling and quite an accomplishment. But remember to be modest about success. Take the same quality, ethical shots that you would in archery season. Should you wound a deer, you can legally trail it with a rifle, but that's not how you want a hunt to end. Simulated practice sessions prior to the hunt should determine your maximum range. Don't let the seduction of a rifle-follow-up compromise your principles. Many firearm hunters believe that a crossbow is much like a rifle, and such attitudes threaten the extended seasons we enjoy.

When you find a big scrape like this, you will want all of your gear with you.

When you succeed, you won't have to tell your buddies that you took it with a crossbow. In most camps word will get around, and you want the focus to be on your hunting skills, such as the ambush you selected, your preparation prior to the hunt, and the substantial practice time that enabled the shot. You know how to bow hunt, so "stick to your guns" and you'll soon understand how little the game changes in firearm seasons. You'll enjoy many more days afield and probably an extra tag . . . or maybe even two.

GEAR TO LEVEL THE PLAYING FIELD

Easy Cock and Shoot

Two of my favorite bows are the Mission MXB-320, because it cocks so easily without a stirrup, and the Excalibur Matrix 310, which is so durable it doesn't have a dry-fire protector. www.missionarchery.com and www.excaliburcrossbows.com.

Mechanical Heads

These broadheads fly like target points, and allow easy practice in a host of situations. My last buck fell to a Rage Hypodermic two-blade, and the blood trail was exceptional. Plus, it flew just like the practice head. www.ragebroadheads.com.

Tree Stands

My opening day stand is a Millennium two-man ladder stand. Although I hunt alone, I love the extra room for gear, food, and comfort. www.millenniumstands.com.

Range-Finding Binoculars

In areas where point restrictions are the law, Bushnell's new Fusion 1 Mile 10x42 binoculars combine two important functions into one device. www.bushnell.com.

ScentBlocker Spider Safety Apparel

During firearm season, you want to spend all day in your stand. It's easy to become drowsy, yet I'm safely harnessed in. www.robinsonoutdoors.com.

LimbSaver Kodiak Crossbow Sling

Carrying a bow over your shoulder keeps your hands free for calls, gear, and navigating steep terrain. The LimbSaver sling grips your shoulder and is very comfortable. www.limbsaver.com.

Easton Carbon

Since crossbow bolts fly at such great speeds, bending an aluminum shaft is always a worry. Carbon solves that problem. www.eastonarchery.com.

Illuminated Scope

A scope like my Hawke, with illuminated reticle, greatly helps eliminate "pin confusion" in low light. If batteries are a concern, consider an Aimpoint red-dot scope whose batteries last, full on, for six years. www.hawkeoptics.com and www.aimpoint.com.

Chapter 25

Tree Stand Safety and Success

A tree stand gives a hunter a strategic advantage over whitetail deer. Posting high in a tree helps to conceal your location and reduce scent detection.

Whether the goal is a big-rack buck or a fat, tasty doe, these shooting tips and practice methods will increase your success.

Always cock your bow on the ground, and then pull it into the stand with a pull-up rope.

Two bucks stared intently toward their back trail. Something *big* was approaching, and my heart pounded in anticipation. A heavy, eight-point buck suddenly stepped into the green field. Then it turned and looked back. I could hardly stand the suspense.

A record-class, ten-point emerged, searching the open field for danger and potential rivals. At one point, the eight-point turned and presented a challenge. But it quickly relented to the dominant male. My pulse quickened as the big buck eventually stepped into "easy" range. At twenty-five yards, I aimed and launched, zipping an arrow cleanly over its back. The trophy deer bounded fifty yards and looked back, oblivious to its near demise. The buck was clueless of the miss. I was dumbfounded. How could I have missed???

Tree stands offer the advantage of sight and scent concealment, yet many archers (myself included) shoot high at known distances. Is this an element of buck fever? Errant shooting form? Or some unknown shooting dynamic at work?

I was hunting the Enon Plantation in central Alabama. Although I'd seen other deer on the three-day excursion, this was my big chance at a trophy-class buck. Another hunter bagged two does that same day, and by the hunt's end he'd tagged two more. Obviously, he had the secret to tree-stand straight-shooting. I eagerly sought his advice.

"I love to shoot does," said C. J. Davis, then public relations director for Mossy Oak Camouflage. "I enjoy bagging a good buck like the next guy, yet when a big female whitetail comes along, I rarely pass one up. They just taste too darned good."

DUMB DOES? NOT!

Tree stands are the most dangerous aspect of hunting. Always make sure that your stand is well maintained, and that it is used according to manufacturer's instructions.

The Enon Plantation consists of fifteen thousand acres of prime habitat, such that harvesting does was part of the property's Quality Deer Management (QDM) plan. Davis was happy to help out. In the world of big-buck testosterone, shooting does is seen by some as "less sporting." However, Davis pointed out a fact I've witnessed many times. "Does are often more alert than bucks," he said. "They spot you right away." Only when a buck reaches full maturity does its alertness surpass that of a female. Does are constantly vigilant to protect their young. The fact that Davis had such consistent success proved he was doing something right. Actually, he was doing a heck of a lot right.

OPENING DAY ACTION

The Enon Plantation has offered bow-hunting-only whitetail opportunities, thereby generating many trophy-class bucks and a wealth of knowledge about deer movements. This hunt occurred in November, which is "early season" in Alabama's Black Belt region. Deer typically feed in acorn draws or woodlots in the early morning and in green fields in late afternoon.

The first morning, Davis climbed into his stand half an hour before daylight, leaving sufficient time for a deer to feed under him at dawn. "When I could see well, two more deer approached," he said. "They fed intermittently as they neared the stand. I dared not draw until both heads were down feeding. Eventually, they got too close to the tree."

Davis's patience was rewarded as two more deer approached, munching on acorns in the travel and feeding corridor. Finally, a large doe stepped behind a pine tree and Davis raised the bow. When the deer stepped into a small opening, he released. "I made a good shot and watched it fall," he said with a smile of satisfaction.

The range was just seventeen yards, and Davis attributes the success to patience and good stand placement. "I never aim at a deer if I can see its eyes," he advises. "Deer should be feeding or looking away before I'll make a move. Usually, I hang my bow on a hanger and sit in the stand. As soon as I see a deer approaching, I stand, pick up the bow, and get into shooting position. The key is to be patient and move only when the deer's vision is obstructed."

DOUBLE-TAKE

The next morning, Davis climbed into a different stand, yet in a similar circumstance. Today he was hunting a travel corridor of red oaks ripe with falling fruit. "A yearling fed under the stand at daylight, and two others soon came along. The lead doe crossed my entrance trail and became enamored with the scent. Step-by-step she slowly walked fifty yards closer to the tree. Eventually she gave up the scent trail,

Wearing a safety harness is essential to your safety. Consider a lifeline that keeps you attached to the tree all the way to the stand.

quartered away and stopped. This one piled up just sixty yards away," he said.

Since Enon allows two deer per day, Davis made sure the deer had expired, then climbed back into the stand. "This tree was a perfect selection," described Davis. "A limb extended above my head, providing the perfect extension to hang a bow. It was conveniently suspended right in front of me."

Half an hour later, two deer approached from the rear of the stand. Again, scent on Davis's boots caught the lead doe's attention. As it sniffed at the spot, an arrow pierced its lungs. Ironically, as Davis was about to climb down, two bucks appeared. One was a big eight-pointer.

A good red-dot scope will give you a definite edge.

EVENING FINALE

The last afternoon of the hunt, Davis seemed destined to bag another large doe. Two deer fed in the middle of a green field, moving steadily toward his stand. At forty yards, they altered course and headed away. "I already had a couple of clumps ranged in and was ready to aim, until they turned away," Davis remembers. "Then a deer entered the other end of the field and joined them. This mature doe fed in the same area, but came ten yards closer. It went just eighty yards and was easily retrieved."

Davis was quick to give credit to the Enon staff for excellent stand placement. "They always put me in great trees," he said. Typically, an Enon stand is twenty feet high with good back cover. Stands are comfortable and very stable. Best of all, they are placed in areas deer use regularly for feed and travel.

Enon stands are typically twenty feet high. Be sure your range finder is handy, and have one that allows for downward-angle readings.

Chapter 26

The Laws of Physics and the Development of the ZEISS XB75

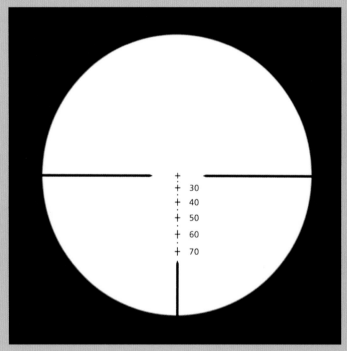

Carl Zeiss Sports Optics introduced a quality scope that may well become a model for the industry.

Joel Harris, now Head of Global Public Relations for Carl Zeiss Sports Optics recently completed a two-year study of crossbows in the development of the new ZEISS TERRA XB75 crossbow scope with a patented ballistic reticle. I hunted with him during the early stages of the process, and he could barely walk from the strain that had been put on his back from frequently cocking crossbows thousands of times. Harris started by shooting most of the popular bows in a variety of poundages and arrow weights. Since he represents no specific crossbow brand, his research is particularly revealing. Here's an exclusive interview about the development process:

> I saw that there was a huge need for a better crossbow optic, as most crossbow packages offered optics that weren't good enough for the guy that understands the need for good optics. We were stuck with models that were inferior to the technology of crossbows, and the technology of crossbows had advanced far beyond the average scope.
>
> For a guy who knows quality optics, I wanted him to have a very good choice. As I looked at this, crossbows have been around for a while, and the guys who really wanted to shoot them were already in the crossbow area. But with the vast majority of states across the country legalizing the use of crossbows, this opened up a huge opportunity. There are guys who are rifle hunters and want to extend their season, but they don't have enough time to dedicate to becoming proficient with a vertical bow. These are the guys and gals who probably don't know a lot about crossbows, or they just walk into an archery shop and pick out a package in the crossbow section.
>
> I thought about this guy or gal who has been a really proficient hunter and comes into the crossbow market already understanding what good optics are. He or she may buy a really nice package bow with an inferior scope, and then they may not have such a great experience, due to not enough light transmission, less clarity, or not a super great reticle. That person will most likely become frustrated and want to replace it with another scope. Whether they understand good optics or not, they now have a choice that is similar to—or maybe better than—the scope that is on their current hunting rifle.
>
> Identifying the need was first and foremost in the development of this scope. I wanted to launch the world's first premium crossbow scope, so I drew from my vast knowledge of archery. I knew what to look for and researched the market and products extensively.
>
> I began by talking with the crossbow manufacturers about any ballistic data they may have had, and I quickly learned that there was no data available. It just didn't exist. It had to be created; so I began looking at options.

At that point I went out to a local archery shop that I had a great relationship with, and they allowed me to go through the several models they had in stock. By experimentation, I found the bows that hit the speeds advertised. I settled on the Mathews Mission line, because it allowed me the flexibility to adjust poundage up and down to hit the various speeds I needed to gather the required data for the ballistic curve I needed to complete this project. There is a large variation among crossbow bolts and broadheads weight-wise. I had to settle on a specific bolt: the Mission crossbow bolt. I decided on a 400-grain total weight setup, point weight included. The shop also allowed me to go through dozens and dozens of bolts to make sure they were all identical in weight, as I needed to use the same weight bolt for every speed, every distance, every shot.

From the beginning I knew that the testing had to precise to get this scope and reticle combination to work for every bow. Using a Bench-Master shooting rest with levels, I first got the BenchMaster level with the surface. Then I placed a Wheeler scope-leveling device on the rail. I leveled the rail with the BenchMaster and used an additional leveling

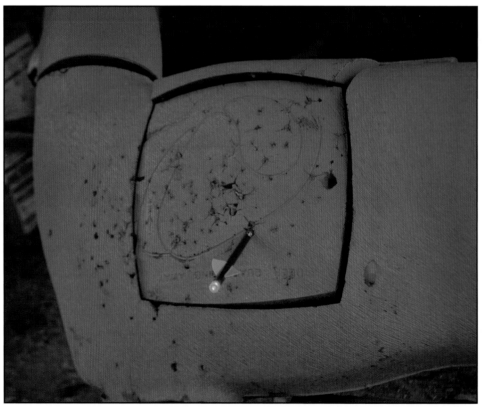

Good optics will help you shoot where you want to shoot.

device on the turret. This way I would have the crosshairs level with the shooting platform. I shot every shot at every distance on that BenchMaster and through a chronograph.

Again, my test arrow was a 400-grain (total weight) Mission crossbow bolt, including vanes, nocks, and points. I started at ten yards to make sure the bolt was hitting dead center. Then I moved to all respective distances. The idea was for the reticle design to work from twenty to seventy-five yards in 2-½ yard increments, so I had to make sure that my speeds were consistent. That kept it very controlled. To get it precise, I kept the conditions the same every time I did my testing, including temperature, wind speed, time of day, altitude, etc.

When the testing began, I never recorded any data unless I had three shots consecutively at the identical speed; and they had to impact the same spot on the target before I would enter a value. That allowed me to base everything off of speed. It doesn't matter if your bolt weighs 300 or 500 grains, it all comes down to speed. The testing process was very time-consuming.

The ability for a crossbow hunter to use a scope is a significant advantage over compound-bow shooters.

When I handed off the data I had gathered to my German engineers, they about fell out of their chairs. Every ballistic program they ran it through was as accurate as it could be. They said that this was the best ballistic data they had ever worked with.

I built the XB75 on a 2-7x32 TERRA ED riflescope platform. The ocular design has both speed and magnification engraved on it. As you go up in magnification, you go up in speed as well. This covers crossbows from 275–425 fps. We had to match the sub-tension of the reticles and magnification to speed. We have the world's best engineers with a vast knowledge of ballistics. We've developed and patented several ballistic reticles, including our Rapid-Z and RZ reticles that can be found in some of our current rifle-scope models.

The XB75 has six individual crosshairs, one each for twenty, thirty, forty, fifty, sixty, and seventy yards. The dot in-between each individual crosshair represents the half-yard increments (twenty-five, thirty-five, forty-five, fifty-five, and sixty-five yards). The top of the vertical post coming from the bottom of the reticle represents the seventy-five-yard mark.

Hunters should use a rest when possible, although at close range shooting offhand can be very effective.

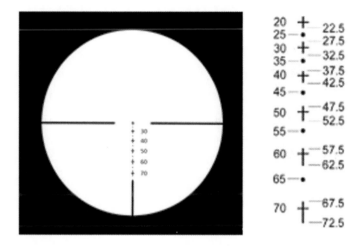

SIGHTING IN THE XB75

Now that the reticle is complete, the sighting process is simple. You start by mounting the scope with the main crosshair as square as you can. Choose a place to shoot your crossbow with a safe backstop, and ensure that no one can step unseen into or in front of the shooting lane. To start the zeroing process, place a target in front of the backstop at a measured distance of ten yards. Leaving the power at the lowest magnification (2X), adjust the fine-focus so you can clearly see the reticle on the target. Now take your first shot at the center of the target. If an adjustment is required, remove the dust covers from the windage and elevation turrets of the scope. Make your adjustment to the turret to bring the point-of-impact (POI) closer to your point-of-aim (POA). For example, if the arrow impact is lower than your aiming point, rotate the elevation turret counter-clockwise to raise the point of impact. A high impact point requires a clockwise adjustment. Both turrets will move the POA one-quarter minute of angle per click. This is equal to one-quarter inch at one hundred yards. After achieving an approximate zero at ten yards, move to a distance of twenty yards and continue adjusting the turrets until the top crosshair of the reticle and the point of impact are the same at this distance. Each click equals one-quarter of an inch, so four clicks are needed to move the impact one inch at one hundred yards. When you are satisfied with the twenty-yard zero, replace the dust covers.

CALIBRATING YOUR SCOPE TO THE CROSSBOW

The ocular ring has engravings for speed and magnification. Adjusting the speed selector also adjusts the magnification. Start by setting it to the manufacturer's advertised speed of your crossbow, and adjust the fine-focus so you can clearly see the crosshairs on the target. Move to a measured thirty yards from the target. Using the thirty-yard marker in the scope (the second crosshair down), shoot the crossbow at the target. If the arrow impacts the target high of your aiming point, turn the speed selector higher, and the next arrow shot will impact the target lower. If the arrow impacts the target lower than your aiming point, turn the speed selector lower and the next arrow shot will impact the target higher. Once the thirty-yard crosshair is sighted-in the scope is calibrated

Just like with arrows, some hunters enjoy combining their crossbow with after-market products. The ZEISS XB75 will be a welcome addition.

to your crossbow and all of the other aiming points will be correct. At this time, the speed/magnification selector will need to remain in this position. Make a note of the position to keep the scope and the crossbow calibrated to each other. If you notice a slightly lower impact at fifty yards, simply turn the speed dial down in small increments until it is dead-on. This will have only a little effect when you go back to shoot at twenty yards, where the impact will only be about a half inch high. Crossbows with speeds over 425 fps, and using a lighter arrow combination may require a main crosshair sight-in point of thirty yards instead of the normal twenty yards. This will require calibrating the scope at forty yards to compensate for the flat trajectory of the crossbow bolt.

I encourage everyone to shoot through a chronograph, which will give you the best starting point for this reticle. But the other really cool thing about this reticle is this: If you don't have a chronograph, after sighting in at twenty yards at 2X, move the target to thirty yards and slowly dial your speed up until you hit dead on. Then look at the ocular, and you can see what your actual arrow speed is, like a chronograph.

Here's a ballistic curve example: Using a 400-fps crossbow with a 400-grain bolt, the drop at seventy yards is thirty-eight inches. Using a 300-fps crossbow with the same 400-grain bolt, the drop of the bolt is sixty-nine inches at seventy yards, dropping one inch for every yard. Understanding what your arrow is doing is very important, especially if you're shooting in a situation where you have overhanging limbs between you and the target.

ONE SHOT SIGHT-IN

Sighting in a crossbow or rifle can be a fun or frustrating experience. Learn this one-shot method, and it will save you precious time and arrows some day. It's best done with a second person and a solid shooting rest. Here's the technique:

Begin with all the safety steps engaged. Have a known target and backdrop, and use shooting glasses and a solid rest.

Lay the crossbow on a lead sled or benchrest type device, so that the bow can be fired and kept in place.

Place a large (24x24) target ten yards in front of the bow. Using your best form, aim at the bull's-eye and squeeze effectively.

Return the bow to the exact shooting position and place the reticle or red dot on the bull's-eye. Note the arrow strike position. While you hold the bow steady, allow the second person to adjust the scope's vertical and horizontal adjustments until the reticle zeroes the arrow. Now your bow will be sighted-in for that distance.

The key is holding the bow still during the scope adjustment. Try it; it's quite simple once you learn the ropes.

For more information on the TERRA XB75 crossbow scope and all the award-winning ZEISS products, please visit www.zeiss.com/us/sports-optics.

Chapter 27

Accuracy Enhancement: Tuning Gear and Shooting Skills

Accuracy with a crossbow is as much about the arrow as the bow.

Want to shoot your crossbow like an accuracy machine? Know how to troubleshoot it when it doesn't? Check out these tips.

Most modestly-priced crossbows shoot at or less than a three-shot, two-inch group at thirty yards. That's accurate enough to put a broadhead through a deer's heart every time with a consistent shot, and some would ask, "What's the problem?"

In a nutshell, *stuff happens,* if you get my drift. There's this thing called Murphy's Law that hasn't gone away like the rotary-dial telephone.

As much as it pains this male ego to say, the best way to get the most from your crossbow is to read the manual and watch the CD supplied by the manufacturer. Or go to YouTube and download videos showing how best to use your bow. Topics usually include cocking the bow; weight, spine, and length of arrows; assembly techniques; and other basic elements about shooting the bow safely and accurately. As suggested earlier, if you are ordering a bow, do this homework ahead of time so that you know the ropes of the bow before cocking it; no pun intended.

ASSEMBLY AND MAINTENANCE

Some bows come completely assembled from point of purchase. If not, you can request that it be done along with any special elements of the process. If you want to fly the bow, pack it into a camp, or otherwise reduce it to its shipping condition, you'll want to know any tricks involved.

My Mission Sniper Lite came in a large box, pre-assembled. In fact, with this model, dismantling the bow voids the warranty, so I saved the box, just in case it ever needed warranty work or repair. My Horton, on the other hand, came in a much smaller, rectangular box and assembled easily, with only one tricky part. The cable slide must be assembled correctly, and that involves close attention. The manual and assembly instructions alert you to this specific installation, though, so it's not a problem.

Recurve bows like the Excalibur Micro are the easiest to assemble, since there are no cams or cables on the bow. Assembly and disassembly requires just a few Allen wrenches, and it's nearly foolproof.

Before you put your new bow together, be sure to check which pieces of gear need lubrication. And remember, more isn't necessarily better. You'll want to

Develop maintenance routines such as lubing your rail every ten shots and assuring that your cables and strings do not dry and begin to fray.

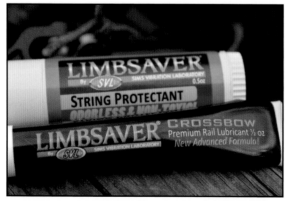

Maintain your bow properly to prevent string and cable wear and ensure consistent accuracy and performance.

You should demand consistent accuracy from your bow and be able to shoot groups under three inches at thirty yards.

lube your rail every five to eight shots as the manufacturer recommends, but don't douse the bow in lubricant, as that tends to make it retain field debris. Doing so may actually gum up the bow and cause more friction than it relieves.

Use your cell phone camera as a memory keeper. Lay all the parts of your bow on a flat surface and take a picture so that you know all of the pieces. Likewise, once assembled, make a digital record of where each part goes and how it fits. Do the same with mounting and dismounting the scope. A quick glance at your phone will show in which groove of the Picatinny rail the scope installs, so it's always exactly consistent with what you are used to.

COCKING: CONSISTENCY COUNTS

Unless you load each arrow with exactly the same process, you won't get accuracy and consistent grouping. Like a scope with a screw loose, arrows will strike inconsistently.

How you cock your bow can affect accuracy. Ropes and cranking devices give the best results.

The bow launches in the same manner, but placement of the nock on the string at various release points will cause variations in point of impact.

Cocking by hand is the usual suspect in the crime of inaccuracy. As you draw the string into the full-cock position, it's easy to pull with one hand more than the other, which places the release point off-center. This is particularly true with compound bows of narrow width, since the string is drawn at a very steep angle during the cocking process.

The most consistent way to cock a crossbow is with a rope or mechanical cocking device. A cocking rope usually reduces the force needed to cock the bow by 50 percent, and this is further reduced by compound crossbows in which the cams reduce the draw weight as the string nears full cock. With recurve bows, you need to pull the string back with force, and more powerful models, with draw weights approaching or exceeding two hundred pounds, may be more than you can handle. For these, you will need a mechanical cocking device, usually one that turns with a crank handle.

Maintain the same cocking routine in the field as you do at home.

Although this tip rarely affects accuracy, it's helpful in the overall sanity of using a cocking rope effectively. My Mission does this very well. First, the handles of the rope are of different color. I always put the orange handle in my right hand, which keeps the string hook facing upward. Next, the string length is just enough to reach the bowstring with a small amount of tension on the rope. In this way, I store the bow

Having an adult assist youngsters will ensure that there are no dry fires or misfires.

with the cocking rope attached to the bow, and I always know where it is. Additionally, Mission bows do not have cocking stirrups, which creates a cocking stroke that mostly uses your legs and thighs, making the process quicker and easier.

More powerful bows will require a mechanical cocking device. One of the easiest to use is the TenPoint ACUdraw 50 system, in which the cocking rope attaches to the stock and the handle nests into it. Other bows have devices that attach to the stock and draw the string by cranking what is basically a winch. As you will soon see, this puts a lot of pressure on the cocking rope, so you want to proceed with care. I once tried cocking a TenPoint bow in the "silent mode." The handle slipped off, and the cocking device busted a spring. I was warned not to do this in the owner's manual, and I paid the price for not heeding that warning.

Finally, TenPoint has the market cornered in the cocking-rope department with the ACUrope. I try to remain neutral on most products, but this cocking rope is hands down the easiest to use, store, and deploy. Like the ACUdraw system, the rope retracts and folds into a handy loop that easily fits in your pocket or on your belt. Best of all, the rope fits most crossbows. Once you try it, you will love it.

ARROWS MAKE THE DIFFERENCE

Most bows of modest or higher price will shoot well right out of the box, and there's really not much you can or should do. Where the accuracy rubber really meets the road is in the arrow department. Of great importance is the match between what you shoot and what the manufacturer recommends. In particular, the length of the shaft and weight of the arrow, including the point, needs to meet manufacturer specifications. Lighter arrows will shoot faster and flatter than heavier arrows. Yet by decreasing the weight below the manufacturer's recommendation, you move closer to a dry-fire effect. A lighter arrow transfers more energy into the bow itself, causing excess wear and more vibration, which also translates into a louder release.

Nock configuration makes a difference too. Basically, crossbow bolt nocks come in three configurations: moon (or concave), flat, and Omni, which is the TenPoint proprietary brand. Moon nocks are concave and allow the string to capture the arrow upon release, reducing the likelihood that the string will slip under or over the nock resulting in a misfire. This nock is very popular, but you must make sure the cock feather goes down during the loading process so that the string slides into the valley of the nock. If you load an arrow with the cock feather canted, the string will strike the sharp edge of the nock, which may cut the string on contact. Normally, arrows with moon nocks are fletched such that having the cock feather down ensures the nock is oriented correctly, but always check to make sure.

Nock configuration can make a huge difference.

Flat nocks give the archer the ability to rotate the arrow in case the spine of one arrow varies from others in the quiver. If you use flat nocks and one arrow flies away from the group, the first attempt at a fix is to rotate it and shoot again.

Each piece of an arrow must fit perfectly for proper flights. If one shaft flies differently than others, check to be sure the nock and insert fit properly.

Flat nocks are also handier to shoot under pressure, since there is no wrong way to load the arrow.

The folks at TenPoint merged these two ideas and created the Omni nock that has a small indentation in the nock for greater string traction, yet provides the ability to rotate the arrow for consistent spine alignment. This provides the advantages of each nock style without the danger of cutting the bowstring.

BUILD THE BEST ARROW

Building an arrow from scratch is a bit like guys who reload ammunition. There's nothing wrong with Hornady or Winchester cartridges, yet some people enjoy the ability to ensure that everything is exactly to their liking. Competitive archers who buy raw shafts weigh them first and discard any that vary by more than a grain. Next, they cut the shaft to their specifications with a high-speed saw specifically made for carbon and aluminum. This gives a relatively square cut and eliminates most burrs on the tube. However, quality arrows always have the interior of the tube smoothed with a device that reduces any remaining burrs.

Next and most importantly, each end of the shaft is squared with a G5 tool. Of all the causes of inaccuracy among arrows, a lack of alignment is the greatest. Unless the ends of the shaft are completely perpendicular to the shaft, the nock will not fit properly, and the insert, which holds the point, will not align with the arrow. This is the reason that archers install a broadhead and then give it the spin test. Placing the tip of the broadhead on a hard surface and rapidly rotating the shaft should show a true spin devoid of wobble. If the arrow wobbles, something is wrong either with the arrow insert or the broadhead. Sometimes the shaft is square, but the insert has glue on only one side, which cants the alignment with the shaft. There are other variables here as well, but you should spin every broadhead on a shaft before using it. If the head wobbles, use a different one that spins true.

NUMBER YOUR ARROWS

Whenever you see an archer, vertical or horizontal, with numbers on his fletching, you know you are dealing with a person of high accuracy standards. Although most arrows,

Number the fletching on your arrow. Number the cock feather so that you consistently shoot arrows with the same vane orientation.

like most rifle cartridges, are very similar, one could be a flier. Luckily, we have an advantage over our firearm brethren in that we can shoot our ammo and test how each one shoots.

Begin with target points and a bench rest. But don't shoot at twenty yards. Many bows shoot so consistently that you may crack or damage the nocks of previous arrows. Either do your tests at thirty yards or shoot at twenty using a target with multiple aiming points. I personally like the latter option, since arrows can crash at thirty yards as well, and that would mean replacing it at some expense.

If you use flat nocks, number the feather you want to use as the cock feather so that your arrow spines will be consistent. For other nocks, number your fletching so that it's easily observed as you load the arrow. As crazy as it sounds, once your arrows have a "name," you'll soon find those you like more than others. Maybe your Number Three arrow seems to shoot the best, in which case you'll want it loaded for opening morning. Conversely, if Number Five seems to fly low or a little left, reexamine the construction. Perhaps by rotating the cock feather orientation it will fly more consistently. But be aware of the nock dangers mentioned above. Despite the cost of discarding a shaft, an inaccurate arrow can have a huge cost in poor performance.

FRONT OF CENTER

Front of Center (FOC) will affect how an arrow flies. For example, Excalibur crossbows come with one of the lightest arrows on the market, the Diablo. Combined with a short power stroke, the arrows are also among the shortest compared to other crossbows. The light, carbon arrows generate high

An arrow with a heavier tip will fly better than one with a lighter tip.

speeds from the recurve-limb designed bows, yet the brand's tests have shown that they fly best with a 150-grain field point or broadhead. That too is heavier than any on the market, yet it gives the Diablo shafts a high FOC which keeps them flying accurately.

This concept is easily demonstrated with a paper airplane. Whatever the design, it will fly better if you place a paperclip on the front. You'll quickly see that the plane flies straighter, with less effect from wind and imperfections in the folding process.

The exact formula for FOC is difficult to predict, since arrow spine weights and lengths vary widely. Suffice it to say that using a weighted insert and a 125-grain broadhead may well increase the consistency of each shot, help arrow flight, and improve penetration due to greater arrow momentum.

FLETCHING LENGTH

Fletching length has little effect at close range unless the arrow launch is unstable, in which case longer fletching will stabilize an arrow more quickly than shorter fletching.

The length of arrow fletching varies from brand to brand. Some arrows use full three-inch vanes, while others opt for much smaller two-inch guidance. Which is better? Again, it depends on the arrow. It can be said that longer vanes have more steering ability, but they can slow the arrow at longer distances. Occasionally, they can make noise as well. Two-inch vanes create less wind resistance and help maintain arrow speed, which results in a flatter trajectory curve.

One way to test the effect of vane length on your bow is to conduct a paper test as vertical archers do. If your arrow cuts a perfectly round hole with short vanes, the shaft will probably fly very well with them. If, however, you get a left or high tear, then the shaft will need more guidance, and longer fletching will improve accuracy.

Crossbow shafts are typically so stiff that fletching plays a small role in the stabilization of the arrow. With longbows, recurves, and compounds, arrows oscillate wildly upon release, and the fletching is needed to keep the arrow on course. Ironically, one of the ways of tuning a compound bow is to shoot a bare shaft. If it flies well, then the fletching is just icing on the cake.

Chapter 28

Crossbows on Safari

Don Wilson took this trophy impala, one of the many animals taken on the trip.

"Do not aim behind the shoulder," I said adamantly to my friends as we finalized our plans and gear for an upcoming African safari. African antelope aren't whitetail deer, and you must make yourself aim differently or you may not retrieve your game. But you will still pay for it."

This trip with Rassie Erasmus of Louwlardus Bowhunting Safaris (contact via email: bowhunt@rassie.co.za) would be my twenty-second safari in Africa, and I can now celebrate two decades of chasing plains game animals from hides and stalking. This time, however, the gear would be crossbow-only, and I had two enthusiastic friends to join in the quest. Don Wilson, a long time hunting buddy and friend had been to Africa previously but always seemed to run into bad luck. Either promising game properties proved disappointing or a successful trip ended with all taxidermy lost. That was a really bad experience in Zimbabwe.

Crossbows were adequate for deer-size game, but what about larger species like a 1,500-pound eland?

Ed Beachley is a local dentist who heard about the trip from Wilson and immediately wanted in. Both men had experience with vertical gear, yet had not taken seriously to crossbows. Since I was writing this book and had access to a variety of new bows and other equipment, we could hunt with the latest gear and do the ultimate performance tests with as many as twenty animals in the mix.

MANAGEMENT SAFARI

I met Rassie Erasmus at the Safari Club International Convention, and we discussed his unique management-safari concept. Erasmus had offered bowhunting safaris for many years and was well-known in archery circles. In addition, he worked with several bow companies and sold equipment in South Africa. He offered traditional, ranch-style safaris with one significant difference. Instead of hiring sharpshooters to cull older animals to keep populations within limits, he offered these management animals for 30 percent of the typical price. If you were willing to harvest an impala with worn antlers, he offered the trophy for $150, about 20 percent of the normal price. Blue wildebeest sold for $550, and an old zebra went for $500, about a third the price of the skin alone at the airport gift shop.

The Ebola epidemic in West-Central Africa really hurt the tourist market for all of Africa. We would be nine hours by jet from the nearest problem, yet reduced numbers of passengers really brought the airfare down. Normally, a person will pay at least $1,500 for a round trip flight from Washington, D.C. to Johannesburg, yet the 2015 price was an incredible $1,040.

All in all, my estimated safari cost would be $5,100 for a bag of five animals, seven days of hunting, all meals, guides, and lodging. That even included airfare. By comparison, the cheapest archery elk hunt you will find in the West will barely touch this price. Most quests for wapiti range from seven to ten thousand dollars, and even then you may well not get a shot. I fully expected each of our group to be within range of hundreds of wild animals with excellent success opportunity.

GEARING UP

With the safari two months on the horizon, I had borrowed four crossbows for testing and evaluation and three sights from Aimpoint, including their new H-2, a 9000SC, and a Hunter model. All of these were world-class, red-dot optics. These scopes are built to military standards, including battery life of 50,000 hours of continuous use, so we didn't worry about the batteries running down. Additionally, Aimpoint scopes are parallax-free so wherever the red dot shines, the arrow strikes. Easton was my primary arrow provider, and I settled on three dozen Full Metal Jacket shafts that were target friendly and considered by many to be the best bet for hunting. The shafts were heavier than carbon shafts; with the significant power of the bows, the extra momentum of a heavier arrow was a benefit. Robinson Outdoor's ScentBlocker came on board with scent-elimination sprays, detergents to wash our clothes, and one of their newest hunting outfits, including base layers. Finally, the tests included several new broadheads, including the NAP Killzone for crossbows, the Rage Kore, and Wac'Em cut-on-contact heads.

The four crossbows included Mission's Sniper Lite, Horton's Legend, Excalibur's Micro, and the PSE Dream season. We had Aimpoint scopes for the first three models and a new Vortex model on the last. I'll touch on the aiming systems in a moment.

As we set up our equipment, including Aimpoint sights, we were amazed at the low total cost of the equipment.

One potential problem was "who shoots what?" Although all bows were similar in some respects, they had important differences as well. How would we divide up such cool bows? I helped out initially by setting up each bow and sighting it in, which was certainly a really fun activity. I quickly learned that this decision would be a win-win-win situation. So here's a quick and dirty synopsis of each model:

HORTON LEGEND ULTRA LITE

This brand had a loyal following up to the time the company was purchased by Ten-Point, at which time the name discontinued for a year. In my humble opinion, TenPoint preserved the shooting performance of the brand and incorporated several of TenPoint's strongest attributes. First, the bow is easily assembled right out of the box by following a few steps. Additionally, the DVD supplied is very informative and offers a number of shooting and safety tips for any bow, not just Horton. Additionally, the bow has excellent customer service, should a person have a problem or question.

The Horton Legend Ultra Lite was very accurate, and the built-in cocking rope gave peace of mind that we wouldn't forget it. Since we used heavier arrows than specified by the manufacturers, our arrow speeds were less than publicized, yet they still provided abundant kinetic energy.

I specifically requested the ACUdraw 50 cocking system, which keeps the cocking rope magnetically nested in the stock of the scope. The bow cocks easily, and the safety engages automatically. My buddy Don "often leaves things behind," to use his words, and I can envision him crawling into a blind with game all around only to realize he left his cocking rope back in camp. For this reason, Don ended up with the Horton, since he couldn't lose the cocking rope and the safety engaged automatically. Horton arrows come standard with Omni nocks, a proprietary brand, and I had his Easton FMJs re-nocked with the Omnis to maintain the warranty and ensure proper launch every time.

Aside from shooting the bows for familiarity and sighting in, I wanted to analyze the true speed and kinetic energy of each bow. It's important to note that the speed ratings of crossbows have no standard convention. When a manufacturer says its bow shoots at 350 fps, that rating isn't with a standard arrow length or weight, so must be taken as an advertised value. As you will see, none of the four bows I tested met their ratings. However, that may be due to my bias.

As an outdoor writer I have used, experimented with, and written about the mass-vs.-speed debate for decades. In other words, is a fast, light arrow better than a slower, heavier shaft? Ironically, I made up my mind by watching my grandson shoot his recurve bow in my back yard. Using the standard, light arrows that came with the small recurve, the arrows barely stuck in the bag target, while using heavier arrows weighing twice as much, each shaft struck and penetrated.

For this reason, I opted for as much mass as I could get within the bow specifications. And I used either 125-grain or 150-grain broadheads for better FOC and increased mass.

Arrow Performance

The Horton Legend Ultra Lite features a draw weight of 175 pounds, an advertised speed of 330 fps, and a kinetic energy of 97 foot-pounds from a power stroke of 12.9 inches. For this setup I opted for Full Metal Jacket arrows, Easton's premium hunting arrow that weighed in at 366 grains for the 20.25-inch shaft. Tipped with a Spitfire or Killzone 125-grain

Dr. Beachley loved the Mission Sniper Lite bow and quickly became adept with it. The Kore broadheads shot well in practice.

head, the total weight approached 500 grains (491 to be precise), much heavier than most shafts. This extra mass slowed the arrow to an average of 272 fps with a kinetic energy of 80.7 foot-pounds. As a comparison, the minimum kinetic energy needed for a Cape buffalo hunt is 90 foot-pounds, so this setup should handle all the plains game animals we would hunt.

MISSION MXB SNIPER LITE

Dr. Beachley is by far the tallest of the group, so the longer cocking and power stroke of the Mission Sniper Lite seemed a perfect match. I had killed two great bucks with the Sniper Lite's predecessor, the MXB-320, the previous year, and the extra power stroke was very appealing.

Although Mission makes a cranking cocking device, I stayed with the standard rope and its dual-colored handles that made cocking the bow very consistent. The bow made a significant clicking sound as the limbs' energy was harnessed, and the safety automatically came on. The Sniper Lite shoots twenty-two-inch arrows, which would be tipped with the new Rage Kore crossbow heads. Dr. Beachley was really excited about this hunt, and I expected that the Sniper Lite would see lots of action.

Arrow Performance

Mission rates the speed of the Sniper Lite up to 310 fps, with a draw weight of 150 pounds and a power stroke of fourteen inches. My tests using the Easton BloodLine carbon shaft of 333 grains with a 125-grain Rage Kore broadhead yielded a mass of 458 grains. As a result, arrow speed averaged 266 fps with a kinetic energy of 71.9 foot-pounds.

EXCALIBUR MICRO

At choosing time, we had just three brands. (The PSE would arrive later.) Yet I had no reservations about the recurve-limb model. In firearm terms, the Micro is a carbine of sorts, with its light weight and short length. This bow is perfect for a ground blind or tree stand, due to its great maneuverability. Excalibur recommends their Diablo carbon shafts with 150-grain broadheads for added FOC and improved accuracy. These arrows shot well, yet I was a bit concerned about the lack of mass and penetration. To be safe, I had a dozen Easton FMJ shafts cut to size for the bow with a thirteen-inch power stroke, and I planned to use both on the trip.

Although small in stature, this bow took all of my strength to cock the 270 pounds of draw weight. Without the mechanical advantage of cams, I needed to bring enough

Arrow performance from all of the bows was excellent. We got deep penetration in targets and excellent accuracy.

force to bend the limbs, and it took two hands full. Unlike the compound models above, cocking the bow didn't automatically engage the safety, but I believed that my experience with crossbows would help me remember.

Arrow Performance

Given the 5.2 pounds of mass and short stature (32.5 inches) of this bow, I expected it to shoot at the lower end of arrow speed. However, it came in second only to the PSE RDX 365 for speed rating. Using the standard Diablo arrows with a 150-grain broadhead resulted in a mass of 400 grains and speed averaging 284 fps. That yielded a kinetic energy of 74.7 foot-pounds. I cut the premium Easton FMJ shafts down to sixteen inches and netted a weight of 425

The PSE RDX 365 bow was the fastest of the four used on the safaris. The tactical style bows made by PSE are among the fastest in production.

or 450 grains using various broadheads. The shafts flew at 303 fps with a kinetic energy of 86.6 foot-pounds.

PSE RDX 365

As mentioned above, the PSE arrived after the other bows were set up and sighted-in. The Dream Season model was the most modestly priced of the four bows, but it still had plenty of benefits. Thanks to the compound limbs, the bow cocked easily and sighted-in quickly using the bow-package scope, which is designed for longer-range shooting. Just as with PSE vertical bows, this model came with PSE's proprietary arrows made of lightweight carbon.

The RDX 365 was a bit on the heavy side, weighing in at 7.6 pounds without the scope and quiver. Conversely, the trigger was set at three pounds, an ideal hunting weight, and the bow shot very well. Sporting 165 pounds of draw weight and a power stroke of 14.5 inches, the bow was rated at 365 fps, as the name implied.

Arrow Performance

Thanks to the split limbs and cam system, this bow shot the fastest of the four, with readings averaging 330 fps. My best performance came from Easton Bowfire carbon arrows that weighed 330 grains for shafts of 20.25 inches in length. They averaged 329 fps, with a kinetic energy of 109.4 foot-pounds.

SPECIAL SIGHTING SYSTEMS

Each bow came with a very competent scope, yet I knew that I needed to stack the deck in favor of success for my friends. Gear for North American whitetails is well suited for African plains game, yet the aiming process is dramatically different. I taught elementary school in a younger life, and I considered having my friends write one hundred times: "Do not shoot behind the shoulder." Antelope are not whitetails, and

The red-dot scopes made sighting easy, and I was emphatic with my friends about not shooting behind the shoulder.

if you take a standard double-lung aiming point on African game, you will not retrieve the animal. The heart and lungs of antelope are *between* the shoulders, not *behind* them. To hit heart and lungs, you must shoot through the front shoulder and the best way to reinforce this is with a single red dot as an aiming point.

If you remember back to the introduction, the buck I killed in that thick river bottom happened due to an Aimpoint scope. African animals rarely drink or travel alone, and a hunter must constantly monitor the movements of the herd. When congregating at a water hole, bulls and cows are often fighting for dominance and first drinking rights. In this context an open scope allows for complete vision of animal activity. These scopes are designed to be shot with both eyes open, providing the hunter with the full view of what's happening in front of him or her. In addition, shots are typically fifteen to twenty-five yards, and a hunter can aim squarely on the shoulder and hit the vitals every time.

The downside of red-dot scopes is battery life. But Aimpoint makes their hunting optics to military grade, so if you leave the scope powered on consistently, the red dot will glow for six years. Not six days or months, but *years*. As a result, I wasn't worried about battery life, even in the high excitement of an African safari.

PREPPING FOR THE HUNT

You only get to live the excitement and anticipation of your first safari once in a lifetime, but a close second is taking friends or family along. In a way, I hijacked the excitement of that first time from Don and Ed, looking at the hunt vicariously through their eyes.

Prior to the hunt we met for hamburgers and hotdogs at my home, where I laid out the gear I had amassed for the hunt. Since the wives were part of the adventure, we tried to

Full-size and compact binoculars both have their place on an African safari.

cover all logistical elements like airline schedules and an overnight in Johannesburg, and answer as many questions as they had.

Two months out, we met again to shoot equipment and try out all of our gear. In the meantime, I'd given each bow a workout, checking for accuracy, consistency, and broadhead performance. Each worked exceedingly well, and by the time of the practice session, each bow and master were nailing the ten ring. Part of the practice including simulated shooting on deer targets. Instead of aiming at the lungs, Don and Ed concentrated on the shoulder, which was a diffi-

The Aimpoint scopes were left intact, since their small size and the padded case made removal unnecessary. Since the Aimpoints were military grade, we knew they would travel well.

cult practice for them. It had been so ingrained in them to aim behind the shoulder that the habit was difficult to break. Back inside, we put up animals on my computer screen, and we took turns practicing aiming points at animals in various poses.

It's a bit unethical to think of shooting in economic terms, yet considering the cost of the hunt and value of the quarry, we'd each be launching $1,000 in arrows, sometimes more. The performance of the arrow and our aiming process would make the difference. If we perform at our best, the animal lives perhaps ten seconds after the shot and we claim a trophy and a job well done. At worst, we pay a significant wounding fee, and the animal must deal with pain until it recovers.

PACKING FOR A SAFARI

Since each bow will enjoy a sixteen-hour plane ride to South Africa, you might think that a hard case would be ideal to deal with vibration and protection. In a perfect world, that might be the case, but I've learned otherwise. First, hard cases for crossbows are large, and they may incur an extra luggage fee from the airline. And I'd need four of them, which could become very expensive. Additionally, whether flying firearms, a compound, or a crossbow, it's best to be discreet about the interior of the package. Firearms require a hard case by law, yet this may lead an anti-hunting airline employee to handle the case in a negative way. Additionally, some airlines charge a significant fee for flying sports equipment, including archery, even though gear fits in standard bags. Lastly, and unfortunately, flying obvious archery gear may land you in the South African police office at the airport, where bribes are the norm to see that your bag is handled properly. This may sound politically incorrect, yet my last flight had included archery gear in a fiberglass case, and the police and the porter clearly wanted a bribe to handle the bag. I refused, and the bag wasn't flown home until the next day. It seemed their way of saying, "I'll teach you."

Three of the four crossbows we would be using disassemble, which makes them very easy to fly. I put three in one Cabela's roller duffle

We double-checked our gear to prepare for the long flight to Africa. We disassembled and reassembled bows and scopes to be sure they would fly well.

along with plenty of padding. I use my hunting clothes to buffer against mishandling, and I don't announce that the bags contain bows unless I'm asked. This isn't being deceitful; you never want to do that with an airline. Yet archery gear requires no special treatment, and what's in my bag is my business as long as it doesn't violate airline regulations.

The Mission does not disassemble, but it came in a padded case, and a large duffle bag should handle it well, especially with additional handling. Scopes can be removed, because they are easily reattached on the Picatinny rail system. It's a good idea to take pictures of the bow with your smart phone before disassembly. In this way you know how each part goes back together. Additionally, reinstall all screws or bolts so that they won't get lost, and place your tools in a place where you will remember them. On long hunting trips such as a safari, taking an extra string or cable system is a good idea. One errant slip with a broadhead can end the hunt, and replacement parts will be difficult to find in the bush.

Chapter 29

Crossbows on Safari: What I Learned

What an adventure! Challenging African antelope with a crossbow.

African plains game animals can be two to ten times the size of a whitetail deer. Can today's crossbows and broadheads handle a challenge of that size? Let me count the ways!

What if you knew of a tree stand where you'd likely see whitetail deer, elk, mule deer, moose, and caribou? "That'd be the best stand *ever*!" you say. Yet it's just another day in an African water hole blind, in a manner of speaking.

"On any given day, you may see two dozen species of game," said Rassie Erasmus, as he described his unique concession in the Limpopo Province of South Africa at the Safari Club International Convention.

"Can I use a crossbow?" I asked, trying not to sound too excited about a prospective hunt.

"Absolutely," he replied. "We always have one or two in camp in case someone's bow fails or they just want to try a crossbow for variety."

Needless to say, I booked the safari for mid-August, a period of new moon and a month when dryness should prompt most game animals to head to a water hold each day for a drink. On August 18th, the "Crossbow Safari" began with a bit more drama than I imagined; however, the results far exceeded expectations.

MANAGEMENT SAFARI OPTIONS

Erasmus operates a six-thousand-acre game ranch five hours north of Johannesburg that has been in his family for six generations, and was purchased from a Bushman tribe three hundred years ago. Unlike most hunting concessions in South Africa, this property has a mountain squarely in the middle, and the landscape features stark rocky outcroppings and giant boulders. In the 1940s, the owners traded leopards for nyala, and the population quickly took

The kudu is one of Africa's most iconic hunting symbols. Blessed with large ears that detect sound like radar and a keen nose, these majestic animals are a fantastic trophy.

hold despite the high predator numbers. The colorful and handsome nyala is more often associated with the Zulu Natal region of South Africa, yet they flourish in the mountain conditions along with other species.

Erasmus offers a management option that can dramatically reduce the cost of a safari, and it's one of the reasons we booked the hunt. I estimated that my cost for a five-animal package and airfare to and from South Africa would be a little over $5,000, which is an amazing price.

"I post trail cameras at each water hole and evaluate the health of my herds in October," Erasmus said. All of my water holes are at least a mile apart, so animals often drink at the same ones on a regular basis and I can post hunters according to what they want to shoot. In this way hunters get a price break, and I help maintain the health of my herds."

Management animals can include antelope with a broken horn or tip, animals well beyond their breeding stage, and in one case a zebra that a rival stallion bit the tail from. "That's a management animal for sure," laughed Erasmus. "Who wants a rug with no tail?"

DAY ONE: QUEST FOR A KUDU

This was my twenty-second safari, so I felt confident that I could distinguish management animals from prime trophy specimens. My first day began in an elevated hide, posting an hour after sunrise as is typical in Africa. Soon, animals began to drink at a natural water hole directly below the stand. Kudu, nyala, and zebra were my primary species of interest, and this stand had frequent visits by all but the striped critters. By 10:00, I had seen fifty nyala, which was more of the antelope than I'd seen in the other twenty-one safaris combined. The females sneaked in through dense brush and drank under a cover of thorny vegetation, with the solitary males even more reclusive. Their shaggy black coats were barely visible in the dense cover.

Next, a kudu bull came to drink at the main water hole followed by another and another. Soon, I had six mature bulls within thirty yards, and my management-evaluating confidence began to crumble. Probably one of the animals was a management specimen, but which one? Normally, I can evaluate horn length well, but suddenly they all looked alike.

Erasmus includes a booklet of 8x10 photographs of his management animals, and I went through it, trying to match an animal with the picture like some *Law & Order* line-up on TV, but to no avail. Luckily, Erasmus sneaked into my blind at noon with advice. "If you saw that many kudu bulls, you probably saw that management bull," he whispered. "It has white tips on its horns and white age spots on it head. Look for those and you'll be OK."

With that he slipped away and my confidence was bolstered. Within an hour, the bachelor kudu boys returned, and I scoured each one with binoculars and finally noticed the white horn tips and age spots. Unfortunately, the management animal chose not to drink, but stood in the shade of

Unbelievably, this is a management kudu, despite its fifty-inch horn length. The old bull had worn its teeth to the gum.

A management impala, identified by its worn tips and shorter horn length. Despite the age, the meat was tasty, and we enjoyed it at each meal.

a tree for nearly an hour before melting back into the bush. My heart sank as I watched it walk away.

The afternoon passed quickly as one species of animal after another came to the water. Suddenly, a set of tall, curled horns with white tips appeared at the water. *"That's him!"* I thought to myself. Glassing the white spots on its head, I sprang into action, switched the safety off on the Excalibur Micro 335, and put the red dot from the Aimpoint H-2 low on the shoulder. I squeezed, and the arrow zipped through both shoulders of the beast, causing it to whirl and run. I saw the Boltcutter broadhead protruding from the far shoulder and knew I'd gotten complete penetration on the six-hundred-pound animal. After a hundred-yard blood trail, Erasmus extended his hand in congratulations "That's the one," he said with a broad smile.

A CHANGE IN TACTICS

The second morning of the safari, we got up well before dawn, had breakfast, and entered the blinds in darkness with the plan of returning for lunch and then sitting a stand until dark. This allowed us to see animals that perhaps came to drink very early or at last light.

Zebra are notorious for showing up at a water hole in the last second of shooting light, and this ultra–elusive animal was high on my list. Zebra are frequently a "second-safari" animal, as most first-time hunters think they are just a horse with stripes. Yet they are one of the most aware animals you can hunt with a bow. For rifle hunters, shooting one at three hundred yards while it stands in the open is no big deal. But just try to slip up on one or even ambush it at a water hole.

"They rarely drink before dark," Erasmus advised. "But I have one blind where they often drink. You won't be able to shoot any other animals, and you'll have to be extremely quiet if you want to see them," he said. "Maybe you'll get lucky."

Normally, South Africa in August is cold at night and up to seventy degrees in the afternoon, but this year's weather was abnormally hot. Climbing into the blind around 1:00, the temperature neared 100 degrees. I unzipped two shooting windows and made the mistake of taking my hat off. Blessed with a shiny, bald head and white hair, my head glowed like a sparkler in the dark blind, quickly alerting a band of baboons drinking nearby. They

Normally, South African nights are quite cold in August. But this year temperatures rarely dipped below sixty degrees.

barked and alarm-called for the next hour, but finally they settled down and other animals came to drink.

The water hole was a hub of activity, with eland, wildebeest, kudu, impala, nyala, and, finally, stripes. A small herd of zebra approached to drink with either a big stallion or fat mare about to foal among the herd. I finally had the shot angle I wanted, but I didn't want to take a pregnant mare. The animals drank for a minute or two and quickly disappeared. As darkness fell, the zebra with no tail showed as well, but it was too dark to shoot.

TROPHY HUNTING IN REVERSE

If you are a fan of TV hunting shows, you know that it's a popular practice to name a particular target buck or two and hold out for those trophy animals. This management hunt was just the opposite. Each day I'd see several high-scoring trophy animals, yet I was looking for management animals with abnormal horns or aged well past reproduction. As I learned, identification of management animals required a lot of patience and visual analysis.

"That large zebra you saw was probably a stallion," Erasmus told me back in camp. He used his smart phone to show me pictures of zebra in various poses. "A male will have a very thick neck and be larger than the mares. Unfortunately, you can't identify sex from a tree stand, due to the higher view. Maybe you'll get another chance."

Professional Hunter (PH) Pieter Otto spent the third day with me, and his experience and help were invaluable. Our quest was for a management nyala bull, and we seemed to be in a honey-hole for that species as one big bull after another came to drink. We easily saw a hundred animals during the day, including a management impala and warthog which we trailed and transported to the meat locker at the end of the day.

Dr. Beachley smiles behind his really old gemsbok cow. This trophy was known for its age, and my dentist friend made a great shot.

Ever since the "Cecil" incident, African hunting has come under scrutiny. You can be assured that every scrap of African game was either eaten on our camp table, shared with the workers on the ranch, or sold in local markets, which is a common practice in rural towns and villages. Animals are taken whole to a skinning shed, where they are butchered in a sanitary facility and the meat hung in cold storage.

SEEKING SAGE ADVICE

By the fourth day I had seen dozens of nyala bulls, and surely some of them were management types. Managements were one-third the price of a prime trophy, and hunting with a guide seemed the best bet. Actually, I doubled up with one of my hunting friends, as we each wanted different game animals and the advice of an experienced pair of eyes would be invaluable.

The water holes were busy during the day, with at least a hundred animals of various species.

We got an early start in the same blind where I killed the kudu bull, and where I remembered seeing numerous nyala bulls. Around 10:00, a dark figure sneaked into the thorn-covered water hole below the stand, and my guide gave me the thumbs up. The nyala bull stepped from the water and passed through a narrow opening. The angle was steep, but the Aimpoint red dot held steady, and the arrow zipped through both sides. The beast ran, but it lay still in seconds.

In the afternoon, my wife Vel and I returned to try for the zebra trophy one more time. The stand hadn't been hunted since I passed the stallion the second evening, and I hoped that things had settled enough to get a shot.

The author poses with his Excalibur Micro 335, which proved extremely effective on the hunt.

As the afternoon wore on, the usual parade of kudu, wildebeest, and a herd of nearly fifty impala drank and dawdled around the water. When animals drink and seem relaxed at a water hole, it sends the message, "The coast is clear," to more wary species. I took great care to be very still and quiet in the stand.

Suddenly, I saw a large zebra standing off to my right, waiting and watching. Holding my breath, I moved the safety to off and got ready. Four smaller animals approached first and came directly to the water, while the larger animal, a thick-necked stallion lagged behind. It took several steps closer and stood almost broadside, testing my patience. Long moments passed as it took several more steps, finally presenting the angle I needed.

On impact, the zebra turned, but he did not run. Awkward on its feet, the animal moved about thirty yards and went down with the rest of the animals standing and watching. The chest of this animal was nearly two feet thick, yet the arrow and Boltcutter broadhead passed completely through.

Five animals with five arrows was exactly the goal I'd set for myself, and the camp as a whole went fifteen animals for fifteen arrows, a testament to quality shot opportunities and to equipment that performed perfectly. I was now confident that I could hunt any North American game with a crossbow and expect short trails and a quick demise. The "Crossbow Safari" was little short of fantastic.

GREAT GEAR THAT DELIVERED

Each day we sprayed down with ScentBlocker spray to reduce scent in the blind. Since African antelope usually travel in herds, you must fool a lot of noses.

My safari ended with five animals from five arrows, and I couldn't have been more pleased with the performance. Here's a quick look at what worked so well:

The nyala is one of Africa's premier trophies, and Erasmus had many on his property, both trophy and management animals.

Excalibur Micro 335 ($900)

With a 270-pound draw weight from recurve limbs, this small, light bow generates excellent arrow speed from a compact package, which accounted for a complete pass-through on every animal. At just over five pounds, it's one of the lightest hunting bows on the market.
www.excaliburcrossbow.com.

Aimpoint H-2

This compact sight was the perfect match for the Micro and gave instant aiming with no pin confusion. Sighed-in at twenty yards, it was an inch high at fifteen yards and an inch low at twenty-five yards.
www.aimpoint.com.

Diablo Arrows ($65); Boltcutter Broadheads ($45)

At first I was a bit nervous about the shorter, lighter Diablo arrows and the cut-on-contact Interlock 150-grain broadheads. No more. The team got incredible penetration and downed game in seconds.
Diablo (800-463-1817) www.excaliburcrossbow.com.
Boltcutter (800-463-1817) www.excaliburcrossbow.com.

TriggerTech

The Micro 335 came with a good trigger, but the custom TriggerTech trigger ($130) had zero creep and helped made quick, accurate shots.
(888-795-1485) www.triggertech.com.

ScentBlocker

Scent elimination is just as important with African antelope as white-tail deer. The Alpha jackets ($260) with WindBrake technology were quiet and helped keep us concealed in secret.

ScentBlocker (507-253-4484) www.robinsonoutdoors.com.

Spending a day at a water hole is great fun and an incredible opportunity for photographing animals in the wild.

PERFORMANCE CHART:

Crossbow	Animal	Shot Distance	Broadhead	Length of Trail	Notes
Excalibur Micro	Kudu	18 yards	Interlock	100 yards	Complete penetration
Excalibur Micro	Impala	15 yards	Wac'Em	250 yards	Blades separated on contact
Excalibur Micro	Warthog	12 yards	Interlock	50 yards	Complete penetration
Excalibur Micro	Zebra	20 yards	Interlock	40 yards	Complete penetration
Excalibur Micro	Nyala	15 yards	Interlock	40 yards	Complete penetration

The author took this old nyala bull on the fourth day of the safari, an incredible trophy despite its management status.

Chapter 30

Quality Plains Game Management

Blackbeard shoots a ninety-pound compound, yet he enjoyed shooting my crossbows as well.

Cecil the Lion cast a spotlight on hunting in Africa, where game ranch management is similar to a whitetail deer concession in the United States. That is, it's similar in some ways; it's very different in others.

"Predators are a real challenge here in Botswana, including cheetah, leopard, hyena, and the occasional lion that passes through," said Professional Hunter and game ranch owner Luke Blackbeard. "My goal is to introduce very few animals and rely on the natural reproduction system to populate my ten-thousand-acre ranch. Predators play such a role that all of the blesbok and black wildebeest are gone," he continued. "They aren't savvy enough with predators, and whatever you relocate will not survive."

Interestingly, Blackbeard does not lament the high population of predators that are completely protected by his native Botswana. He began his career as a Professional Hunter with Jeff Rann Safaris, and he has worked for and managed several hunting operations since that time. As a PH, he has taken many dangerous game animals, and clients often request his skill and tracking expertise. Now married with a young family, he's putting his talents to work on his Botswana game ranch, offering five miles of river frontage along the Limpopo River.

"When I bought this property three years ago, there were thirty cow eland, but no bulls," said Blackbeard. "The previous owner had hunters take all of the males, so I bought several bulls to allow the herd to reproduce. Ironically, the day after those animals arrived, two big bulls broke through the fence to breed the cows, and another followed suit a month later."

Rassie Erasmus operates a game ranch a hundred kilometers south of the Limpopo, but he faces many of the same challenges. Whereas Blackbeard's concession is flat with river frontage, Erasmus hunts a mountain that provides a unique habitat, especially for nyala. "We believe that we have a population of about fourteen leopards, and they are tenacious predators that kill a lot of game to survive," he says. That predator factor changes the way he manages game animals. "We don't shoot any baboons, as they are favorite foods of leopard," says Erasmus. "Hopefully, every baboon a leopard kills helps take the pressure off of plains game animals." He also tried to introduce blesbok on his property by purchasing six males for his heard of ten females. Five of them quickly fell to predators, but one ram survived and has sired a second generation of the species. "Although we manage animals for trophy horns, it's more important to protect those that will survive," he reasons.

Since game animals have a market value in South Africa, not all culling need to be lethal. "We are in the midst of a drought, and I quickly saw that our zebra population was grazing too much grass," Erasmus said. "As a result, I brought in a helicopter, rounded up thirty head of zebra, and sold them at auction. Our drought is continuing, and my grass would have been in trouble had I not taken action."

GOOD-NEIGHBOR FENCES

Many deer management properties in the United States are fenced, which is occasionally a controversial element with game ranching. Fences become less significant on very large ranches that contain thousands of acres. African game ranches are often ten to fifteen thousand acres in size, and once hunters enter a property they rarely see the boundary fence again.

Game fences offer a containment factor that allows managers to control the numbers of animals on their land and provide data on populations, species, size, and age diversity.

Game fences are typically ten feet high, but that doesn't mean African game can't cross them. Most eland and kudu can jump a game fence, and warthogs wage a constant excavating war with the barriers. Once they burrow through, other animals can follow, often using their horns to pry up the wire to enter or leave. I hunted a free-roaming area in Namibia two years ago, where the owner had seen a sixty-inch kudu, which is comparable to a 170-inch whitetail. Driven by breeding urges, the big, spiral-horned antelope jumped from the free-ranging area onto a game ranch, where it made one hunter very happy.

Game fences protect many grazing animals from neighboring cattle farmers, who will shoot them on sight for competing with livestock for food.

African antelope are both browsers and grazers, the latter causing them to compete with neighboring cattle ranches. "They'd shoot all of our wildebeest on the spot if they crossed onto their land," one ranch manager told me. "Wildebeest are grazers and eat the same plants as cattle."

Drought is a problem for some game ranches in the United States, but it is a fact of life for concessions in southern Africa. In South Africa,

Poachers cleverly place snares near water where animals must travel. Even large animals cannot escape the strangling effect of a poacher's wire.

Namibia, Botswana, and Zimbabwe, the rainy season ends in March or April, and barely a drop of rain falls again until October or November. In the African rainy season, vegetation can grow to a height of four feet or more, but during the dry season that same vegetation can completely disappear.

Game ranch owners manage their game in several ways to deal with the annual drought. First, they scatter water holes throughout the property. Since even creeks and rivers dry up, this allows game animals to disburse and access natural food sources while still having water within walking distance. Otherwise, they'd congregate around a single water source and quickly overgraze and overbrowse the resource.

Secondly, many ranches provide supplemental food for game. Kudu and warthogs are among the most vulnerable species, and their health can quickly deteriorate in years of severe drought. One manager told me he'd found fourteen trophy bulls dead one season due to malnutrition. Like mule deer in the West, some African antelope have a difficult time digesting commercial feeds, and some won't eat it at all.

POACHING: THE SCOURGE OF AFRICA

Game fencing is required by law in South Africa and Botswana for commercial hunting operations, and the wire both contains and protects the animals inside. My last safari took me to the Limpopo River, which forms the border between Botswana and South Africa. That trip provided a glimpse into the grisly world of poaching. In the United States, poaching is often done with a small-caliber rifle, and the criminals are either looking for meat or prized antlers that give them monetary gains or bragging rights with their scumbag buddies.

African poaching is much worse. Since few natives own firearms, they resort to using snares. They basically set up a length of wire that forms a noose and hangs their victims. They attach one end of the wire to a solid tree or bush, and make a loop with the other end. Poachers are cagey and place the loops in small openings on game trails where an unsuspecting animal will attempt to walk through the wire loop. Once caught, the

The author pauses beside an animal taken by poachers but never recovered. We found about fifty snares ready to unleash their deadly attacks.

noose tightens around its neck. As the doomed creature fights to get away, it draws the noose more and more tightly around its neck until it strangles. As if this practice weren't sinister enough, the practice is magnified by the placement of dozens, maybe a hundred snares in a single area.

Luke Blackbeard's anti-poaching crew poses for a picture with the many snares they have found on local farms.

If the poachers catch a wildebeest, they cut it up and pack it out of the area, leaving an unknown number of other animals lying to rot. What's more, once set up, these deadly devices have no expiration date. Like ticking gallows landmines, remaining snares can catch an animal months after they were first set, leaving it to die and rot away.

Quality management depends upon fees from hunting that support the overall game population as well as the perpetuation of the business and its infrastructure. Poaching robs all elements of this practice. It is a heinous criminal enterprise.

For more information on Rassie Erasmus Management Hunts, e-mail bowhunt@rassie.co.za.

Luke Blackbeard Safaris is at www.bowhuntbotswana.com.

Chapter 31

Crossbows on Safari: Mission Sniper Lite Field Test

Dr. Beachley, a dentist, took a lot of ribbing from his friends about going to Africa and hunting with a crossbow after the "Cecil the Lion" incident broke internationally.

The African bush and dust are tough on equipment, not to mention huge, wily animals that have survived predators for thousands of years.

One month before the safari began, Dr. Ed Beachley, a local dentist, brushed the last strokes onto his preparation for the African safari. With "Cecil the Lion" all over the news, he got quite a ribbing from his friends. But he could not have been more excited about his first African safari, which was entirely on the level.

Beachley hunts with both compound and vertical bow, but he dedicated this trip to a thorough test of Mission's new Sniper Lite crossbow. Other new gear included the Aimpoint 9000SC red-dot scope and Rage Krossbow Kore broadheads, an interesting new design from a company known for two-blade heads.

"I'm usually a two-to-three-hours-in-a-stand kind of hunter," said Beachley, as our group of three sat around a raging Mapony fire on the eve of the hunt. "I understand that we may be in a blind all day, and that sounds like a long time."

Any reservations about boredom quickly vanished as "Doc" began seeing animals in the first hour, including a trophy impala. "That's a good ram," whispered Pieter Otto, his PH. His client clicked off the safety and Mission Africa got its first test. The shot was broadside at twenty yards, and the Easton Arrow zipped through the deer-size animal, which bounced away in a typical heart-shot manner. "Good shot," whispered Otto, containing his excitement.

PRIME AND MANAGEMENT

This safari was conducted by Rassie Erasmus (bowhunt@rassie.co.za) and included both management and prime animals, combining an opportunity for the owner of the game ranch to take out some of the oldest animals, and with a chance for us to take a trophy animal, like the impala, Erasmus uses trail cameras at water holes to identify management

One of Dr. Beachley's hunting objectives was a trophy kudu, and as you can see, he succeeded.

specimens, as well as the advice of an experienced PH to identify animals that are then discounted 50–75 percent in price.

Interestingly, Beachley would see a management wildebeest drinking at the same blind in late afternoon, and he quickly collected that specimen as well. "We watched it go back and forth to water, and eventually we made the decision to shoot at the end of the day when it came broadside at twenty-five yards. The Kore hit it squarely on the shoulder, and the PH said it was a great shot. The old bull went no farther than fifty yards, which is a remarkably short distance for one of Africa's toughest antelope. This was a great first day; it far exceeded my expectations," remembers Beachley. "When whitetail hunting, I've gone days and not seen a deer or had a shot. This African hunting is quite a thrill."

KUDU QUEST

The second day, Beachley wondered if the excitement of the hunt could continue at the previous day's incredible pace. Two animals on Day One. Incredible!

Next on the dentist's wish list was a trophy kudu bull. He posted in an elevated hide near a water hole where numerous kudu often drank. Beachley and his PH climbed into the hide in the dark to get maximum potential for success.

The early morning tactic brought dozens of animals into view, including impala and nyala, but not the kudu bull he sought. At lunchtime, they raided the cooler box for a sandwich and a drink. Shortly after, activity at the water hole began to increase. Several kudu bulls approached the water, but they slipped back into the bush as a band of baboons came to drink. "My adrenaline was pumping," remembers Beachley. His PH expressed optimism that the group would return once the monkeys left.

About thirty minutes later, a bachelor herd of seven kudu bulls appeared again and

Management hunts allow hunters to harvest old animals before they die of natural causes, which can often be a death much more painful than an arrow through the ribs.

cautiously approached the water. "The one at the back is the best trophy," whispered Otto softly, as Beachley's heart pounded in anticipation of the shot. Tension mounted as one by one, the kudu drank and walked back into the bush, leaving only Mr. Big. He drank, facing the blind at twenty-five yards, presenting no shot. Beachley could literally feel his heart pounding as the bull drank for long moments. All the while, Doc struggled to remain calm.

Suddenly, the baboons returned, and the bull moved back from the water and slowly stepped away. "My PH and I had talked a lot about shot angles, and I knew I had to shoot quickly or pass," remembered Beachley. In an instant, the Kore broadhead buried behind the shoulder of the kudu and passed out the other side. Otto assured his client the hit was good, and they celebrated softly as the bull piled up just thirty yards away. "It was a great trophy, and I was equally thrilled with the shot and the animal expiring in mere seconds," said Beachley.

MAKE IT A DOUBLE

With three animals in two days, Dr. Beachley took the next morning off and had a leisurely breakfast with Betsy, his wife. Evening campfires had been dominated by such exciting tales that Mrs. wanted in on the action, and they spent the afternoon at a blind where a monster warthog had been drinking. The beast had tusks of fourteen inches or longer, and the doctor and his wife wouldn't need a PH to pick it out.

Betsy and her husband thrilled to the approach of a variety of animals as the afternoon wore on. "A monster warthog came to the water in midafternoon, and he literally became Boss Hog, fighting with other animals and establishing dominance," reminisced Doc with

Beachley's Mission Sniper Lite performed superbly on safari.

a chuckle. Despite the big pig's activity, it managed to avoid presenting a shooting angle. "As the sun set, the porker finally turned broadside, and Dr. Beachley took the shot. "We heard it crash about thirty yards away, ending an afternoon that was a great experience for me and my wife," he said.

SWAN SONG

The safari had gone amazingly well for Beachley and his gear. Not only had the Mission Sniper Lite and Aimpoint scope put the arrow exactly on target each time, but the Kore broadheads had performed amazingly. "Each head could have been used again," said Beachley, who examined the head after every shot. "The mechanical aspects of the blade were tough enough to handle even large game animals without damage."

The final day of the safari, Beachley and Otto went back to the place of their initial success. Several gemsbok often drank at that water hole, including an old cow that was well past her calving years. In early afternoon, two bulls and the old cow came to drink. But the female, which had the longest horns, held back from the water. Finally, it came to drink, and Beachley exercised patience and put the Mission to its final test. Just like the other animals, the gemsbok piled up within fifty yards. Beachley could barely believe his success.

"This safari was absolutely amazing!" he said with great enthusiasm. "It was my first time to Africa, and we had a fantastic time. The variety of game far exceeded my expectations, and it was challenging to be selective and patient. Hunting from a water hole was new, but the days went by quickly due to the interaction between game animals. The Professional Hunter made the hunt much more enjoyable, answering questions on

"The safari was absolutely amazing!" was Dr. Beachley's assessment of the experience.

the spot and expanding on the characteristics of each animal. Betsy and I had a great time, and this first safari probably won't be our last," he said, flashing a white smile that any dentist would love.

HORTON PERFORMANCE: HOLY COW!

Don Wilson had hunted with a crossbow before, yet never for game larger than a white-tail deer. He'd been to Zimbabwe and South Africa on rifle safaris, and now he was keenly interested in the bowhunting adventure.

In preparation for the safari, Wilson bought a copy of *The Perfect Shot,* which should be mandatory reading for any prospective safari-goer. Regardless of the weapon you use, the book shows in graphic illustrations the vital organs of African game, so a hunter can plan to make the most lethal shot possible.

"You were right," he said to me as we got on the plane for Africa. "You do have to shoot African game through the shoulder."

I wanted to say, "Duh! What have I been telling you and making you practice!" But I did not.

THE SAFARI BEGINS

As excited as a trio of three-year-olds on Christmas morning, Wilson, Beachley, and I headed for our blinds. You've read about the exploits of the author and a dentist. Now here's how a retired school counselor did.

Wilson hunted with a Professional Hunter the first morning, and the duo saw a pile of game, including a management impala. He'd planned to take one of each, management and trophy, so when the worn-horn ram turned broadside, Wilson put the arrow directly through the shoulder. The beast went just fifty yards. Since this was his first harvest with the Horton gear, Wilson was impressed with its accuracy and the per-formance of the NAP Spitfire head.

Beachley loved the Mission Sniper Lite. The light, tactical-style stock helped make the bow more manageable.

In early afternoon, a large impala ram drank close to the water hole and Wilson signaled that he'd like to take that animal as well. The animal was just ten yards away, but Wilson forgot both his "master's" teachings and the contents of *The Perfect Shot*. "I knew I'd made a mistake as soon as I shot," he said later. "I aimed behind the shoulder like a whitetail."

Realizing that the hit was behind the shoulder, the duo suspended the trailing process until Rassie showed up. Wilson and Erasmus began trailing the impala, but the outfitter quickly spotted it lying down not far from the blind. "If we leave it alone, it will quickly die," whispered Erasmus, and that's exactly what happened.

SAFARI MONSTER: THE ONE-EYED ELAND

The second morning of the hunt, Beachley and Wilson traded blinds, and a bit of friendly rivalry began. One of the first animals that Beachley saw was an enormous eland bull that had one eye, qualifying it for the discounted management list. Since Beachley's safari was only an hour old, he passed on the beast, but Wilson was more aggressive.

"We watched the big bull around the water for nearly an hour, but it would not give me a shot," Wilson said by the fire that evening. Eventually the bull walked away from the water, and Wilson believed his chance had passed. Then suddenly the beast reappeared and gave a quick, quartering away angle for a few seconds. "You must shoot now if you want the shot," his PH whispered, and Wilson pulled the trigger.

Despite its giant size, the animal went just thirty yards and collapsed, the Horton and Spitfire doing their work in quick fashion. This animal was so large it produced eight hundred pounds of meat. Double that if you want to figure the on-the-hoof weight.

QUICK KUDU

I hunted the duiker stand, one of the most remote on the property, and each time I was there, I noticed a lone, bull kudu come to drink at precisely the same time. Since I'd already taken a kudu bull, I told Wilson about the sighting, and he expressed an interest in this one. I shared a picture from my camera, and the image showed a really old bull with modest horns and all of its ribs showing, exactly the kind of animal Rassie wanted to cull from his herd.

Wilson was in place the next morning, and like clockwork, the bull showed up. Anticipating the opportunity, Wilson made a perfect shot and the bull went down in sight.

The preparation and practice prior to the hunt paid big dividends in the field and accounted for a perfect fifteen-for-fifteen record.

Later that afternoon, he changed hides again and took the only bushbuck of the trip, an old ram with worn horns. I was able to follow a blood trail that looked like a paint bath, and the animal went just thirty yards.

Overall, Wilson couldn't have been more impressed with the performance of the Horton. Combined with the Easton FMJ shafts and NAP 125-grain Spitfire broadheads, the package was pure lethality.

At the risk of repeating Beachley's performance, here's the result of our shots in one chart for comparison:

THE GREAT CROSSBOW SAFARI: PERFORMANCE DATA FOR BOWS AND BROADHEADS BY HUNTER

Joe Byers

Crossbow	Animal	Shot Distance	Broadhead	Length of Trail	Notes
Excalibur Micro	Kudu	18 yards	Interlock	100 yards	Complete penetration

Excalibur Micro	Impala	15 yards	Wac'Em	250 yards	Blades separated on contact
Excalibur Micro	Warthog	12 yards	Interlock	50 yards	Complete penetration
Excalibur Micro	Zebra	20 yards	Interlock	40 yards	Complete penetration
Excalibur Micro	Nyala	15 yards	Interlock	40 yards	Complete penetration

Ed Beachley

Crossbow	Animal	Shot Distance	Broadhead	Length of Trail	Notes
Mission Sniper Lite	Impala	17 yards	Rage Kore	30 yards	Complete penetration
Mission Sniper Lite	Wildebeest	24 yards	Rage Kore	30 yards	Broke the arrows
Mission Sniper Lite	Kudu	25 yards	Rage Kore	30 yards	Complete penetration
Mission Sniper Lite	Warthog	20 yards	Rage Kore	50 yards	Complete penetration
Mission Sniper Lite	Gemsbok	21 yards	Rage Kore	40 yards	Broke a rib on far side

Don Wilson

Crossbow	Animal	Shot Distance	Broadhead	Length of Trail	Notes
Horton Ultra Lite	Impala	13 yards	NAP Spitfire	50 yards	Complete penetration
Horton Ultra Lite	Impala	10 yards	NAP Spitfire	50 yards	Complete penetration
Horton Ultra Lite	Eland	27 yards	NAP Spitfire	35 yards	Full penetration
Horton Ultra Lite	Kudu	20 yards	NAP Spitfire	50 yards	Complete penetration
Horton Ultra Lite	Bushbuck	14 yards	NAP Spitfire	40 yards	Complete penetration

Chapter 32

The Big Picture: Plan to Hunt the Whole Season

Young Sawyer Rowe and his grandparents smile behind his special buck, taken with a Christmas present.

Like football, deer season has four quarters that require persistence, performance, and an eye on the end zone.

A fullback plans to score every time he touches the ball. That rarely happens, yet he's prepared to maximize every snap until he eventually succeeds. Blessed with months of hunting opportunity, bowhunters should do likewise, using the full season. From opening day through the rut, at winter's onset, and into the post-season, hunting pressure differs. Habitat modifies, and even deer behavior changes. To maximize potential for each segment, begin with the big picture in mind, and prepare for what lies ahead. Are you looking for a fat, tasty doe? A trophy buck at the time they are most vulnerable? A late-season venison bonus to last until summer? Or to spark the hunting fire of a newcomer? Whatever your goal, pace your season and make the most of each part.

UNIVERSAL PREP

Like any athlete preparing for a full season, you must be physically and mentally ready. Crossbows level the playing field among archers so that you can shoot a powerful bow regardless of age, sex, or physical stature. Build and strengthen your core by walking or jogging. Work out moderately, and practice on a 3-D target to boost your overall fitness, muscle memory, and kill-zone concentration.

Sawyer was all smiles after recovering his first buck with a crossbow.

Repetitive practice is important for vertical archers, while just the opposite bodes well for horizontal folk. Once you have sighted-in at known distances, practice intermittently, shooting one arrow before work, maybe another over a lunch break, and again at the end of the day. Getting a second shot with a crossbow is very difficult, so it's absolutely critical that you make that first shot count. Instead of launching lots of arrows, intermittent practice puts you in a pressured circumstance, building absolute confidence in your shooting ability. Also, practice shooting offhand, since a bench-style rest is unrealistic in most hunting situations. "Aim small, miss small," is a rule that applies to crossbow and vertical archers alike. Aim precisely in the heart area, and expect to hit there.

GEAR SELECTION

Scent elimination is another universal preparation. It won't matter if you are basking in the sun on opening day or shivering in a blizzard on the last, a deer's nose is an equal-opportunity detector. Luckily, there are application sprays to suppress human scent, including options from ScentBlocker, ScentLok, Ozonics, Scent Killer, and others. One

Scent control is important year round, even when scouting in summer months. A pair of rubber boots will help control human scent.

The gear you select can make a huge difference when you discover that special rub or other deer sign.

of the most effective habits a deer hunter can develop is to take a shower with unscented soap before the hunt and to dress in clean, scent-free clothing. Storing your boots and outer layers in a plastic tub is a great way to begin and end each hunt.

As you shoot your crossbow in practice sessions, be sure to check for signs of wear and tear. Lube your rail every five or six shots, and be sure that your broadheads fly like the target points. As your hunt draws near, begin using all of your gear, and store it consistently. I use a day pack with dedicated pockets, where I always carry a cocking rope, a grunt tube, camo face paint, a head net, camo gloves, a bow hanger, knife, latex gloves, and other gear. In the long days of early season, it's easy and productive to hunt before or after work, and a well-organized day pack allows you to "grab and go."

Clothing is key when looking at the full season ahead. You may hunt in light pants and shirt in the early season, need rain gear and a variety of layers as the rut kicks in, and wear a full set of down insulation in late season. Do your research online at Sportsman's Warehouse, or plan a trip to a major sporting goods store like Cabela's, Gander Mountain, Bass Pro, or another major outlet. Ensuring that you have the right clothing ahead of time will give you greater flexibility as the weather and hunting conditions suddenly change.

EARLY SEASON

"Early" means August 15th in South Carolina, September in the mid–Atlantic states, and October in others. Environments and deer activities vary widely depending on location.

Key characteristics of the early season offer excellent opportunities to score on opening day. A lack of hunting pressure is number one, since animals will react to food, weather, and cover sources as they have in previous days, perhaps weeks, barring some major crop harvest or human intervention.

Early-season hunting is fun because the foliage is brilliant and the temperatures are moderate.

Midday scouting, trail cameras, and long-range observations are savvy elements in determining deer patterns of vulnerability. A spotting scope or 10X binoculars can not only show where deer are feeding, but pinpoint the exact position where they enter a food source. Bean fields and freshly-cut corn fields are prime examples in the Midwest, where crop fields are large in size and bedding cover more limited.

Trail cameras, both motion-sensor and time-lapse, are the go-to scouting gear for many hunters before and throughout the season. Motion-sensor optics are excellent where deer travel is in fairly restricted corridors, such as a pinch points, fence crossings, or heavily used trails, while time-lapse cameras are best to cover food plots and other large areas, showing exactly when and where deer enter or travel.

Frederick's Jeff Harrison is the mid-Atlantic's early-season specialist, with more than ten Pope and Young bucks to his credit, many taken on opening day. A working dad with two children, Harrison deals with all of the family time constraints many hunters identify with, yet he makes a

Jeff Harrison loves early-season hunting and often scores on the first day of the season.

point to cruise suburban neighborhoods before and after his work day. Ironically, he often finds good bucks in neighborhood yards, where he asks permission, hangs clandestine stands, and scores on day one.

RIGHT ON WITH THE RUT

In late October and early November, whitetail behavior changes, and those nocturnal bucks that were only seen on trail cameras suddenly appear in daylight. This gives you the chance to outsmart your adversary with rut tricks such as grunt calls, rattling antlers, deer scents, and decoys. If you are new to bowhunting, you can anticipate some of the most exciting hunting on earth.

Before does begin breeding, bucks rub trees, make scrapes, and expand their core area. Posting a stand or ground blind along a fresh rub line can be very effective, especially in late October and early November. Grunt tubes and rattling horns work well in this early phase of the rut when bucks are primed to breed, but does are still resistant.

During the rut, midday can be as effective as an early morning sit. Last fall, I caught a good seven-point buck on my trail camera near one of my main stands. I hunt the western

In late season, find a scrape line like this and then post a stand nearby. Be patient and you will score.

region of Maryland, where mountain deer don't grow the massive antlers like they do in the Midwest. But they are still exciting to hunt, and they taste just as good.

On the way to my stand one morning, I put doe urine on my boots and lay down a lengthy scent trail, but I got no action. The next afternoon I returned to pull the camera media card, and I decided to spend a few hours, since fresh sign was nearby. I was barely in the tree ten minutes when that seven-point buck chased three does over the ridge and followed the scent trail right down the hill.

DAY PACK AS DESKTOP

The desktop of your computer stores the items used most often so that they are easily located and quick to use. Organize your daypack in the same fashion, so that you can grab it and go hunting without forgetting critical items. Once you establish a storage pattern, you'll know the location of each piece of gear even in the dark. Here are six pieces of gear to always have with you:

Extra Cocking Rope

You may be able to cock your bow with your hands, but a cocking aide will increase consistency and assure accuracy.

Knife and Latex Gloves

Unfortunately, whitetail diseases are on the rise. You'll want to protect yourself against harmful bacteria.

Grunt Tube and Calls

Buck-grunt and doe-bleat calls seldom spook deer. They may not always work, yet they will definitely increase success in the long run.

Cell Phone in a Zippered Pocket

Safety, not entertainment, is the issue here. If you have a problem, or a buddy does, help can be summoned.

Pull-Up Rope and Safety Harness

Quality safety vests are best. Yet a harness, like those supplied by tree-stand manufacturers, works well.

Small Binoculars and Range Finder

You need the range finder for obvious reasons, yet the binoculars allow you to identify deer at a distance and enjoy your natural surrounds and critters close-up.

CROSSBOW SAFETY: THREE IMPORTANT TIPS

Like the Rowes, many hunters are buying crossbows to archery hunt for the first time. Crossbows are somewhat like firearms in that you should never point one at a person. But unlike a gun, firing a bow improperly can be very dangerous to the user. For example, if you're not careful, it could amputate a thumb. If you are new to the sport keep these three tips in mind:

Before buying that special bow for yourself or another, go online and read the safety materials. This will help you learn to shoot more quickly and assure you do so safely.

Before Buying

Before you buy a bow, go to one of the leading crossbow websites and review their safety video, like that offered by TenPoint at www.tenpointcrossbows.com. Aside from safety, you'll learn tips and techniques about maximizing the effectiveness of the bow, and you'll be well informed for that first exciting shot.

Buy Two Targets

You'll practice much more effectively by using a bag-style target for target points and a foam or 3-D target for broadheads. Today's bows have such power, that you can hurt yourself trying to extract a practice bolt from foam. Practice sessions should be fun, and the two-target approach is a great asset to performance.

Cocking Is Critical

If you plan a morning hunt, cock the bow in the cabin or even your garage before you leave. Make sure the safety is off before cocking and that you have complete visibility for the process. During daylight, cock the bow on the ground before you climb into a stand, and use the pull-up rope.

Chapter 33

Build Your Own Record-Book Bucks

In early season, Neil began seeing more game as his adaptation to the forest took hold.

Like water on the desert, the right application of quality forage and deer management can have big bucks blooming all over the place.

"Kindred Spirits" has no electricity, yet the insulated walls of this mountaintop hunting camp incubate camaraderie and family bonding like no penthouse on earth. In 1990, Craig Dougherty purchased 150 acres of the poorest deer habitat imaginable. The abandoned farm on the western slope of a New York mountain was overgrown with scrub brush, its productivity in complete decline. Mast was limited to a few surviving hardwoods and an old apple orchard, abandoned by its owner thirty years earlier. The few surviving fruit trees faced stiff competition from upshooting saplings and an over-story that shut off incoming light.

Today, thirty years later, the property has gone through a metamorphosis that rivals a monarch butterfly, thanks to scientific wildlife management and plenty of hard work. In fact, as the twentieth century came to a close, Dougherty's son Neil made a life-altering decision. He chose not to go back to college the fall of his senior year. Instead, he spent the deer season at Kindred Spirits, hunting as often as he wished, imbibing huge quantities of mountain air, and fermenting his soul like grapes among autumn leaves and bright sunshine. Can you imagine how difficult this situation was for father and son? No doubt Neil was enthusiastic about the prospect, but given the expense of college, dropping out one year before finishing must have been maddening.

Planting food plots can involve large equipment, which can be leased or borrowed.

"I had three goals for the season," remembers the lad, reflecting back upon the experience. "To take a Pope and Young buck, harvest a wild turkey, and see a black bear." During the '90s, the Doughertys had spent many weekends and summer vacations working on the property, practicing the techniques of quality deer management. Neil's goals were ambitious. In ten years of hunting, no one had seen a record-class deer on the property. Turkeys? Yes, a flock was often seen and Kindred's dense cover seemed hospitable to a bear's liking. Ironically, striving for these goals provided an outdoor education with an unanticipated impact.

THE SEASON BEGINS

Opening day, October 1, the Kindred Spirits environs seemed more like the Deep South than Northern Tier. Neil, his dad, and three friends hunted the camp and their reports were promising. Although no one unleashed an arrow, everyone saw deer, and several archers passed year-and-a-half bucks. Increasing the age structure of resident deer was one of the first objectives of the camp. It was not a hard and fast rule ("We were a camp, not a school," said the Dougherty's), yet guests were encouraged to pass on year-and-a-half old bucks.

Throughout the month of October, as one day rolled into the next, Neil increasingly came to understand the movements of wildlife, and he relished the opportunity

Food plots benefit many kinds of wildlife and ensure that whitetail deer have the nutrition they need.

to experience the outdoors on such a personal level. As the month drew to a close, he had found many bear tracks and seen several flocks of turkeys. But he had not yet located the big antlers he sought.

Finally, the big day came, when Neil and a friend spotted the deer of their dreams. Chasing a doe in terrain called "the hole," the big buck's hangout seemed to be a steep, thick section that was rarely hunted. Rather than risk spooking the buck from the area, they chose to hunt its perimeter. That strategy that did not succeed, but they did not spook the buck.

During the next week, Neil hunted the "hole" area several times, choosing stands that had a favorable wind. Gone was the need for immediate success. He sought to understand the habits of his quarry and close the distance for a shot. Late in the week, Neil spotted the buck for a second time, coming from the "hole" and reeking of rut odor.

Saturday morning, Katie, Neil's girlfriend, and a buddy joined forces, but the morning and afternoon hunts were uneventful. Sunday afternoon, Neil dropped to the lowest point on the property and hunted the hole.

About forty-five minutes before dark, he heard a deer approaching, but he thought it was a six-point that had passed his stand several times. "Suddenly, the deer appeared, and my heart stopped," he remembers. "That's him!" The deer walked below the stand about forty yards away, hit a logging road, and turned directly up hill.

> He was moving quickly down the logging road and would pass through a shooting lane at about thirty yards. I had the tree ranged in and felt confident. When the buck passed behind a mass of grape vines, I drew silently. Two steps before the opening, the buck turned toward me, side-stepping the shooting lane. Then, for whatever reason, it turned and walked away. I was still at full draw as the deer passed through a small opening, and I released.

After the shot the buck raced out of the hole, and Neil and his friends were soon on the track. Seventy-five yards along the spore, the hunt came to a crashing crescendo. Not only did the 136 Pope and Young buck lay still in the leaves, it expired just ten yards from the only access point to this dastardly location. Recovery was swift and jubilant.

A NEW MAN

Young Neil Dougherty accomplished two of his goals. His Pope and Young whitetail will be a trophy to remember into the twenty-second century. And on a windy afternoon, he spotted a flock of turkeys feeding in the BioLogic. Craftily using a thin peninsula of pine trees, he snuck up to the flock and arrowed a tasty hen. Although he didn't see a bear, he frequently found tracks, trails, and scat, all signs indicating that the elusive animals were thriving in an environment inviting to all wildlife.

The lad wanted to live in the woods, hunt every day, and witness the change of the season from late September to mid-December. "On a personal level, you reach a different way of moving," said Dougherty of his experience. "When I returned to the city, people would comment that I was *different*. 'What's changed?' they'd ask.

"On the mountain, I seemed to be able to move at will among the animals, rarely alerting them. After a week at home, I returned for the late muzzle-loading season and spooked three deer in the first hour."

Food plots also provide a year-round activity for friends and family. By planting food plots, "hunting" becomes a four-season activity.

FROM BARREN TO BIG BUCKS TO DEMO SITE

"Hugely rewarding in many ways," is how Craig Dougherty describes his habitat improvement program. "It's a happy camp when everyone is seeing bucks, but the satisfaction runs much deeper than big antlers. Doing things with the land keeps you there all year long. You seed it, fertilize it, and get great satisfaction from watching a blanket of brush change to a field of green."

Craig and Neil have taken their QDM program a step further by creating the NorthCountry

The food plots on the Kindred Spirits camp have changed the mindset of hunters. Now they see lots of game.

Food plots can be planted for a variety of purposes, offering nutrition in the summer and extra holding power in the fall and winter.

Whitetails Demo Center for hunting and habitat development. Drawing on a decade of experience, the latest research, and Mossy Oak products, Neil has become a widely sought after seminar speaker, sharing habitat development strategies.

The Dougherty property has twenty designated hunting and habitat stations, and visitors can sign up for a four-hour tour. Neil explains the habitat improvements at each station using areas that have been created specifically for whitetail habitat improvement. Topics include creating habitat with chainsaws, creating a sanctuary, working with log roads, timber stand improvement, creating property access, creating approach cover, and fourteen more. The Doughertys don't offer commercial hunting, yet they use their years of habitat improvement to demonstrate how to grow bigger bucks and hunt them effectively. Neil also provides individual site evaluations to meet the habitat-improvement goals and objectives of landowners.

Kindred Spirits began as a dream. Through time, hard work, and proper management, a small, unproductive tract of land has transformed into a haven for wildlife and those who love it. Where once an occasional spike buck passed through, thirty-three antlered bucks were seen by hunters during the past season, only one of which was harvested. Neil Dougherty's decision not to return to college was gutsy for him, and no doubt stressful for his father. Of all the classes he'll ever take, though, none will impact his character or life-building philosophy like that fall in the woods

Author's Note: For information on the NorthCountry Whitetails Habitat Development, phone (716)388-6990 or www.NorthCountryWhitetails.com.

MAXIMIZE WILDLIFE THROUGH FOOD PLOTS

"We are very much in favor of food plots to benefit wildlife," says Jimmie Bullock, Manager of the Sustainable Forestry and Wildlife Programs for International Paper (IP). "A good planting program may or may not draw animals from neighboring properties, but food plots will make them more visible, especially in late afternoon. Planted food sources make harvesting does

Food plots can be grown in various sizes. Starting small is a good philosophy until you learn the ropes of farming.

easier and hunting in general more successful for youngsters and spouses. Wildlife is much more visible and club members get a feeling of accomplishment," he said.

Planting a food plot may sound like a very expensive project, yet Bullock suggests ways that make the process effective for hunting without depleting timber resources. "On IP land, we allow up to 1 percent of the land to be used for food plots, and we encourage plantings that facilitate hunting and the tree harvest," he said. "Widening sides of interior roads is an excellent and extremely accessible practice that produces a long, linear plot with maximum edges. Additional sunlight to roads often reduces maintenance, because they dry faster. Power lines and utility rights-of-way also make excellent plot sites without cutting trees. Streamside management zones and logging-loader sets make ideal locations for small plots, especially if adjacent to

Food plots can be planted for hunting, with narrow field edges and funnels that provide good shooting lanes for archers.

thick cover. Widening roads and planting them was one of the Dougherty's first planting practices. Increased sunlight also increases browse growth.

Hunt clubs should select food plots with tree stands and wind direction in mind. If brush piles will be created, use them to funnel deer entry effectively to stand sites. "Always conduct a soil sample," advises Bullock, to determine the proper pH for the best growth and use of fertilizer and lime. Deer prefer to browse any plant that has been fertilized. They have the ability to pick a fertilized plant from one that has not been supplemented.

"We recommend planting plots that will benefit wildlife year round, as opposed to providing large grain supplements," says Bullock. "However, quality supplemental feeding during stress times can be very beneficial in late winter, when natural food is at its scarcest, and late summer, when natural vegetation loses some of its nutritional value."

Finally, Bullock recommends fencing a small section, roughly a square yard, of any wildlife habitat improvement. This acts as a barometer of feeding activity. Often the inaccessible, fenced vegetation shows dramatic growth, which gives an indication of the amount of food the plot is providing.

Chapter 34

Elk On Your Own: Wyoming

Because elk bugle during the archery season, making them sound-off is a critical skill. It can also be a hair-raising experience.

The Cowboy State has become a premier destination for elk hunters, with a predictable license situation and tons of public land. Our group of four hunters took three bulls in five days, and it was only a deflected arrow that ruined a perfect score. If you can camp, you can hunt elk in Wyoming.

Elk legs waved and wagged in the air like some wapiti Jedi saber battle. It would have been almost comical had my pulse been under two hundred. The bull with heavy, chocolate antlers wallowed seventy-five yards away, and I was spellbound waiting for its next move. Suddenly, two cows left their stream drinking spot and moved back up the mountain, a signal that the bull would soon follow. I gave a brief cow mew that grabbed the bull's attention and coaxed it thirty yards closer, where it drank at the wallow in front of me. Originally, this had been a crossbow hunt, but my bow's cocking device got trashed by the airline, so I had resorted to my Hoyt compound.

I've hunted water holes for decades, and watching an animal drink should have been old hat, yet as the beast kept slurping liquid, both of my hands tingled with excitement. This was not some tiny sensation; I had full-fledged bull fever. Could I even draw the bow? On and on the bull drank, until I began filling the time by counting antler points. *Dude, you know better!* chastised my inner voice.

Finally, the bull had its fill, and without pausing a moment, he turned, directly following the cows. Anticipating the problem, I gave a brief mew with a diaphragm caller, and the bull paused. In an instant, the shaft was away and seemed to be on target, yet the sound on impact was soft and muffled. Had I missed? An hour of daylight remained, and I knew I needed to at least begin trailing the animal before darkness fell. After waiting a few minutes, I carefully approached the shot location, when I saw the bull standing eighty yards up the mountain. I watched as it staggered and fell. Suppressing any celebration, I sneaked to the beast to make sure it had expired. Woohoo! It was my second year hunting Wyoming public land, and a dandy bull was mine.

WESTERN HUNTING: WHY IT'S SO DIFFERENT

"The most exciting big game hunt in North America is a mountain-state elk hunt during the rut."

Certainly this is a controversial statement, yet in my mind there is no greater excitement than stalking wapiti in spectacular mountain scenery with the potential for a six-hundred-pound beast, with daggers on its head, screaming and blowing snot in your face. I once had a mature bull stand three yards behind me, so close I could hear every breath and rutting gurgle. Eventually, the bull walked away, but I was so unnerved that I blew the shot.

Aside from the excitement, elk hunts are incredibly fun and adventurous, especially if you form a group and hunt the same area each year. Our guys began hunting in Idaho seven years ago, and I joined the team midway through that tenure. Despite hunting on our own, the camp usually filled to about 15 percent, about the state average for archery hunters.

Our last year in Idaho, I rented a car in Boise, expecting to upgrade to an SUV upon arrival. "I'm sorry," said the lady behind the rental counter. "There is a golf tournament in town, and every 4x4 has been rented." For five days, I drove a Dodge Charger up ten miles of mountain road, no doubt to the hysteria of other hunters, yet it got me into elk country, and I downed a good five-by-five. I shot the bull at 8:00 and had the last piece of boned-out meat in the vehicle by noon. That may sound impossible, yet Western public land is so accessible, that you can literally just park a vehicle (even a Dodge Charger) and hunt.

A quality campsite makes the nucleus of any hunt, and you will build bonds of friendship that last a lifetime. When everyone pitches in to cut wood, cook, do dishes, and pack out meat, the camaraderie accelerates exponentially. Planning menus, gear, and hunting strategies make the hunt a year-round adventure. Driving to camp, even from the East Coast, helps save costs and allows for the transport of tents, stoves, and other large objects. Once there, you can rent a small commercial storage unit for the next year.

Elk hunting in Wyoming is synonomous with camping. Often hunters can find success without a guide if they hone their mountain-man skills.

WHY WYOMING?

The Cowboy State has an estimated elk population of 120,000 with a bull-to-cow ratio of about 1:4, and age is generally well distributed among the herd. For crossbow hunters, Wyoming is your best bet for elk, because it treats crossbow hunters just like bowhunters. The rut usually peaks the third week of September, and focusing on this period will have you in the woods when bulls are most vocal. Don't worry about being an expert caller because most big

A backpack is your lifeline to the many pieces of gear you will need.

bulls are call shy by this time. If you can make a squeaky, little-bull bugle and a soft cow call, that's all you need. Begin each day by hiking uphill with the wind in your face, and when you hear elk, sneak in, always checking the wind. You can't drag an elk out, yet with this strategy all the packing is downhill.

Last year our group of eight killed one bull and missed another in six days of hunting. That 25 percent shooting rate ranks up there with about any archery area in the country, especially considering that this area was totally new to us. Wyoming's overall hunter success is 44 percent, which includes rifle hunts, guided hunts, and ranch hunts. For a first time group, we fared pretty well. Biologists say that mature bulls continue to thrive in most hunting units, especially in the western and southern sections of the state where elk populations are "over-objective," meaning there are too many elk.

Wyoming does not discriminate between vertical and horizontal archers.

Some ranches and units are overpopulated such that Wyoming Game and Fish has instituted a "middle-man" between hunters and landowners. If a landowner has elk he doesn't want around, he calls up the rep, who then calls hunters to help reduce the surplus. You can sign up on the WY Game and Fish website.

Wouldn't it be great if you knew where the most archery bulls were taken last year? It's all online. Go to the Game and Fish website www.wgfd.wyo.gov and look under "Harvest Info," where you'll find all 130 elk units listed with the harvest information for each. They even break it down by "Harvest Tool," so that you can focus on archery success. Wyoming has eight elk districts, and the forecast for each region can be found under "2015 Statewide Hunting Season Forecast." If these statistics are overwhelming, you can always call WY Game and Fish and ask to speak to an elk biologist. He or she can quickly identify the herds with the best elk populations, and the hunt begins.

Once you select an area of National Forest, stop by the local Forest Service office for more detailed information. It's their job to give you as much information as they have, and they will be happy to help. Finally, talk to the people you meet along the way. A sheepherder told me about a small, dynamite water hole that's a quarter-mile

Scent control is important in elk hunting as well. Elk don't sniff the ground like whitetail deer, but they can smell a human half-mile away.

from a paved road, and I found no human tracks there. Some rifle deer hunters may be in your area, and they will often open up about what they have seen since they have a different license. This sounds so simple; and it is!

ADVICE FROM A PRO

Mike Clark is a native of the Cowboy State and an experienced outfitter in western Wyoming on a variety of big game species. Ask him the top three things a do-it-yourselfer needs for success, and he doesn't waste a second. "Be in shape," he says emphatically. "Hunters have to be ready for the altitude and the ruggedness of our terrain. And it's extreme." Next, Clark urges archers to practice in a wide variety of situations from five to fifty yards. "You may have to draw slowly and release, kneel down to shoot under

Mechanical heads are a good archery bet, since they fly the same as target points and make practicing easier.

timber, or take a steep uphill or downhill shot," he says. "Practice at a variety of distances and shooting positions." Thirdly, and not surprisingly, Clark advises practicing range estimation:

> So many fellows rely on laser range finders today that judging distance in the field has gone by the wayside. Archers should practice as soon as they get to Wyoming, estimating distances to trees, rocks, and logs whenever they can, using their range finders to verify their best guess. Often a bull only gives a moment or two to shoot, and being able to determine an accurate range with the naked eye can spell the difference between a good bull and next year.

Weather is as fickle in Wyoming as it is in any Rocky Mountain state, and Clark advises all of his hunters to dress in layers and carry raingear or a poncho. "Temperatures can range from ten below zero to eighty in a day's time, and you have to be prepared for whatever comes from the sky," he says. "Likewise, break in your boots well before the hunt, and select foot gear with plenty of ankle support. Side-hilling can quickly cause blisters unless your boots fit well with a well padded pair of socks."

Clark's clients are usually guided, so he doesn't require them to know elk talk, yet it doesn't hurt to know your way around a cow call. "I carry a necklace with several calls,

Since elk are easy to miss, you'll want a full quiver. Many hunters carry the quiver in their pack to avoid contact with brush while stalking.

If you are doing a spike camp, you'll want to follow Mike Clark's advice on gear and include a good map of the area.

and I sometimes partner with another guide to sound like a herd of elk making noise," he says. Finally, carry a wind puffer, one of those spray bottles of powder that lets you determine wind direction. "You can fool their eyes and ears, but you can't beat an elk's nose," he says.

Clark offers drop camps, where he packs your gear in and your game out, for those hunters who don't want to do everything on their own. This tactic may be a good stepping-stone, especially if you are new to elk hunting. Clark can be reached at mikeclark_hunt@yahoo.com or by phone at (307)884-6356.

GEAR TO GET IT DONE

My first season in Wyoming I carried a TenPoint crossbow, and I had every confidence that I'd bag a bull if I could get within forty yards. And I came within a coin flip of doing so. I found a small, secluded water hole, and my buddy and I flipped to see which side we'd watch. Two bulls came in from his side, but he blew a shot.

A crossbow in the 330-350 fps range is perfect for elk.

Bow-Power

A crossbow in the 330–350 fps range provides sufficient power to down the biggest bull, yet you must shoot it in the proper spot. Many archers have gotten only a broken heart, and the bull a sore shoulder, by putting an arrow squarely in the muscle of the front shoulder. Practice aiming behind the shoulder so that the arrow strikes the lung cavity, and your trophy will go down in short order.

Arrows

The shaft you shoot will be just as important as the bow. Since an elk shot may average thirty to forty yards, it's easy to flatten out with light arrows to reduce the aiming arch. However, you want momentum on your side, and a heavy shaft will penetrate much better, especially if you hit a

Select gear carefully for an elk hunt. You need the essentials, but every ounce counts in the high country.

rib or catch the muscle of the near shoulder. Personally, I like cut-on-contact heads for large animals, but be sure they fly like your target points, or sight the bow in using the broadheads.

Broadheads

Two of our bulls fell to expandable broadheads: NAP's two-blade, 100-grain Killzone, and the FUSE Kumasi. I used NAP's Big Nasty, and it flew and impacted perfectly, gaining complete penetration at forty yards. I actually practiced with the head in camp and then re-sharpened it.

Decoys

Montana decoys are so realistic that a glimpse of one often relaxes cows and entices bulls. It's the elk you don't see that bust you, and deploying one among elk helps cover sound and movement.

Packs

A half-empty large pack is better than a full smaller one. You'll need room for emergency gear, knives, meat bags, and other supplies in a pack that hugs your hips and transfers weight to your legs. Extra space can be used to pack out meat when successful, which can save an extra trip up the mountain.

Binoculars can be your best friend, saving miles and hours of stalking for an animal that's too small or not legal.

Not for guys only. A crossbow allows a slender female to hunt with the same gear as a muscle-bound mountain man.

Boots

Waterproof, breathable footwear is a must, as you will be walking in wet vegetation and crossing streams. My Danner Ridgemasters were sturdy and rugged. Other guys opted for lightweight hiking boots to save weight. Both work, but be sure yours are well broken in before the hunt, whichever you choose.

Clothing

You can take several hunting outfits, yet you'll probably wear the same one every day. I opted for a ScentLok base layer that wicked moisture very well and defied scent contamination. As an outer layer, a water resistant ScentLok Full Season top and bottom were quiet and warm.

Calls

Bugling in the dark, hours before daylight, can be an excellent scouting tactic, but sounding little and foolishly aggressive lights up the competition. Most public-land bulls are call-shy, so I rely on a Sceery cow call and a Primos Hoochie Mama. Sometimes I'll use them together to simulate a herd. I also use a Wayne Carlton diaphragm for bugles and the single mew that stopped my bull in its tracks.

Maps and GPS

Quality maps from the US Forest Service are invaluable in planning a hiking route and scouting for game. Generally, elk bed on northwestern slopes, and any steep, timbered area often contains game. A GPS is ideal for logging isolated trails, water holes, wallows, and overland routes in the dark and for finding your way back to camp. Be sure to carry extra batteries.

The Miscellaneous Extras

Finally, bring a real pillow, a warm sleeping bag, and a comfortable pad as well as your favorite cooking gear. Whether using a gas stove or a charcoal grill, make sure you know how things work before you leave. The first year is always the toughest, yet once you establish a routine and learn the area, success will follow.

BULLS ON A BUDGET: SEVEN STEPS TO SUCCESS

1. Plan ahead. Preference points can save $500 off the special license price. Get in shape. You'll hike and climb most of the day.
2. Buy used camping gear, but test it in the back yard. Consider renting a camper or small cabin.
3. Tow a small trailer and drive, sharing travel expenses among the group. Buy your food and pack it in coolers according to a planned menu.
4. Arrive a day or two early to allow your legs and lungs to adjust. Your elk license may include fishing privileges.
5. Expect success. A bull is worth at least $1,000 in groceries, so bring meat bags, coolers, knives, and freezer bags to utilize every ounce. Arrange for processing back home before you leave, or do it yourself.
6. Use the Internet to research the units that produce well. Generally, the higher and more remote sections of a forest hold the most elk. Hunt in pairs for safety and to make field dressing easier.
7. Finally, consider bivouacking. Carry a light tent and enough food and water for three days, and camp where the elk are. This is often very effective.

A bull elk is worth about $1,000 in groceries, so get in shape and prepare for success.

WAPITI AIN'T WHITETAILS: DON'T MAKE THESE ROOKIE MISTAKES

If you've never hunted elk before, team up with a buddy who has experience, and keep these tips in mind.

First, Find the Elk

Don't tip-toe around as you would with whitetails. Cover lots of ground until you find fresh sign.

Once Buggered, They're Gone

Elk have no core territory like deer, so if you bust a herd, they rarely return.

Natural Noise Is a Good Thing

Elk are noisy animals, and they expect to hear noise from others. If you snap a stick, undisturbed elk may think you are part of their herd.

Never aim at an elk's shoulder. Even quality arrows, such as these FMJ shafts from Easton, won't penetrate the heavy muscle and bone.

Don't Over-Call

Many successful elk hunters rarely call. They sneak in on bugling bulls. Raking a tree with a limb often excites a rutting bull, and that's hard to mess up.

Never Aim for the Shoulder

Your gear may punch through a deer's shoulder, but rarely will that work on an elk. It's lungs or nothing.

Learn how to use your scope and select yardages quickly. Elk shots can be very close or out to fifty yards.

Enjoy Where You Are, Jeremiah Johnson

The average archer bags a bull every six or seven years, so breathe deeply pilgrim. Embrace your surroundings, and have fun.

Chapter 35

Backyard Bucks: There Goes the Neighborhood

Jeff Harrison has taken a wall full of bucks like this one from the suburbs of Washington, D.C. and Maryland. He specializes in backyard bucks.

Record-book deer may live closer than you think. Here's how a group of guys find great deer, boost their enjoyment, hunt close to home, and even make a few bucks in the process.

"Giant! Giant!" whispered Jeff Harrison excitedly to his video partner Troy Knoll as the two men stood in a suburban stand not far from Washington, DC.

"I'd been taping Jeff for years, and he never got that emotional," remembers Knoll. "Giant? I was almost afraid to look."

"The huge nine-point was tailing a doe while trying to keep smaller bucks from sneaking in," remembers Harrison, who had taken fourteen Pope and Young bucks from similar suburban situations. "We were at the head of a funnel, and if the buck kept approaching, I knew I'd get a shot." Unfortunately, the distractions from the other bucks caused the doe to retreat, and the estimated 160-class whitetail slipped out of sight.

Harrison and Knoll were hunting Halloween morning on a five-acre lot in suburban Maryland. Although Knoll had accompanied Harrison on numerous hunts, he'd never filmed one of Harrison's real trophies. Two hours later that luck seemed about to change when the "giant" returned and bedded down with a doe eighty yards away.

"Troy and I were getting antsy," said Harrison. "This was Halloween, and we each had trick-or-treating obligations with our families. The prospect of bailing on the huge buck was maddening, yet we'd have to leave by early afternoon. Unfortunately, the doe began feeding shortly after lunch, and once again, she backtracked, keeping her pursuer out of harm's way."

Jeff Harrison works as a painting contractor, a job that brings him into contact with many homeowners in the suburban area.

SUNDAY SECOND CHANCE

Early the next morning, the duo was texting about their plans for the day. Fortunately, this was one of Maryland's Sunday-hunting days, and the men were debating strategy and the best stand to hunt. "In nearly twenty years I've never seen a big buck twice," reasoned Harrison. "So there's no urgency about returning to that spot." At the time, rain was falling in torrents, but it was expected to abate in early afternoon. They agreed to try a different, but nearby, stand at noon.

This stand overlooked three one-acre lots that adjoin a flood plain, forming a natural corridor.

Rain fell as the men climbed in, however the skies were clearing and things seemed promising. Suddenly, Harrison noticed movement behind him. He nudged his partner who immediately sighed, *"Oh my God!"* The same, or a similar buck was standing fifty yards away in one of the yards. Apparently it was bedded in a thicket when the hunters arrived, and it got up to follow a doe.

"The buck was fifty-eight yards away," said Harrison, who had memorized the distance to every section of the yard. "The doe milled around for nearly forty-five minutes, in a standoff of sorts that really had me nervous and on edge. Finally, the two deer came toward us. They were about to jump a low fence when I came to full draw, gave my signature "hey!" to stop the buck and released, catching it right in the heart. The buck jumped the small fence and skidded to a halt within fifty yards. Troy caught the entire segment on tape."

NEIGHBORHOOD NUANCES

Despite having a Pope and Young 150-class buck a stone's throw away, Harrison knew he needed to keep his cool and act respectfully. He quickly circled the yards and knocked on the door of the home where the buck fell. When he got no answer, he went to another neighbor so that someone familiar could accompany him. As the three men began retrieving the deer, a house sitter emerged. The lady hadn't answered the door because she was deaf, and she didn't know Harrison or that he had permission to hunt the adjoining back yards.

"It took some creativity, but we wrote notes and she texted the homeowner who gave us the go-ahead to remove the deer," laughed Harrison. "Then we went about removing the huge deer which green-scored 159 inches, had a twenty-one-inch inside spread and weighed 220 pounds field dressed. That was twenty pounds larger than any deer I'd ever shot. It was a giant, yet not "The Giant." The buck we'd seen the day before is still out there."

SILENT SCOUTING: KEY TO SUCCESS

Andy Cuttitta killed his first urban deer in 1985, and he became an enthusiastic member of the Harrison group, especially since his Ultimate Camo blended so well with tree bark, and all their hunts occurred from trees. "Some of the most fun is scouting with a trail camera, which is especially easy to do in urban settings," he says. "Two years ago, I photographed a particularly good deer, which really sparked my interest. I began setting

A rutting buck can ruin thousands of dollars in decorative trees in a single night. Some homeowners want all deer killed.

Andy Cuttitta uses trail cameras extensively. He finds a special tree and then posts a camera to learn what types of deer pass by.

up cameras in July, and after eighteen-hundred pictures, I had only two of that good buck. I post cameras on the edge of fields or thick cover, so that I don't have to go into the woods and deer become used to seeing me in certain locations."

Like a scientist, Cuttitta is very methodical when hunting urban bucks, using the data he collects to maximize success. Once he begins to photograph a target animal, he'll wait until he has some consistency during daylight, and then he'll wait for the perfect wind. Although urban deer live near humans, mature bucks can be very crafty.

Cuttitta hunted his special buck for the first time on January 2nd, a blustery cold and windy day, from a stand that had yielded great success, especially in late season. The stand was located in a small woodlot adjacent to a horse farm, and deer traveled regularly along the fence line. He saw thirty to forty deer the first day. He'd mostly photographed Mr. Big in the afternoon, so he climbed into his stand at 2:30 and got set.

He hunted the stand again on January 4th, but the buck didn't show, so Cuttitta went back to his camera work. Images from the 5th showed the buck with a doe on two occasions, and the forecast for the 6th held a favorable wind. In late afternoon, the buck came past the stand and stopped broadside. The big typical-ten-point scored 157 with great mass. Cuttitta estimated it at 5-½ years old. When setting trail cameras and setting stands, Cuttitta looks for trail intersections. "I've learned that deer usually stop naturally at such places to scent the movement of other deer. Nine times out of ten they stop to see which way to go."

Andy Cuttitta took this great buck in the suburbs of Baltimore. He and his friends film their hunts and have made a series of the events.

Deer in suburbs quickly learn.

CITY BUCKS, COUNTRY BUCKS

Like the old mouse fable, differences exist between small urban patches and big rural farms. "I hunt a couple of large farms in rural Maryland and spend weeks glassing large fields, looking for good deer," Cuttitta says.

One farm is nearly a mile long, and deer don't seem to move in a pattern. One day they enter at one spot, the next another. Also, feeding on a large farm, deer have many food options, from corn to beans to acorns. One bean field is six hundred acres, so pinpointing where a deer will feed is difficult.

In urban areas food sources are less varied and more restricted, and deer often pass through small pinch-points to access them. Also, I feel deer get less pressure in urban areas. On the big farms we have trespassers, while people aren't so brazen to go through a person's backyard or into parks. On big farms we often "catch" people on our cameras.

Urban deer don't necessarily see humans as a threat, whereas, unless you are on a tractor, farm deer are usually running. Finally, the biggest difference is the square footage you have to hunt. On big farms exact deer movement is difficult to predict, while in urban areas it's easier to figure out.

Deer movement is much easier to figure out in suburban areas than in large wood lots.

With respect to tree stands, both Harrison and Cuttitta use lock-on stands. "You want to get into your stand as quickly and quietly as possible," Cuttitta says. "Big deer will probably be bedded nearby, as it was in Harrison's case, and you can position the stand for the best shot. In the big woods, deer can come from any direction."

Cuttitta uses rut tricks, but he prefers to let nature take its course. He uses bleat cans, grunt tubes, and rattling horns, in that order, choosing to begin subtly and work toward moderate aggression. "Bucks are looking for does, not a fight," he says.

Finally, neither he nor Harrison field dress a deer in the area in which it is killed. They strive to leave as little evidence of their presence as possible. Should a neighbor's dog bring home a piece of viscera, your hunting privileges could be jeopardized. In any neighborhood where deer are present, some people will love them and some will want you to

The size of a deer rub is directly proportional to the size of the deer that made it. Find one of these on a tree in a front or back yard, and you will find an unhappy homeowner.

kill them all. Showing respect for the land and neighbors can keep the camo carpet rolled out for you. The buck of your dreams may be bedded in the next yard, right behind the barbecue.

GETTING PERMISSION AND KEEPING IT

"We like eating does and hunting," says Cuttitta. "Any property can be a gold mine. Put a trail camera out and see what comes along." If you've never tried urban hunting, here are some tips and strategies to get started.

Field dressing a deer in the field is a no-no. Eventually neighborhood dogs or other animals will move the viscera around and cause objections from neighbors.

The best locations are lots of one to five acres with wooded and/or brush sections, especially if they border a park or creek drainage where building is restricted. Once found, look for lots with deer deterrents, such as wire around bushes, obvious browse lines on shrubs, or high fences around gardens. Harrison often recruits new properties by asking permission to hunt for sheds. Often, residents don't know what they are, so it can be a great icebreaker. Additionally:

- Make a friend. Share your camera photos. Always ask permission. Identify your car, and ask the best place to park.
- Be discrete. Don't scout in camo clothes or use flashlights in the dark.
- Shoot does, and donate some of your venison to food banks.
- Barter your services. Offer to mow grass, trim trees, perform a trade service, or shovel snow in return for hunting privileges.
- Place stands for maximum invisibility, as far from human traffic as possible. You don't want a child testing his courage.

- Know the facts: You are feeding the hungry, fighting Lyme disease, reducing traffic accidents, putting organic food on your table, and humanely balancing deer populations. That's about as "green" as it gets.

By visiting people with large lots and small farms you may get permission to hunt great bucks in unlikely places

THE OVERKILL TEAM

In the same spirit as *Brotherhood Outdoors,* the *Buck Commanders,* and other TV show groups, Harrison and several friends began to videotape their hunts. At first, the challenge was, "Can we do this?" But that soon developed into, "Wow, this is fun!" and eventually, "Hey, let's make a video."

"I'm self-taught with big dreams but not big money," laughs Troy Knoll, the technical guru of the group. I enjoy shooting video as

Team Overkill earned its name by going overboard on taping deer, doing whatever it took to succeed.

much as hunting, and I've always been fascinated with Jeff's deer. Operating as *Team Overkill* we are very giving with our hunting spots and sharing with the video job. We are close friends, and we try to accomplish everything without sacrificing the family."

"Our gear isn't the most expensive," continued Knoll. "I use a Canon GL2 I bought on eBay, and it's done well for us. Also, I carry a Panasonic GS250, a camera you can get for about $500. We needed a three-chip camera for TV quality, yet now things are changing to HD. I edit on my home laptop and do it all on a $100 program called Pinnacle Studio. Our idea was to show what friends can accomplish together with minimal dollars. It's not totally professional, but it's obtainable for the average guy."

Currently the group has tape of twenty does, thirteen bucks, and two sika deer hunts to be used for the next video. "I'm a magazine junky, and now with the video, I put my "story" in video form," Knoll says. "We get together and have a blast reliving our hunts over and over. You don't have to spend a fortune to make a quality tape and tell a story."

Author's Note: *There Goes the Neighborhood* is the group's first video. It can be seen on the website vimeo.com/teamoverkillmd. *Also*, check out Troy Knoll's photo and text blog, which he updates three times each week.

Jeff Harrison practices extensively and has changed from a compound to a crossbow on many hunts, opting for its excellent accuracy in situations where he can use a rest.

Chapter 36

Crossbow Organizations: Join the Club

Like-minded people who enjoy sharing an experience have spawned the National Rifle Association, Rocky Mountain Elk Foundation, Ducks Unlimited, and a host of other organizations that help promote particular sports, conservation practices, or species. Fortunately, crossbow enthusiasts can choose from regional and national associations to stay on top of local and national trends and developments. Here is a look at several, along with websites for additional information. Thanks in advance for permission to include these organizations, and I urge you to visit each of their sites:

THE AMERICAN CROSSBOW FEDERATION

> The American Crossbow Federation is dedicated to the promotion and preservation of *all* forms of hunting with *all* weapons, especially the crossbow.

The American Crossbow Federation (ACF) was formed in 1996 as an umbrella group within the shooting sports industry, with the mission of educating and promoting additional crossbow hunting opportunities. Since its inception twenty years ago, dramatic changes have occurred in attitudes toward crossbows and crossbow hunting thanks to a continued educational process from the hunting industry. Many exciting new opportunities have fallen into place across the United States and Canada, as more hunters become educated about the benefits offered by crossbows to the hunting community. Now is the time for those pursuing crossbow hunting opportunities to join together and exchange knowledge on their shared interest.

The ACF focused on game managers, legislators, and the general public to promote a positive image of crossbows and crossbow hunting. The continued proliferation of

America's favorite big game species, the whitetail deer, has facilitated this acceptance. Initially, many traditional bowhunters and the general public believed that crossbows would so simplify deer hunting that populations would plummet and increased regulations would be placed on all archers. By consistently presenting evidence to the contrary, those initial beliefs have changed. By providing a proactive fraternity dedicated to uniting individuals from all across the continent who believe the modern crossbow should be just one more legitimate option for hunters in their pursuit of big game animals. The ACF's prime objective is to educate game managers, legislators, and the general public about the crossbow and its positive attributes as applied to modern hunting and effective game management.

Every organization needs a central vehicle for information dissemination and in the fall of 2001, the American Crossbow Federation launched its Individual Membership Program, along with a new quarterly publication entitled *Horizontal Bowhunter*. This magazine focuses on hunting and includes input from the full spectrum of the industry, including personal stories from day-to-day members. Additionally, leaders in the crossbow industry, such as TenPoint, support the magazine and its information dissemination in general. Leaders from the crossbow industry contribute regular columns that cover an array of crossbow topics such as technical tips, crossbow politics, crossbow-hunting adventures, and repudiation of many popular crossbow myths.

ACF members are invited to share their ideas, opinions, and successes with other members in the pages of *Horizontal Bowhunter* magazine. This publication has become a forum much like those posted online, and publishes a variety of opinions about tactics, gear, hunting seasons, and other matters of interest to the sport.

Members receive a membership card with each membership package and a new, updated card each time they renew their membership, as well as a bumper sticker that proudly proclaims that you are a Member of the American Crossbow Federation. Members receive four quarterly issues of *Horizontal Bowhunter* magazine with each year of paid membership.

HBM BIG GAME REGISTER

Although hunting is not a competitive sport, most hunters enjoy comparing their prowess via game harvested using the Boone & Crockett club for firearm hunters and Pope & Young for archers. The ACF launched the *Big Game Register*, which is the official crossbow big game record-keeping system that accepts entries of any animal taken with an arrow, regardless of what kind of archery equipment was used in its harvest, from any paid ACF members. It includes categories for every animal in the world, even including one for the wild turkey.

Crossbows aren't just for hunters, and a committee of ACF members designed and released the ACF "Official Crossbow Shoot Rules" for family tournaments. These guidelines have been designed to stress the fun and family value of shooting your bows together, rather than stressing the competition aspect. It encourages members to share their knowledge with their fellows in an effort to make them better shooters and hunters.

THE NATIONAL CROSSBOWMEN OF THE USA

The National Crossbowmen of the USA, Inc. (TNC) is an organization of people interested in supporting the crossbow sport. Their aim is to perpetuate the history of the crossbow, and enhance its use as sporting instrument for target shooting as well as for hunting. TNC has similar goals to those of ACF, and promotes the acceptance of crossbows for recreational purposes and seeks ways of reaching this end.

TNC Membership

TNC annual dues are $15.00 for an individual membership and $18.00 for a family membership. Corporate membership dues are $20.00. Overseas subscription to the organizational newsletter "The Chit-Chat" is only $20.00 per year.

Hunting with crossbows in the United States is much more popular than competitive shooting, and TNC helps to expand awareness of all aspects of crossbow recreation. TNC membership is open to anyone interested in supporting the crossbow sport. It is not necessary to own a crossbow, nor that you shoot in actual competition or hunt, although participation in the use of the crossbow is the group's main objective. Members of TNC may compete in the annual US indoor and outdoor national championship tournaments, where they are eligible for the rotating championship awards of TNC and the championship awards of the NAA and the NFAA. www.crossbowusa.com.

CROSSBOW NATION

This is a very cool website for those who hunt and includes a forum section where you can ask questions and chat with other hunters about gear and hunting techniques. It also contains a library of articles and videos to help with any problem you may experience. Here's their mission statement:

When we decided to build the Crossbow Nation website, we had one goal in mind: to give the crossbow enthusiast a place they could come to, free of ridicule, to find the resources they need to get up-to-date information regarding crossbow hunting and shooting, and to provide a community for people who share the common interest of the crossbow. We were fed up with other archery and hunting sites, which disregarded the crossbow as a viable choice for hunting.

Until recently, many forums about bowhunting were either negative toward crossbows or gave very limited access and coverage. Visitors who wanted to share experiences or learn from others had a difficult time locating such data in a nonjudgmental atmosphere. Because crossbow shooters amounted to only a small percentage of total members on those sites, we were often left feeling hopeless and abandoned by the moderators and administrators. Crossbow Nation is a place where crossbow hunters and shooters will feel welcome, engaged, and appreciated. It is family oriented and promotes all forms of hunting. It is a place where crossbow enthusiasts can feel like they belong. This philosophy will grow the organization, because it meets the needs of members. Now they have a group they can belong to, share ideas with, and learn from. Crossbow Nation is all crossbows, all the time. Working hard to help support, help inform, and help promote the sport of crossbow hunting and shooting. www.crossbownation.com.

WORLD CROSSBOW ASSOCIATION

This site offers information and conducts crossbow shoots around the world, in several categories such as:

Target

The more familiar type of competition event where a sixty-centimeter target face is placed up to sixty-five meters from the shooter, and up to ninety bolts are shot.

Target Match Play

This competition is shot at the target venue, but the shooter is shooting against a direct competitor. The winner progresses to the next round.

Indoor

This competition is similar to Target, but with thirty bolts being shot into a forty-centimeter face, usually over an eighteen-meter distance. The event is conducted indoors.

Forest

Similar to a 3-D competition, this event is usually shot in a forest environment, where twenty-four targets are laid out on a course (similar to golf). Each competitor shoots two bolts at each target before scoring and moving to the next target.

3-D

This competition is similar to Forest, but it uses life-size, three-dimensional models of various types of game.

www.worldcrossbow.com.

NORTH AMERICAN CROSSBOW FEDERATION

Mission Statement

The North American Crossbow Federation's (NACF) purpose is to advocate for the use of the crossbow for recreation and as a legal hunting tool for any licensed hunter during all seasons in which archery equipment is permitted. The goal is to promote safe and ethical hunting, supporting sound game-management practices, and cooperating with wildlife agencies and other officials to recruit, retain, and educate participants in all aspects of crossbow shooting and hunting.

The NACF functions like many conservation groups, such as the National Wild Turkey Federation, the Rocky Mountain Elk Foundation, and the National Shooting Sports Foundation, to promote crossbow hunting with wildlife agencies at the departmental level. The NACF supports the unification of all hunting-rights advocates in the fight to preserve our hunting heritage and seeks to partner with like-minded organizations and manufacturers in the effort to grow hunting and recreational shooting as a beneficial form of outdoor recreation.

One of the main goals of the NACF is to collect, develop, and distribute accurate information about the use of crossbows both for hunting and recreation. In the late 1990s and early 2000s, crossbow hunting was dominated by anecdotal and very emotional arguments, and the NACF has effectively sorted the wheat from the chaff. Much time and effort has been given to gathering accurate data concerning all aspects of crossbow use. Much of this data deals with the use of crossbows as a hunter recruitment and retention tool, as well as a game management tool for state game-management agencies around the country.

Although crossbows are safe when used properly, NACF continues a consistent education process to promote the safe and effective use of crossbows. www.northamericancrossbowfederation.com.

Chapter 37

Young and in Love with Hunting

Hunting doesn't have to be a solitary activity. Taking your significant other along for the fun can lead to great things.

Hunting is often a solitary, one-on-one commune with nature, or at least an escape from everyday life. Yet TV couples like Lee and Tiffany or Ralph and Vicky command a loud and loyal, enthusiastic following. What's it really like to live with your hunting partner 24/7/365? Could you and yours transform a hunting lifestyle into an income and status

Ralph and Vickie are one of the most popular couples on television, and their competitive humor becomes addictive.

as a outdoor celebrity? Since we've covered crossbow hunting comprehensively, here's a look at another advantage of the crossbow, it's versatility and adaptability for hunting couples. Three outdoor-media couples share their experiences, with tips of how you can share your passions indoors and out.

"We are like yin and yang," laughed Vicky Cianciarulo about Ralph, her husband and co-host of the very popular *Archer's Choice* TV show. "A lot of people couldn't spend 365 days together, but Ralph gives me crap and I give it right back," laughed Vickie. "We're partners in business, in crime, and as husband and wife, and we're so used to being together we almost know each other's thoughts."

Ralph and Vicky have been married seventeen years and recently celebrated ten years with their award-winning TV show, in which they constantly try to outdo each other, always with great humor. Vicky's quest for an Alaskan brown bear emphasized their togetherness, as they spent more than twenty days in tiny camping tents. One stretch lasted a solid week in howling wind, horizontal rain, and lightning such that they were completely tent bound. "We collected water in a tarp and survived on ramen soup," she said with a shudder.

After two attempts with a bow and no shots, Vicky opted for a Thompson/Center icon in a .300 Winchester Magnum, a rifle she'd learned to love and fired effectively. As always, Ralph, a veteran bear guide, had very specific instructions for his wife. "Only take a standing broadside shot under a hundred yards, and a bear is illegal if it's standing in water."

As so typically happens with this couple, they encountered a large bear walking toward them along a stream at 130 yards, and Ralph said, "Take him!" A good shot, Vicky put two lethal rounds into the animal before it fell into the water and expired. "I didn't listen to anything you told me," she said, "but I got my bear."

THE LIFE OF A HUNTING ROADIE

Every guy has fantasized about quitting a day job and hitting the road, hunting North America from east to west, but how do you bring your wife or girlfriend along? Could you deal with the pressures and frustrations of hunting and make a living?

Ralph and Vicky's schedule includes trade shows from January to mid-March, then turkey and spring bear season, fol-

Having your spouse with you is a huge help when videoing hunts. One can shoot while the other runs the camera.

lowed by consumer shows in July and August. That leads into antelope, caribou, and other big game adventures through the end of the year, all the while producing TV shows and raising a family.

"I learned I was pregnant in an outhouse over a fifty-five-gallon drum in bear camp," said Vicky. "It opened a new chapter in our lives."

Vicky first met Ralph in his archery shop, where she went to buy a new bow. The two became friends, fell in love, and eloped in Africa, where they spent a two-month honeymoon. In 1995, Vicky quit her job and began working for Ralph, just as the fledgling hunting-video market began to grow.

When thoughts turned to children, the couple knew they could not carry out their grueling schedule and also raise a child, so they spoke with their parents and worked out a plan to share the parenting responsibilities.

Ralph's mother had no other grandchildren and was thrilled when RJ was born. She soon became "Nani" and the chief caretaker when the hunters were on the road. "RJ loves Nani like an angel, and without her I couldn't hunt and partner with Ralph," said Vicki with intense sincerity. "Nani has been there since Day One, and RJ is her life. Everyone back home knows who Nani is; she even became a pack leader for the Cub Scouts."

Today, RJ is eleven years old. He's becoming old enough to join his parents and even be part of the show. Recently, the lad took a spring gobbler hunt in Florida and bagged his first turkey with a guide he called Uncle Hoppe. When the tom went down, Vicky suggested that RJ call Nani to tell her the news.

Andrew and Katie Howard met while hunting and worked together before getting married. I met them during their courting stage, and it was easy to see that they were a very compatible couple.

Who-decides-what is as much a dilemma for a hunting couple as any other partnership. Generally, sharing is better.

"Oh that's so exciting," Nani said. "What did your parents say?"

"Me and Uncle Hoppe are the only ones not crying," he said in bewilderment.

MUST HAVE AND TO HOLD

Andrew Howard and Katie Hill have teamed up to bring *Must Have Outdoors* to the Pursuit Channel, an innovative concept that combines an in-depth look at outdoor products in an informative and entertaining manner. Andrew graduated from the University of Missouri, where he took a wide variety of courses including sales and marketing. Katie spent her college career in Hannibal, majoring in business administration, and she spent the last half of her senior year as an intern with Howard Communications, which is where the two met.

Physically, both Andrew and Katie could be magazine cover models. And with common interests and proximity at work, it's no wonder they soon became an item. Although *Must Have Outdoors* could be produced by a man or a woman, they believe that their partnership and relationship adds greater viewer appeal. "Some of the draw is that guys want their wives to be involved in hunting in some way," said Andrew.

"We get lots of comments like, 'I wish my wife hunted,'" said Katie.

"Guys want their wives or girlfriends to relate to what they are so passionate about. From a woman's standpoint, it's interesting to see how hunting works, and it's more interesting if it's a couples-show or a boyfriend and girlfriend. Viewers think the interaction between Andrew and me is really good," Katie says. "They can definitely see our chemistry."

WHO DECIDES WHAT?

Disagreements easily arise in any partnership, whether it's a business or personal relationship. The Cianciarulos capitalize on their seemingly adversarial relationship because it is so entertaining. Each spouse openly vies to out-achieve the other, which often leads to comical results. Since every couple faces conflict, outdoor TV viewers can easily identify with the challenge and the reality of opinion diversity.

A great hunting team, requires sharing and commitment to make it work.

Andrew and Katie use their passion about their TV idea as a guiding force toward decision-making. "We are both comfortable with bringing up ideas, and reaching a decision is easier because we know each other so well," Katie says. "We worked with each other before starting this project and got along very well," she laughed, noting that their respective office cubicles are defined by boxes of products used on their show.

A loving and viable relationship underlies their business plan, an image they share through social-networking sites such as Facebook. "We created a fan page for *Must Have Outdoors,* where our fans can go and see what we are up to," Katie says. "We can post videos and post our blog there, and they can follow us as well as the products and the show. It's a more personal and intimate relationship with people. We have about 2,200 fans and expect to have many more."

Social media makes getting started easier. You can post a short subject, build an audience, and look for sponsors.

Keep at it. Making hunting video is difficult, but keeping the feelings in your work helps viewers to relate.

"We take one question at a time and respond individually which has been well received," says Andrew. "We each want to be an outdoor person just like you, and we can relate to your needs as a hunter or outdoor person. We check our sites every hour at work and carry web-phones with us at all times. In this way, the job isn't 8:00–5:00. The show *is* our personal life, which is good because we are so involved and passionate about it. We talk about stuff at night, even when we are watching a movie, Katie may say, 'OMG, we need to do that.'"

LEE AND TIFFANY: UP CLOSE

If you have attended a consumer-sporting show lately, you may think that somewhere at the head of that huge line, someone is giving away a free hi-def television. Yet a closer look would reveal a petite, attractive lady with long, blond hair and her tall and handsome husband. They are Lee and Tiffany Lakosky, hosts of the *Crush* TV show. Fans stand in lines hundreds deep and wait patiently for hours on end to have a photo taken and chat with their hunting idols.

"I don't know exactly why we have so many people come up to us and say, 'It looks like you are having fun and make hunting fun. "Yes," says Lee Lakosky emphatically. "Isn't that why we all hunt?"

Whether the Lakoskys have struck a vein of golden outdoor interest among women, or whether they are creating a role model for hunting couples is unclear, yet the chemistry of the dynamic couple is definitely having an impact. "So many young women come up to us and say something like this: 'We have been married for twenty-one years, and I never even thought of hunting. But it looks like you are having a good time. I think I'll try it.' That's been phenomenal for us," says Lee. "It's not something we tried to do or

Lee and Tiffany have a huge following on television and on social media. They moved to Iowa where the big deer live.

People stand in line by the hundreds to speak with Lee and Tiffany, along with taking a selfie.

promote, husband-and-wife or couples hunting, it's just what we do, and it's been great to see."

Tiffany believes that she and Lee have a relatability factor, information she gathers from fan input. "We are married, we like to hunt, and now viewers have something in common, because for a long time there weren't many hunting couples on TV," she says. "One thing about us, I'm not perfect, and I have a million things going on. One of the biggest jokes in our household is that I have no sense of direction whatsoever, and I feel that a lot of people who are watching can identify. But ultimately, they enjoy being out there, and I kind of laugh at it and the patience we have. I think we are relatable with people in their relationships."

ALL THE RIGHT MOVES

The Lee and Tiffany story began ceremoniously at their wedding, yet three weeks later Lee quit his job as a chemical engineer and asked his new bride to move to Iowa. "I just couldn't hunt as much as I wanted, so I walked in and quit," Lee said. "I didn't know what I was going to do, but if I moved to Iowa I might be able to get a job in the chemical industry. At least I could be living where I could hunt after work and on weekends. When I asked Tiffany if she wanted to move to Iowa, she said, 'Sure.' That was her personality; most wives would have probably killed you. But, 'Sure that sounds fun,' she said, and she was thrilled that I quit my job, because I was getting crabbier and crabbier as we went along because it just wasn't what I wanted to do."

"Anything we ever did was built around hunting and the outdoors. It's what brought us together," Tiffany says. "After moving to Iowa, we knew no one there, but began filming each other and enjoyed that very much. David Blanton was good enough to put some of our hunts on Realtree's *Monster Buck* video series. We were such huge fans of those hunting shows that it was like Christmas Day for me when they came out in local stores. I was so thrilled. We never got paid, never asked for money, and never wanted any money. We were just thrilled that someone wanted to use it."

As Lee-and-Tiffany hunts were seen by the public, they began to create interest such that ScentLok offered a chance to host their *Gettin' Close with Lee and Tiffany* TV show.

From the very beginning, we were going to show misses. All the stuff, because Tiffany had never hunted before. We were not going to come off as professional hunters that never miss or make a mistake. Hey, we are just people like anyone else. There are a lot of hunters out there better than me, better than Tiffany, and we honestly never wanted to set up as great hunters. Not at all. I'm just like you guys. I think that struck a chord with people too.

Finally, the reality show concept seems to fit the Lakoskys very well, because neither partner seems to have an ego. "We never set out to be a TV show. I mean, really, we are redneck farmers with great spots to hunt," laughs Tiffany. "Really, neither of us likes being the center of attention. It's amazing that either of us has a show, because neither of us actually like to be on film. If we didn't have a reality show, we'd be in big trouble. We never set out to do this."

"Actually, we are kind of private people and are overwhelmed with the celebrity," says Lee. "I have loved whitetails since I was three years old, and having people stand in line is so flattering. We never dreamed in a million years it would happen to us. Now that we are on TV, it's great to let people into our lives and experience what we do."

Author's Note: For information about these couples check their websites:
Ralph and Vickie: www.archerschoicemedia.com
Andrew and Katie: www.musthaveoutdoors.com
Lee and Tiffany: www.thecrush.tv

Chapter 38

Conclusion: Have Fun Out There

Have fun out there. Crossbows are ideal for the entire family and can be used easily in the back yard.

I'll turn seventy years of age in 2016, and I have been blessed with a life filled with adventure and outdoor ambition. My father, who survived the Pacific campaign of World War II, was a drill instructor who raised me with a positive, can-do attitude. Many of the adventures of my life were achieved because I didn't believe there was any other way. My mother was a schoolteacher who raised me with compassion and an uplifted spirit. My reverent hope is that she will live long enough to read this book when published.

Hopefully, you have learned many things about crossbows and hunting in general, with safety afield as a primary objective. By now you should have a good understanding of the potential and limitations of a crossbow, as well as how to use one effectively on big game animals of all kinds. You've heard lots of advice from experts like Stan Potts, Bob Foulkrod, and Bill Jordan. Equally, I hope you will remember the achievement of young Connor, Sawyer's Christmas bow, and the decision of Neil Dougherty and how a semester in the outdoors changed his life. Finally, I'd like to leave you with Jenna's story.

The daughter of a good friend, Jenna and her dad go turkey hunting each spring, which is a time that Dad absolutely cherishes. Teenagers are so consumed with schoolwork, sports, and interactions with their friends that many will not so much as be seen with their parents. In two seasons, Jenna has taken two gobblers with two shots from her crossbow, and her dad literally glows when he speaks of the quest.

Young Jenna smiles behind her great spring gobbler. Each year, she and her dad have a bonding session with a crossbow.

A 3-D target makes a great present for any aspiring hunter. Follow the safety precautions mentioned earlier, and you will develop a lifetime of outdoor adventure.

Jenna plays softball and field hockey year round. She's fifteen now and busy with friends, The hunt together really is such a special bonding time, and our time together creates a memory she will have for the rest of her life. Everybody remembers their first hunts. She shoots a bow and arrow, but to be proficient on wild turkeys, the extreme accuracy of a crossbow fits her schedule. Teenagers are so busy. You have pinpoint accuracy and that's what you need. None of her friends hunt or have family members who hunt, and it's funny to see her enthusiasm. She enjoys being outside and seeing the things she sees. Last year we saw a coyote, and the things you see as a hunter opens your eyes to the whole different world out there.

Crossbows are the perfect outdoor connection for a youngster, and like with young Connor, by gearing equipment to the size and age of the shooter, boys and girls can have fun and develop shooting skills and safety habits that will last them a lifetime. Likewise for those interested in hunting, but who don't have a mentor. The more we help each other, the more hunting and our wildlife populations benefit. I wish you good luck, good shooting, and most of all, good fun.

Appendix

The History of Crossbows

Detail from "The Martyrdom of St. Sebastian," Circa 1475.

CROSSBOW TIME LINE

Sixth Century B.C.

The earliest known handheld crossbows are unearthed in two tombs found in East China.

Fifth Century B.C.

The earliest reasonably reliable date for the crossbow in the Greek world.

500–300 B.C.

Sun Tzu's influential book, *The Art of War*, refers to the use of crossbows.

341 B.C.

Earliest reliable record of the use of the crossbow in warfare at the Battle of Ma-ling in China; also famous for first use of the illusion of retreat-and-ambush to gain the upper hand in battle.

228 B.C.

Earliest factual evidence in the form of a bronze lock mechanism from the tomb of Yu Wang.

400 A.D.

Evidence of use as war instrument in the Mediterranean.

Fourth to Seventh Centuries A.D.

Reliefs on structures in Roman Gaul show crossbows used for hunting.

947 A.D.

Belgian attack on Senlis near Paris driven off by crossbowmen.

986 A.D.

Lock bows are used in the Battle of Hjorungsvåg, Norway.

1000 A.D.

The crossbow comes into wide use in pageantry, crossbow clubs, and among royalty.

Eleventh Century

The rail or tiller is grooved to hold a bolt.

1066

Crossbows are likely used in the Battle of Hastings, and may have been the weapon that killed English King Harold, a pivotal point in the battle with the Normans.

1139

Pope Innocent II condemns and forbids the use of the crossbow by Christians against Christians by saying they are "deathly and hateful to God and unfit to be used among Christians."

1180

Mardi bin Ali al-Tarsusi of the Middle Eastern Ayyubid dynasty records the different types of crossbow and the use of the belt and claw for spanning, also called cocking.

1199

English King Richard I, "The Lion Heart," who had found a loophole in the Pope's decree against the crossbow, is killed by a crossbow in a battle at Chalus, France.

First Half of Thirteenth Century

Matthew Paris, English chronicler and monk, illustrates crossbows.

Thirteenth Century

The stirrup is introduced for cocking crossbows.

1277

200,000 bolts are ordered by the English for use in campaigns in Wales.

1346

English longbowmen defeat a force of 6,000 Genoese crossbowmen at the Battle of Crecy in Northern France during the Hundred Years' War.

Mid-Fourteenth Century

Crossbows now can cast bolts approximately two hundred yards.

1387

Book of the Hunt, a treatise on hunting by Gaston Phoebus, includes crossbow technique.

1435

Record of the cranequin, a rack-and-pinion device for cocking, is used by the English army in Rouen, France.

1480

In England, crossbow prices are set at no more than three shillings, four pence.

1486

Leonardo DaVinci designs a giant crossbow that would have been more than eighty feet across.

Sixteenth Century

Stonebows, two-stringed crossbows used to shoot stones or baked clay, become popular, especially for bird hunting.

Sixteenth Century

Record of first crossbows made specifically for target shooting.

1503

First of many laws in English restricting the use and possession of crossbows.

Mid-Sixteenth Century

Highly decorated, heavy-draw-weight crossbows are used widely for deer and boar hunting in Europe.

Eighteenth Century

The Chinese develop a self-loading, repeating crossbow.

1901

Sir Ralph Payne-Gallwey, military author and engineer, shoots a sixteenth-century crossbow 450 yards.

1956

The International Armbrust Union, now called the International Crossbow Shooting Union, is formed as the governing body for crossbow target competition.

1958

Alpine Crossbows, founded by Bernard Barnett, begins production in England's West Midlands. The company, now known as Barnett Crossbows, later moved to the United States.

1969

A very young Bernard Horton appears on Welsh national television showing off his latest creation.

1969

Holless Wilbur Allen is granted a patent for the compound bow.

1973

Arkansas makes crossbows legal during bow seasons. Wyoming had always allowed crossbows during archery season.

1976

Ohio legalizes crossbow hunting in bow seasons.

1970–80s

Crossbow hunting pioneers like Ottie Snyder of Ohio, Bill Hilts, Sr. of New York, Bill Troubridge of Ontario, Canada, and David Barnett of Florida, champion crossbow hunting in archery seasons.

1981

Barnett International opens a factory in Odessa, Florida.

1982

PSE introduces the popular Crossfire compound crossbow.

1984

Barnett International introduces the Thunderbolt compound crossbow.

1984

Proline introduces the ZX-7 compound bow.

1986

Tom Jennings, pioneering developer of the compound bow, releases the Jennings Devastator crossbow.

September 1998

Bobby L. Beeman takes the Safari Club world-record non-typical Northwestern whitetail deer with a crossbow. It scores 281-⅛ inches.

2000

Barnett sells more than a million crossbows.

November 2004

Brad Jerman takes the Safari Club International world-record typical whitetail deer with a crossbow. It scores 206-⅛ inches, and is also the Ohio state record for any weapon.

November 2004

The Bryant Buck is accepted as the second largest whitetail deer ever taken by a hunter, according to the Boone & Crockett Club.

2005

Seven US states allow crossbow hunting archery seasons.

September 2005

William Brown takes the world-record pronghorn antelope with a crossbow. It scores 77-⅜ inches Safari Club International.

April 2005

Amid support and criticism, archery's Pope and Young Club rejects crossbows as a legitimate hunting bow.

May 2006

Gordon Scott takes the world-record North American bison with a crossbow. It scores 65-⅞ inches SCI.

September 2006

Jake Carter takes the world-record typical Rocky Mountain elk with a crossbow. It scores 362-⅞ inches SCI.

March 2007

State Rep. Cy Thao, with crossbow proponent Daniel James Hendricks as spokesman, introduces a bill in the Minnesota Legislature to allow crossbows in firearm, bear, and turkey seasons. It passes, and also allows physically disabled hunters to use them.

October 2007

Ken Loya, Jr. takes the world-record black bear with a crossbow. The bear scores 20-¹³⁄₁₆ inches SCI.

April 2008

Stan E. Christianson takes the world-record Eastern wild turkey with a crossbow. The turkey scores 49-2/16 inches SCI.

June 2008

The Archery Trade Association adopts a policy that states, "Crossbows are viable shooting and hunting equipment."

2009

Inventor James Kempf receives a patent on a Reverse Draw Technology crossbow.

January 2010

PSE unveils the TAC-15 crossbow, which uses an AR-15 lower as its trigger group and stock.

August 2010

Then-chancellor Vladimir Putin uses a crossbow to shoot an endangered gray whale for research purposes.

March 2011

The Illinois General Assembly fails to pass a bill to allow crossbow hunting for people younger than sixty-two, and those without a handicap.

August 2011

Nebraska, Indiana, and parts of New York allow crossbows in archery seasons, bringing the number of pro-crossbow states to eighteen.

November 2011

Jerry Bryant takes the world-record crossbow deer, a 304-3/8-inch, 37-point Illinois buck called the Bryant Giant. Bryant was allowed to use a crossbow in Illinois thanks to a medically-disabled-hunter permit.

2011

Crossbows sales rise 70 to 80 percent in five years, according to the ATA.

Read more: www.gameandfishmag.com/gear-accessories/a-look-at-crossbow-history/#ixzz3dQ8Npi2t.